# Ready for the Defense

# READY FOR THE DEFENSE

## by Martin Garbus

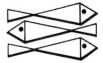

FARRAR, STRAUS AND GIROUX

NEW YORK

*To Ruth*

# Author's Note

I thank Peter Mayer, my dear friend, without whose involvement and encouragement this book would not have been started or completed.

My thanks go also to Basil Heatter and to Henry Robbins, Elizabeth Wallace and Carmen Gomezplata of Farrar, Straus and Giroux, and to Claire Cooper and Elinor Klein, for their editorial help and advice.

Most of the court testimony and legal arguments are taken from the transcripts of the trials. In a few instances I have edited the transcripts to make them more readable. I have not changed the substance of what was said in the courtroom.

# Contents

# Prologue

IN THE PAST DECADE I have devoted most of my working
time to the area of civil rights. I was one of many attorneys
making an attempt to move the battle from the street to
the courtroom. Although many of us considered ourselves
radicals, and were so considered by society, our struggle
for a just community was fought within the context of the
system. We were long on faith—seeking radical change by
representing the people whose conflict with the system
might result in the creation of new rights and the clarifica-
tion of old ones.

But much was altered by the election of Richard Nixon
and Spiro Agnew. A great deal of that faith is gone. The
replacement of Ramsey Clark by John Mitchell in the office
of Attorney General, the Chicago conspiracy trial, the attempts to appoint Clement Haynesworth and G. Harrold
Carswell to the Supreme Court—all indicate the new path
we are traveling.

The civil-rights struggles of the sixties, particularly those
which took place in the courts, could only have been fought
in a country which accepts dissent and change. By this I
do not mean that change was not bitterly resisted. But there
seemed to be, even in the most repressive situations, a na-

tional awareness of the need to remake America. I saw it even in a Mississippi courtroom, where a judge paused to thank me for having come all the way from New York to argue against discrimination, saying that just my presence had made a difference in local customs and attitudes.

My legal career began in a conventional fashion. Attracted by the excitement of the courtroom, I specialized from the start in jury-trial work. I enjoyed the competition, the clear-cut wins or losses, and the financial rewards of a successful practice. But trial by combat soon made me intensely conscious, even within the confines of the courtroom, of the glaring injustices inherent in our society, and I found myself becoming increasingly involved in the defense of society's customary victims.

The cases I have argued in the past few years have covered a broad span—from men condemned to die in Sing Sing to others condemned to cruelly underpaid labor among the grapevines of California. I joined with other lawyers in a Columbia University project to fight George Wallace's attempt to use the welfare system to discriminate against blacks, a case that took me to the Supreme Court. It became apparent that the individuals we represented were also the embodiment of principles affecting us all, and in representing them we were seeking to win a case not only for one man but for many.

Winning or losing, my colleagues and I experienced first the exhilaration of being active in a period of promise and change, and then disillusionment when we saw how deceptive were the promises and how superficial the changes. Through it all, I continued to place my hopes in the courts. Courtroom procedure is the best method we have for resolving disputes. I knew that if it failed—if we failed—the alternative was to take the conflict to the streets.

Some of the people I represented in those years are in these pages. Others, like Cesar Chavez, are not, though meeting them affected my life deeply. If revolution is to come about in this country, it will be because of men like Cesar, who, through torturous undramatic day-to-day organizing, create a mood of peace and faith that will not be resisted. The cases chosen for this book are those in which drama combined with constitutional principle. The resolution of each case makes a point about our society.

Through Cesar Chavez I learned at first hand about people who previously had been little more to me than statistics. Other clients—like Timothy Leary—I was able to defend but could not so easily identify with. But Leary opened my mind to new experiences and I felt richer for knowing him.

In each case the drama in the courtroom was a reflection of daily life outside. The structure of power and privilege was revealed in court for all to see.

I hope this book communicates some of the terror and pity we felt in these struggles. When we came to trial, the prosecuting attorney would declare, "Ready for the People." When my turn came, I often answered, "Ready for the Defense." These are the time-honored formalities of the courtroom, but they are often misleading. I like to think that the clients I represented, in the stories told in this book, more truly stood for the people.

# One

*The State of Mississippi for the Use
and Benefit of Henrietta Wright against
Wages*, et al.

AT 4:00 P.M., AUGUST 26, twenty days after the Voting Rights Act of 1965 was passed, Mrs. Henrietta Wright, wearing one of the first "Black Power" buttons Mississippi had seen, went to the circuit courthouse in Winona to register to vote. This was an act of exceptional courage, for few Winona blacks had tested their new power. It was not until the following year that the Mississippi Freedom Democratic Party succeeded in enrolling large numbers of blacks as voters.

Winona is about two and a half hours north of Jackson by car. It is a small, ramshackle town of 2,000 people, evenly divided between whites and blacks, sitting at the east end of the Delta in the center of one of the most rigidly racist areas of the country. The black middle class of Winona, like the black middle class of many Mississippi towns, consists of the funeral director, teachers, and the janitor in the post office. The funeral director, whose funeral home dominates Main Street, earned his money in the major enterprise the whites traditionally leave to the blacks, and he is the most prominent black man in town. On the outskirts of town is the usual marginal factory whose owners were drawn to Mississippi because of the low wages they could pay.

In his office two doors from the courthouse, Sheriff Wages,

the High Sheriff of Winona County, watched Mrs. Wright as she began the registration process. She filled out the form, then drove home to the Last Chance Café, a restaurant which she and her husband owned and from which they made a meager living, selling hot meals, potato chips, popcorn, and candy. The Wrights lived in a two-room building in the back of the restaurant, at the end of a dirt road called Greensborough Street. Mrs. Wright, a bulky woman in her late forties, left her car and started toward the café.

Before she could walk the twenty-five feet, Deputy Sheriff Miller pulled into the driveway, stopped behind Mrs. Wright's car, and said, while still seated: "Henrietta, you're under arrest."

"What for?"

"For reckless driving and passing a stop sign."

"I didn't pass no stop sign. Where is there a stop sign on the way I traveled?"

"You passed the stop sign on Avern Street."

"I did not."

Sensing trouble, Mrs. Wright's husband walked out of the café.

"What's the problem?"

"She passed a stop sign."

"Well, let me pay the fine."

Miller got out of the car with a pistol and blackjack. "No, I'm taking her to jail."

"Jail? For passing a stop sign? Let me just pay the fine."

"No, I'm taking her to jail."

"There's no reason for that."

Miller yelled, "Henrietta, come here with your hands up."

"I didn't do anything. I'm not going to jail."

"You walked away from me. That's resisting arrest and that's a felony."

Mrs. Wright continued on into the restaurant.

Just then Sheriff Wages and Deputy Sheriff Donald Cross

pulled up into the driveway. Following them came Highway Patrolman Billy Morgan, who parked across the road and removed his gun from its holster. Sheriff Cross drew a pistol and blackjack. Sheriff Wages took a long-barreled shotgun out of the back seat and started to walk into the restaurant with the gun drawn.

"Come on, Henrietta, you're under arrest for reckless driving. Don't do anything to make me shoot you," Wages said.

Mrs. Wright was standing at the far end of the counter on the left side of the restaurant. Wages walked the fifteen feet from the door. He first put the shotgun a few inches from her face and then put the gun hard in her back. As soon as she stepped outside, Miller and Cross grabbed her arms, bent them behind her back, hands pointing up, and handcuffed her.

"She hasn't done anything wrong. If it's just a traffic ticket, let me pay it," Mr. Wright said to Sheriff Wages.

"No, we're taking her to jail."

Mrs. Wright was half pushed and half carried the twenty feet to Wages's car, with Cross and Miller on each side of her, their hands grabbing her upper arms.

She was shoved into Wages's car. Miller and Wages sat in the front, Cross in the back with Mrs. Wright. Wages kept his shotgun across his knees. On the way to the jail, Cross beat Mrs. Wright. Her hands were still handcuffed behind her.

They arrived at the jail at 6:05 P.M. Mrs. Wright was booked and put in a cell, charged with assaulting an officer, resisting arrest, and reckless driving.

"I want a doctor . . . Let me see my husband . . . I want a lawyer."

"Now, Henrietta, you just don't give us any trouble. Just be quiet."

Wages put his hands on Mrs. Wright's breasts, thighs, and backside, saying, "I want to see if you have any weapons."

Because of the possibility that some jailed blacks may have seen him, Wages was later to testify that he did have his hands on Mrs. Wright's body, but he stated that Mrs. Wright had taken his hand and said, "Do you want to feel some hard black titties? If you want to feel something hot, put your hand in my crotch. Just ask like a man for what you want and you can have it. There's no need to put me in jail." At the time, Mrs. Wright still had her hands bound behind her.

C. W. Wright went to the jail at 7:30 and asked to see his wife. Wages refused; Wright went home.

Henrietta Wright's handcuffs were removed. She spent that night in jail, with no offer of dinner. The next morning Wages, Miller, Morgan, and Cross entered her cell, dragged her off the cot, and slammed her head and back against the concrete floor. They kneed her in the stomach, thighs, and mouth, knocking out two front teeth, her mouth filling with blood. She resisted as best she could. They tried to handcuff her to keep her from fighting back, but they were not able to get more than one lock snapped on.

"Henrietta, you're a bad nigger. We're gonna take care of you. You're crazy if you think you can vote," Wages said. "She's crazy," he told Miller. "Let's have a lunacy hearing and put her away."

Miller went to the chancery clerk in the courthouse, a few doors away.

"We have a crazy nigger in jail, a lunatic, and we want to put her in Whitfield. Get two doctors down here, and let's have a lunacy hearing."

Whitfield, a one-and-a-half-hour drive from Jackson, is one of the state mental hospitals. The law requires that before a patient is committed to Whitfield, two doctors, after a complete examination, must certify that the patient has a mental disorder. The law also requires that after the doctors' examination there must be a full hearing at which all interested parties (including the patient's spouse) have an opportunity to testify either in favor of or in opposition to the commitment.

The chancery clerk began the process after a few words from Miller. A letter was immediately written to C. W. Wright notifying him that a lunacy hearing was going to take place that same morning, August 27, at 10 A.M. The notice, received by Wright three days later (after his wife had been in the hospital three days), was mailed *after* the "hearing" took place. The hearing notice said that C. W. Wright could submit any evidence he desired to show that Mrs. Wright was not in need of medical care and treatment.

The law also requires that the alleged lunatic be served with papers telling him of the hearing. Under the law, Mrs. Wright could then call her own doctor, husband, or any other witness she had, to give facts to prove she should not be committed. Miller said, "I threw the notice on the jail floor. I don't know if she saw it or read it."

The examination was conducted in the jail by Doctors Howard and Middleton, two general practitioners from Winona. Dr. Howard, a short, fleshy, florid man, had participated in dozens of similar hearings. The state of Mississippi paid him $5 for the hearing, plus reimbursement for medical expenses. He gave Mrs. Wright an injection to quiet her down. He was later reimbursed $2.40 by the state, the cost of the needle.

Wages gave the doctors a history to justify the lunacy hearing. "She's been violent ever since we arrested her, cursing and hitting. She wouldn't let us take her from her home after we arrested her for reckless driving. She threw herself off the bed and made her cell into a mess. Won't take food."

Dr. Howard walked back to the cell. "I want to examine you."

"What for?"

"These men told me about you, and maybe it would be better if you went to Whitfield."

"Whitfield? What is this? There's nothing wrong with me! I'm not going."

"I just want to examine you."

"Get away from me. Let me see my husband. He can get me a lawyer."

C. W. Wright, meanwhile, had come to the jail while the examination was in progress and he asked to see his wife. He was not told about the examination. Wages said he had no right to be there, so Wright left.

Dr. Middleton, a short, myopic, balding man in his thirties, entered the cell. "Let me examine you."

"No."

"Will some of you give me a hand?" He called Morgan, Cross, Wages, and Miller into the cell. Two men stood on each side of Mrs. Wright and pinned her to the floor while the doctor gave her a second hypodermic.

The drug acted instantly. Mrs. Wright sat quietly on the bed while the doctors, in less than three minutes, concluded a "visual examination." Dr. Howard was later to say on the witness stand, "We didn't have to do no more because of the history Wages gave us, and the way she behaved convinced us she was crazy."

Mrs. Wright sat quietly for ten minutes, until the effects of the drug wore off sufficiently so she could walk. She was taken out of the jail and placed in a car for the ride to Whitfield, her arms rigidly and painfully in front of her body. A belt was attached from each arm to the side of the car to hold her upright. The car, generally used to transport dangerous criminals, had two rings on the floor. Mrs. Wright's legs were held by the rings.


C. W. Wright, a shriveled man several years older and at least fifty pounds lighter than his wife, returned to the jail. He saw his wife trussed up in the car, her mouth bleeding and a glazed look in her eyes.

He stuck his head through the open back window. "Are you all right? Do you need any money?"

The car drove off before Mrs. Wright could answer. Two hours later Henrietta Wright was admitted to Whitfield, examined, and found normal. But she was kept at Whitfield for seven weeks, until October 14. All this happened because Henrietta Wright went to register to vote on August 26, 1965. Immediately after Mrs. Wright was released from Whitfield, she was convicted on the original criminal charges (reckless driving, assault, and resisting arrest) and sentenced to ninety days in jail. The Lawyers Constitutional Defense Committee of the American Civil Liberties Union found out about the case in October 1965. A week after she was released from jail, Mrs. Wright went to LCDC's Jackson office, met with Alvin Bronstein, then its Chief Counsel, and told him what had happened. At first he couldn't believe her story. He investigated the case and early in 1966 filed a complaint.

Mrs. Wright's suit sought to punish the arresting officers and doctors for the beatings and wrongful commitment by making them pay damages. The complaint alleged that these defendants "individually and in conspiracy beat Mrs. Wright because she was a black voter and intended to thereby discourage other black people from voting." Mrs. Wright sought $50,000 from each of the defendants.

Three years after the suit was filed, on February 28, 1969, Armand Derfner, LCDC Chief Staff Counsel, called me (LCDC was then a part of the American Civil Liberties Union and I was the ACLU's associate director) and asked me if I would try the case for Mrs. Wright. Mrs. Wright's case had been on the docket for two years. Armand told me the delay had been ours because there was no one to try such a case. "Jim Lewis knows the case and he'll help you prepare it. He was here back in 1965, knows the witnesses, and just finished a trial before Judge Keady, the judge who's going to try this case. I think you'll need a week's preparation." The case, a federal one, had been called for trial in Oxford, Mississippi, and, according to Armand, was to be tried the week of May 11.

I told Armand I could do it. He gave me a copy of the Mississippi statutes and codes and I began to prepare.

I had last been in Mississippi two summers before and wanted very much to go back. I was then counseling local black leaders and civil-rights lawyers in Jackson who were dealing with the county, state, and federal governments, trying to clarify the rights of blacks in the criminal and welfare areas. Dozens of the leaders had been locked up during demonstrations; I had sought to point out those tactics that would forestall arrest and those that would not.

I sat one day in a steamy room and met over two hundred people arbitrarily turned away from welfare offices and another hundred unlawfully jailed. I listened to people who had been abused and humiliated, and even as I told them what to do and not to "take that" from this cop or that judge, I felt how helpless I was to do anything about it. I longed to be involved in one meaningful confrontation—to be able to make some white Mississippians feel that their actions could not forever go unquestioned. The Wright case was that confrontation for me.

Many suits had been filed by private agencies and by the government in an effort to help blacks make their power felt at the polls. In 1963 the United States Civil Rights Commission, after years of lawsuits sponsored by the Department of Justice, concluded:

> After five years of federal litigation it is fair to conclude that case by case proceedings, helpful as they may be in insulated localities, have not provided a prompt or adequate remedy for widespread discriminatory denials of the right to vote.

In 1961 the Department of Justice had filed a suit in Panola County, the county adjoining Oxford, where Mrs. Wright's case was ultimately tried. The first few lines of the court decision in the case, *United States v. Duke*, tell the story:

> When this suit was filed by the United States on October 16, 1961, Panola County, Mississippi, had 7639 white persons and 7250 Negroes of voting age. At least 5343 white persons were registered to vote. The only Negro registered to vote in Panola County was R. H. Hightower, 92 years old, who had registered in 1892.

The Southern states argued in the case that the Negroes throughout the South had abstained from registering, without any particular reason. "It seemed," they said, "that Negroes were not interested in voting." That was probably true; they were more interested in staying alive.

If Negroes sought to vote, they and their families might be killed or maimed by the rope, gunfire, or burnings. When courageous Negroes tried to register, they were asked to interpret and explain provisions of the Mississippi Constitution, such as Section 212, dealing with the interest rate on the Chickasaw School Fund; Section 228, dealing with alluvial land; Section 266, dealing with restrictions on state office holdings; and Section 282, dealing with "the validity of recognizance and other obligations entered into before the adoption of the 1890 Constitution." Even the best law professor in the state probably could not have passed the test. Needless to say, white registrants were not asked these questions.

On August 6, 1965, the Voting Rights Act was passed, eliminating many of the devices applied to Negro voters to keep them from voting. The result was that more Negroes registered to vote in those five years than had registered in all the years prior to 1968. This was still a pitifully small number. The South, through force and threats of force, had been largely successful in keeping Negroes from the polls. As I left New York, I thought about the tent cities built to house Negroes in

Fayette County who were evicted because they tried to register, and about other brutalities and hardships, killing and maiming suffered throughout the South in the sixties during the time of voter registration. The Wright case, I felt, could be a small step toward eliminating intimidation by law.

I arrived in Oxford early Monday morning, May 5, 1969, and went to the offices of the Northern Mississippi Rural Legal Assistance Program. Jim Lewis told me the program's library and secretarial services would be available to me for the duration of the trial. Oxford, the home of William Faulkner and the University of Mississippi, was beautiful that cloudless day. Located in the middle of flat land stretching as far as I could see, Oxford seemed warm and genteel. At the center of Oxford, as in all other Mississippi towns I've been in, there was a statue of Johnny Reb facing North to fight back the invaders, paid for by the town in commemoration of the Civil War dead. White-fronted stores circled the eleven-foot gray stone statue of a soldier on horseback. The streets were immaculate.

But my first impression of peace and gentility was shattered as I rode around Oxford and recalled that, during the Freedom Summer of 1964, this was one of the towns that civil-rights workers most feared to enter. I saw: the red-brick, white-columned, bullet-pocked university building where James Meredith sought to enroll; his apartment at the end of the long, two-story dormitory where he stayed; the mall where the voting began and where Ross Barnett and the federal government had their confrontation. The week before I arrived, the university had tried—and failed—to stop Julian Bond from speaking at the school. The campus atmosphere was still so charged that, as my car turned each corner, I expected to see mobs.

All federal cases arising in Winona are tried in Oxford, which is part of the Delta Division of the Mississippi Federal Court. The courthouse, facing the Confederate soldier, is a roomy, two-story building with the chancery clerk's offices on the first floor and one courtroom on the second.

Jim Lewis called John Maxie II, a lawyer in charge of the Holly Springs poverty office. At Jim's request, John had obtained a list of the sixty jurors comprising the venire. John Maxie II is a soft-spoken, twenty-seven-year-old, mustached native of Mississippi, a graduate of "Ole Miss," and a descendant of a long line of Methodist preachers. He said to me: "We're an old family, but not Natchez or Vicksburg. We were always poor. My great-great-grandfather was not a general but a private in the Civil War."

The twelve jurors who were to sit on the trial were to be selected from the list John gave me. The practice in Mississippi, unlike that of many other states, is to furnish the lawyers a venire list (in Mississippi it's called the "talisman list") a day or so in advance of the trial. The list describes the jurors by name, occupation, and address, so the lawyers can investigate before the trial and start deciding whom they want as jurors and whom not. The list does not describe jurors by race. However, since all the lawyers opposing us had been in this district fairly often, they knew who the Negroes were and could be expected to challenge them solely on racial grounds. They did.

John cautioned us against merchants from Grenada, who had recently been boycotted by the Negroes; against anybody from Panola County—one of the most bigoted areas in Mississippi; and against one man whom he believed to be a member of the White Citizens Council.

"We have a lot of brutality claims but haven't yet filed suits," John said. "You can't get a good enough case to make it worth a trial. It takes a lot of time to prepare and try these cases, and one of the things the law-enforcement people have learned is not to beat anyone in front of witnesses. They're getting sophisticated. That alone is progress. Let's see what happens to your case."

I then called Bob Fitzpatrick of the President's Committee, for Jim told me that Bob had recently been in Oxford and was familiar with the judge and the court. The President's Committee, formed by the American Bar Association and the federal government in 1965 to provide legal services to the Deep South, had only recently started to become actively involved in the Southern movement. Since President Nixon took office, it has been more often called the "Lawyer's Committee," to avoid linking Nixon with its more militant activities.

Bob and I discussed the selection of the jury. Federal-court procedure is different from the state practice that sees lawyers engaged in long, detailed questioning of prospective jurors. In federal courts, the judge asks the jury nearly all the questions, allowing the lawyers only one or two questions. He might simply request that the lawyers submit written questions for him to ask. Bob said Judge Keady would follow the federal practice of doing the questioning himself. But what of racial attitudes?

"I'd like to get into them," I told Bob. "The problem's there and I'd rather put it on the table than make believe it doesn't exist."

"I don't know if Keady will ask those questions for you," Bob answered. "The questions have limited value unless they are asked of each juror, and I don't think Keady will let you spend that long on jury selection."

I decided not to give Keady the written questions. Instead, I would ask the questions myself. If Keady was more liberal than most Mississippi judges, he might agree. Bob said Keady had a full docket, would be anxious to move the case along, and would, in the interest of speed, not allow the lawyers too much leeway.

"He runs a tough courtroom, knows everything that's going on, and is as good a judge as there is for your case."

Jim Lewis and Mike Trister gave me a short lecture on the technicalities of Mississippi practice, what the various trial motions are called, and how Judge Keady reacts to various trial problems. Mike, a Yale Law School graduate, was dismissed from his teaching post at "Ole Miss" because of his involvement in the federally sponsored Legal Services Program. Suit was filed against the school, claiming he was wrongfully fired. A few months after the Wright trial was over, he won, but a year later he left Mississippi.

We discussed the work of lawyers in 1969 and how it had changed since 1964. Northern civil-rights workers were not spending their summers in the South any longer, so lawyers were no longer needed to defend them in the harassment cases that constituted the bulk of the dockets in the mid-sixties.

The thrust of the legal program now was to put most of our energies into helping black political power develop. Our Mississippi office was acting as counsel to the Mississippi Freedom Democratic Party in the political infighting. We represented them in the credentials challenge at the Chicago Convention in 1968, gave legal advice to the black cooperative movement, and filed welfare and other poor law cases. Many felt voting power was the single most significant area, and Jim thought we ought to place a primary emphasis on implementing the 1965 Voting Rights Act.

Jim went to the office of the clerk of the court and asked the clerk if we could look at the questionnaires from which the jurors' list had been prepared. The questionnaires gave more detailed information. For example, the list indicated that one of the jurors, a Mrs. Mercy, was a cashier in the Welfare Department cafeteria. She probably often talked to social workers and maybe to Negro welfare recipients. She might be a good juror. The questionnaires also told the extent of each juror's education. We wanted as highly educated a group as possible.

The questionnaires gave the occupations of the husbands of some of the women who described themselves as "housewives." A woman whose husband was a law-enforcement officer would tend to identify with the sheriffs and patrolman. A woman whose husband was a doctor would tend to identify with Drs. Howard and Middleton, the doctor defendants.

Knowing in advance which of the jurors we need not bother with allowed me to spend more time and energy on the jurors we wanted.

The trial was to begin at 2 P.M. Jim and I went to the courtroom about fifteen minutes early to absorb some of the court's atmosphere. The room was small. It seated fewer than 150 people, on dark, mahogany benches. The witness chair, unlike the witness chair in any other jurisdiction I had ever been in, was about twenty-five feet from the jury box. Ordinarily, it is much closer. The lawyers would ask their questions from a lectern at the jurors' box, so the witnesses would be forced to face the jury directly, and the distance between the lawyer and the witness would force both to keep their voices up. This would discourage the technique used by many lawyers of putting the questions rapidly when the cross-examination gets tense.

Word of the trial had spread throughout the area. The courtroom was filled with about a hundred spectators—students from the University of Mississippi, Office of Economic Opportunity lawyers, and townspeople. Some of the Mississippi Freedom Democratic Party people had come in from the rural areas. The town square was deserted as the trial began.

The prospective jurors filed in. The first twelve took seats in the jury box, and the rest sat together in a corner of the courtroom. Judge Keady, a tall, imperious figure, swept in wearing a long, black robe. He immediately indicated the time court would start in the morning and finish in the afternoon, and then said, "I'd like the lawyers and their clients to come into my chambers."

The chambers were off to the right of the courtroom. I took Mrs. Wright's hand and walked with her into the chambers. Most of the spectators observed with undisguised revulsion this contact between black and white. The chambers was a small olive-green room containing a dozen chairs. The practice of having clients in chambers during the preliminary discussions was new to me. Judge Keady felt that the clients should be present at all stages of the proceedings. I understood this to be standard in Mississippi.

"How long will this case take? I'm only here for two more weeks and then I move to Aberdeen. I ride circuit here, Mr. Garbus. I don't think the New York judges do that. I have other cases pending and I want to advise the jurors and lawyers what to do. How long will the case take?"

"Our direct case will be two days. I don't know how long defendants will cross-examine," I answered.

Four lawyers appeared on behalf of the defendants. Grover Harris of the Jackson bar represented the doctors. Attorneys William Leith, Hunter Hobbs, and James Naughton appeared for the sheriffs and patrolman. Harris, one of the best trial lawyers in the South, immediately took charge. He was a distinguished-looking, gray-haired gentleman in his early sixties. He was to come into court each day in a freshly pressed suit with a three-pointed handkerchief in his breast pocket. In appearance, manner, and ability, he was far superior to any of the other defense lawyers. It was apparent minutes after he began talking that Harris would be the chief defense lawyer.

"Your Honor, we never made a motion to dismiss this case against the doctors, but we do so now. The doctors were directed to make their examination of the plaintiff by order of the court—"

Judge Keady bristled, "You never made the motion in time, so let's not hear it now." Harris tried to press the point, but the judge stood firm. "Is there anything else, Mr. Harris?"

"There is, Your Honor. Each defendant should be entitled to three peremptory challenges for a total of fifteen. I make a motion for that."

"Comes now Mr. Garbus and states in opposition," intoned Judge Keady. It took me a few seconds to realize that this was the Mississippi way of asking me if I opposed what Harris had said.

"The complaint alleges a conspiracy of the officers and the doctors. It is only one claim, one incident, one incarceration, one beating. Plaintiff is entitled to three and the defendants should not have more than plaintiff. They stand together," I said.

Judge Keady had read the complaint earlier. "As I read the pleading, I see two sets of claims. One against the doctors for the faulty examination and the other against the officers for the beatings."

Judge Keady awarded the defendants six challenges against my three. We went back to the courtroom and started the jury selection.

I addressed the twelve jurors sitting in the box: "Do any of you believe that Negroes as a people are less truthful than whites?"

The twelve jurors started. This question had probably never before been put to jurors in the Oxford courtroom. Harris got up to make an objection, and the remaining jurors in the courtroom sat up. Jurors, judge, defendants, and their counsel now knew we were out to attack the racial issue directly. Many of the jurors also knew that, if they wanted to stay on the jury, they would have to answer the rest of the questions I put to them in a manner inconsistent with their real bias—they would have to lie if they wanted to remain. They might be able to walk outside and say differently, but in the courtroom the answer they would have to give was that Negroes as a people were not less truthful than whites.

I asked each of the twelve to answer. They all said they could trust a Negro as much as a white man. I asked each of them in a slightly different way: "Do you look upon Negroes as being less capable of telling the truth than white people? Would you believe a white person before you would believe a

Negro? Do you feel that Negroes have a greater tendency to lie—to exaggerate?"

Some of the jurors were so hostile that I had to ask them three and four times for answers. Often I could not hear the answers. I tried not to alienate any of them but knew I failed with at least four.

"Could you believe a black lady when she tells her version of what happened if believing her means that you are going to have to disbelieve a white witness? Can you believe the testimony of one witness although that one witness is contradicted by five or six other people? For example, if a white person tells you a story that is contradicted by six or seven black people, can you discount the weight of numbers and believe the white person? Conversely, can you believe a black person when she's contradicted, as she probably will be in this case, by six or seven white witnesses? Can you evaluate the witness solely on the basis of her demeanor on the stand and what she tells you there, and not on her social standing? Can you put aside any prejudice you have against her or any member of her class? Does the mere fact that two of the witnesses are doctors make it more difficult for you to disbelieve their testimony? Do you think because a man is a doctor he is necessarily telling the truth, or can a doctor, like anyone else, be inaccurate, make mistakes, and sometimes lie?"

The first twelve included four Negroes. I decided to ask the Negroes the same questions I had asked the white people. I wanted to show those present that Negroes could and would judge them here or at some future time and that a jury that included Negroes was a jury of their peers. On the surface, the questioning indicated a desire on my part for fair play.

"Merely because a white sheriff tells a certain version of the facts, does that mean, because he is a white sheriff, he can't be telling the truth? Can you take this testimony and listen to it openly and honestly? If a black lady is testifying against a white man, will you, of necessity, come down with a decision in favor of the black lady? Do you think whites less capable of telling the truth than black people? Do you think whites have a greater tendency to lie or exaggerate than black people?"

Josephine Tucker, an attractive black twenty-four-year-old who worked for the local OEO agency and held a bachelor's degree, answered each of these questions with a smile. She understood the reason for my questioning. She was also aware of the increasing annoyance of the white jurors, not only because we were asking a black person to judge a white person but also because we were asking a black person to be fair. Miss Tucker answered each question slowly, aware that she would be challenged by the white lawyers whatever her answers. She rolled the answers around, enjoying the roles we were playing.

I then asked the white jurors whether any of them were members of the White Citizens Council, the Americans for the Preservation of the White Race, or the Ku Klux Klan; whether they belonged to any group or organization which has among its tenets or bylaws the notion that the white race is superior to the black. One juror raised his hand and was excused.

"Do any of you believe that the white race is superior to the black race? Do you believe there is something wrong with black people, so that they can't tell the truth? Do any of you believe that merely because a woman went out to register to vote, the sheriff had a right to beat her up? Do you believe that Mrs. Wright has the right to vote and that a beating or abuse should not necessarily flow from it?"

I went back to Miss Tucker. "Do you believe black people have a right to vote?"

"Yes, sir."

"Do any of you here know Mrs. Wright? Do any of you here know the sheriff or the deputy sheriff or the doctors?"

William Hodges, juror number 12, square-jawed and crew-cut, said he knew each of the defendants. I asked him whether he could believe Mrs. Wright's testimony and could conclude that each of the defendants was not telling the truth. He said: "Because I know the defendants doesn't mean that I would always believe them."

"Mr. Hodges, in this case a black lady is going to claim that all these people that you know are telling lies. If she proves that to your satisfaction, can you come back with a verdict against your friends?"

"Yes."

"Can you give a favorable verdict to a black lady and substantial money damages against white defendants?"

"It'll be hard to believe that one person could be right and seven people could be wrong."

"Generally, if more people say one thing than another, you tend to believe the larger number of people? Would it be impossible for you to believe the one person?"

"Not impossible."

I then went to the next juror and asked the same questions and got nearly the same answers. I asked the women on the jury panel whether they had cleaning ladies, whether the "help" was black, and whether anything in that relationship made it difficult to evaluate this case fairly. All the jurors answered they could trust a black lady as much as a white lady.

The jury was impaneled early that afternoon—twelve white residents of Mississippi. The defendants had exercised every challenge they had against black people and I exercised every challenge I had against white people. I outlined Mrs. Wright's case to the jury and then called her to the stand.

As she seated herself, I saw her body tense. The witness stand faced the jurors' box; she looked at the twelve white people who had just sworn to be fair and impartial. I asked the first questions in a soft voice, trying to soothe her nervousness. She kept looking at her husband for reassurance. After I asked a few preliminary questions to help calm her, William Leith, one of the defense lawyers, interrupted.

"Your Honor, Mr. Wright is a plaintiff in this case too, and he should be excluded from the courtroom." The practice in Mississippi, unlike that of any other state I've ever been in, is to exclude the principals in a civil case. Generally the people suing and those being sued stay in the courtroom. It is common to exclude witnesses in criminal cases, so they don't testify on the basis of what they hear.

"In that case," I replied, "I ask that all the defendants be excluded from the courtroom and they be directed not to discuss their testimony with each other." It was not to our disadvantage to have Mr. Wright excluded. He knew every fact leading to his wife's jailing—he would not learn anything in court. But the exclusion would do damage to the defendants' case because I intended to examine each of the defendants at length on the same issues; they would not have the chance to dovetail their stories on the basis of what they heard in court.

Mrs. Wright's testimony was sufficient. The jury would not be more inclined to believe Mrs. Wright because her husband swore that what she said was so. And her constant glances toward him as she answered questions might indicate to the jury that she was telling a story he had helped create.

Judge Keady ordered Mr. Wright and all the defendants to leave the courtroom and directed them not to discuss their testimony.

Mrs. Wright was a difficult witness. I was not allowed to direct her on my examination and, although we had previously discussed her testimony at great length—including the questions I would ask and the pattern of my examination—she froze on the stand. I told her the evening before she took the stand that I would ask short, open-ended questions and I wanted her answers to be full and long. "I would prefer to ask you one or two questions about what happened and then sit down and let you describe all that happened, but I can't. Let's get as close as possible to it."

Instead of giving full answers, she responded with a short "yes" or "no." The flatness of her delivery made the examination sound rehearsed. We got into a boring, deadly rhythm. I tried unsuccessfully to loosen her up. I suggested, in my questions, some of the answers I hoped to get, but she continued to be unresponsive. I was frustrated. I could not go too far, or the jury would think I was putting words into her mouth.

I had intended to examine her for at least three hours, to give her time to describe what had been done to her the night of the arrest and in the mental hospital. There were four women jurors on the panel, and if she could communicate the outrage perpetrated on her, she might get through to some of the women—not enough to win, but enough perhaps to affect their attitudes, to make them realize that Mrs. Wright was a woman entitled to protection from brutal assaults; in short, that Mrs. Wright was a human being.

But we were failing and I knew it. Mrs. Wright knew it too. She knew she was falling into just that pattern of testimony I had told her we must avoid. The more she felt it, the worse it became.

I asked for a recess half an hour after Mrs. Wright took the stand. Judge Keady looked surprised at the request but granted it.

The first days of a trial are usually the most intense. The relationships between the judge, the jury, the court clerks, and the lawyers are beginning, and the way they begin often determines the way they will end. The tension in this case was compounded by hatreds barely kept under control by the formality of the courtroom.

The jury filed out during the recess, passing behind me on their way to the jury room. They didn't believe a word Mrs. Wright had said. She and I could feel their hostility boring into our backs. Wasting the time of white folk in a case like this! A sharp New York lawyer! Well, the South might not rise again, but they would show us it was still a very lively place.

Mrs. Wright didn't leave the witness stand. She sat staring straight ahead. She saw much of what she had fought for in the last few years, much of what she had spent two months in a mental hospital for, going for nothing. I went over to her after the jury left and I asked her to walk outside in the corridor with me.

We walked around the green-walled corridor as I tried to put her at ease. I went to the three-foot-high water cooler to fill a paper cup full of water for her. A courtroom spectator, with his head lowered and his mouth at the spout, raised his eyes, saw me coming, stopped drinking and abruptly left the fountain.

I gave Mrs. Wright the water and tried to calm her. "You're doing fine. Try to really tell the jury what happened. I'll just ask short questions. I want you to give long, full answers." She said yes by moving her head up and down. Her jaws were locked with tension. She was so nervous she could barely hear me, let alone answer. We walked and talked until the clerk called, "Court's back in session."


Mrs. Wright resumed the stand. After the first few questions, we lapsed into the same pattern as before the recess. I tried to break it by asking her to demonstrate to the jury how Wages had pinned her arm behind her. I hoped this might animate her to show graphically what had been done to her. If I prodded, she might lose herself in the experience of what had happened.

She got up and was as rigid in body as she was in speech. She appeared not to hear the simplest directions. It didn't work. She was stiff, unconvincing, and was starting to become inaudible. I decided, some twenty minutes after she had resumed the stand, not to ask any more questions. Perhaps I could get some information before the jury from Mr. Wright. He could testify about his wife's treatment at the mental hospital, as well as about the arrest itself. It would not be as good secondhand, but it was the best we had.

There was another aspect to the problem. Mrs. Wright had

been involved in three incidents prior to this case, and I had planned for her to testify about them. The facts, if clearly explained, would not hurt us. If I did not bring the incidents up, the defendants were sure to, and both judge and jury would feel we had tried to hide them.

In 1962 Mrs. Wright, while moving a shotgun from a table, accidentally released the trigger while standing four feet from her husband and put a pellet into his thigh. In 1963 she was twice arrested by Wages for disorderly conduct. The first time, she and some friends had played music in her home and, according to Wages, a neighbor had complained. (The identity of the neighbor was never known.) A month later, she was arrested outside Wages's office. She had protested when Wages told her that her license to run a restaurant was being revoked because of her first arrest.

Mrs. Wright was in no condition at that moment to explain these incidents. I decided not to bring them up. In leaving them to the defense, I was giving away an important point, but I saw no alternative. I could, if necessary, call her back in rebuttal.

I left Mrs. Wright to the mercy of the cross-examiners. Jim Lewis looked at me in despair as I said, "I have no more questions at this time. That concludes the direct examination."

If the case went very badly, it would do all of us great harm. Jim and the other LCDC lawyers had previously appeared before Keady and would certainly be there again. It was important that Keady at least believe what they said. Their credibility before him could be impaired if they were trying an apparently worthless case. Mrs. Wright's response also made it seem that we had not prepared her and were trying the case cold, without a full investigation of the facts. Keady viewed a lawyer's responsibility to the courts seriously and would feel that the LCDC had been negligent.

The cross-examination began. I had no way of telling how good the defense lawyers would be. They had not asked questions of potential jurors in the jury selection, but simply exercised peremptory challenges. I didn't know how they felt about black people and whether their racial prejudices—to the extent they existed—would make them less objective in the handling of the case. Mrs. Wright's testimony had not hurt them, and they could produce six white witnesses each of whom would brand her a liar.

Grover Harris asked a few questions, got a few flat answers, and then, when Mrs. Wright did not understand some questions, made it seem that she was being evasive. He turned to the jury with his "what do you expect, she's black, can't believe her anyway" expression and sat down.

James Naughton rose, said, "I have no questions," and sat down. Judge Keady looked at the attorney sitting next to Naughton to see if he would question. William Leith got up to cross-examine, took some papers from his desk, and went to the lectern four feet away. I thought he would take the same line and ask as few questions as Harris had. I looked at the big-faced clock in the back of the courtroom. It was 4:20, and it looked as if Mrs. Wright would be through that afternoon.

I began to think about the next day's testimony. Tomorrow we had Mr. Wright and Dr. Jaquith, who had examined Mrs. Wright at Whitfield. Their testimony would take half the day. I could let the defense lawyers put each of the defendants on in defense, or I could put them on as part of plaintiff's case. If I called them, I would upset the routine of the defense case, probably rattle several of them, and, because of the uniqueness of the approach, get the jury involved and perhaps sympathetic. I could call them in the sequence I desired and throw hostile questions at them before they were fully prepared.

On the other hand, if I allowed the defense lawyers to question their clients first, I would hear in full the story they had contrived and then be able to examine them, rather than have the story sprung on me during my examination. Also, if they testified first in direct examination in response to their lawyers' questions, there would be more testimony and a greater possibility of inconsistencies in the defense testimony, and I would be in a position, as I watched each defendant testify, to judge if I would gain anything by cross-examining him or if I should let him go without any questions. I decided not to call the defendants to the stand.

Leith, a man with a round, froglike face, started to ask questions about Mrs. Wright's movements after she had left the voting booth. She didn't remember how long it took to drive the first three blocks, did not know how fast she was going one mile before she allegedly passed the stop sign. She didn't know how many minutes it was from the time she got to the car to the time she was at the stop sign. The rules of cross-examination permitted Leith to keep after her. He wouldn't let the questioning end with an "I don't remember." Mrs. Wright had just begun to react when Judge Keady said, "It's 4:30, gentlemen. Court will begin at 9:30 tomorrow."

Jim and I sat in the courtroom after everyone left. Jim said he would call Dr. Jaquith and have him in court by 10:30 tomorrow.

I said, "I can't believe that Leith is foolish enough to try and provoke Mrs. Wright. Nobody believes her now. He has nothing to gain by working her over, other than the pleasure he may give some of the people in the courtroom. If he starts to bully her, he may confuse her—she'll give some wrong answers; but the jury may identify with her as a badgered witness."

Leith, I think, believed he could humiliate and degrade Mrs. Wright. The cross-examiner bearing down on the witness has all the advantages. Leith had examined hundreds of witnesses; it was only the second time Mrs. Wright had been in a courtroom. He knew all the ground rules and the exceptions; she could barely understand them. Being abusive (to a point) is accepted practice.

You can abuse almost any witness into telling "the truth." You can take a witness who tries to hide behind "I don't remember" and make him feel so stupid about not remembering that he will give answers about things he never knew and about facts he could not possibly remember—anything, so that the cross-examiner will leave him alone and not hold him up to ridicule in the courtroom.

And when a witness guesses or starts to make up facts, it's easy to make it appear that he is lying. "Do you want this jury to believe that you can't even remember if the light was red when you came to it on Green Street, the street before the stop sign?" Thirty questions like this, if answered "I don't remember" (and how *could* Mrs. Wright remember minute details four years later), would make Mrs. Wright feel stupid, and the jurors would feel they were justified in doubting the truth of what she was saying.

Jim and I spent Tuesday evening at the Last Chance Café, preparing Mr. Wright's testimony. I hoped he could fill in the ground we hadn't been able to cover with his wife.

We returned to court Wednesday morning. Mrs. Wright took the stand and Leith got up to continue his cross-examination. He asked one or two questions about her driving out and returning home, and then, with a sardonic smile, started firing questions about what happened at the time of the arrest. His solid build lent sincerity and strength to his questions. This cross-examination should have taken five more minutes. It took five hours—all that morning and part of the afternoon. He leaned forward, hurling questions at Mrs. Wright with the full force of nearly every white person in the courtroom behind him, the full force of the towns of Oxford and Winona and the state of Mississippi. Each question was an accusation and each answer opened up avenues for more and more questions. Leith's goading cut through Mrs. Wright's nervousness. She stopped her "Yes" and "No" and "I don't remember" responses. Her pride was stung by the bullying lawyer. She started to give thoughtful answers.

A lawyer who feels he has to cross-examine a witness who

has damaged his client's case will often conduct a lengthy cross-examination and attempt to trip up the witness on minor points so that the jury will forget the critical facts revealed in the direct examination. This is called "a geography lesson"—a cross-examination of a witness at length about where he was when the murder or accident occurred, how many feet from one corner to another, how far from the street light, how far the street light was from the ground, and so forth.

A lawyer can destroy his own case by an extended cross-examination that fails, as he makes believable what had seemed false on direct examination. The lawyer's alternative is to leave the damaging witness alone, let his own witness tell a contrary version of the facts, and have the judge or jury decide which version is true. Here, Leith had six witnesses who would directly contradict the Wrights. Only perversity goaded him on. His voice rose.

"Now, is it not a fact that when Wages told you that you were under arrest, at that time you told him, 'I'm not going with no country bastard'?"

"No, I didn't say that."

"Is it not a fact that at that time, after he had told you that you were under arrest, you said, 'I'm not going into this case. I may have a gun in here and I might use it'?"

"I did not say that."

"Did you have a gun in the café at that time?"

"No, I did not."

"Did you have a gun in your living quarters?"

"I did not—"

"Now, when the sheriff came in the door, did you have your hands up on top of the counter or were they down at your side?"

"Down at my side."

"Did he tell you, 'Don't come out from behind that counter with any weapon or I'll have to shoot you if you do'?"

"No, he did not."

"He didn't say anything like that to you?"

"He didn't say anything to me; he did not say anything like that."

"What did he say to you?"

"When he poked the gun in my face, he said, 'Shut up your damn mouth and come on out behind there.' My husband said, 'Go 'head,' and he followed me down the counter with that gun in my face, and it's a little gate at the west end. When I opened the gate he leveled that gun down in my back, and one of the deputies, I don't know just which one, opened the door while he held the gun in my back, and just as I entered outside the door, Wayne—Deputy Miller—grabbed this arm right here—"

"He grabbed your right arm?"

"Right arm, and Deputy Cross grabbed the left arm, and twisted them up my back as far as they could get them and handcuffed me and shoved me in the back of the sheriff's car."

"Which car was it, the one that Wages drove up or the one that Miller drove up?"

"The one that Wages drove up."

"How far was it parked from your front door?"

"About as far as from the door is to that little fence over there where they are sitting, just about that far from my door."

"Now, you say that they grabbed your arms and handcuffed them behind your back?"

"They did."

"With one pair of handcuffs?"

"One pair of handcuffs."

"Is it not a fact that before and as they were leading you out of the door, and grabbed your arm, that you attempted to hit Deputy Cross?"

"I did not."

"Is it not a fact that during all of this occurrence, after you moved out the door, you were cursing and using vile and bad language to these officers?"

"I did not."

"Do you deny that?"

"I deny it."

"Now, where were you put in this car, on the front or back seat?"

"On the back seat. They shoved me into the back seat."

"Now, who drove the car?"

"I disremember who drove the car—"

"Now, is it not a fact that on your way from the café to the jail you continued to curse these officers, using such language as 'the sorry goddamned law around Winona'?"

"I did not."

"Is it not true that on your way from the café to the jail, that when you weren't cursing, you were singing a song that goes like this: 'It's going to cloud up one of these days and rain on you white son-of-a-bitches in Winona'?"

"I did not—"

"Now, you testified yesterday that Wages searched you in the booking room at this time?"

"He did."

"Are you positive about that?"

"Yes, I am."

"Do you deny that Mrs. Wages was the one that conducted the search on you?"

"After Sheriff Wages searched me and I told him—asked him for a searching warrant, then he sent Mrs. Wages to search me again. I was double-searched."

"All right, so Mrs. Wages did come in and search you."

"She did."

"Or she attempted to search you?"

"She searched me."

At this point, Leith turned to the judge: "May it please the court, reluctantly I am going to have to use some language that is profane, but in the interest of my clients I have no other choice."

The court gave him permission. He resumed his questioning.

"While Mrs. Wages was in the booking room, who else was there with you?"

"Sheriff Wages and Deputy Miller."

"Was Deputy Cross there?"

"Cross."

"So, in the booking room there was you, the sheriff's wife, Mrs. Wages, the sheriff, and Deputies Cross and Miller?"

"Right."

"And at the time Mrs. Wages was searching you, tell me where she first started to search on your body."

"Here."

"At that time did you tell Mrs. Wages, in the presence of these other people, 'Here, feel these big tits'?"

"I did not."

"You deny that?"

"I deny it."

"Do you deny at that time in her presence and in the presence of these officers that you placed your hand near your crotch and said, 'Feel down here, this is what's hot'?"

"I was handcuffed. I deny that because I was handcuffed."

"Is it not true, at the same time, and in the presence of Mrs. Wages and these officers, you said, 'If Mr. Miller wants some of this,'—patting your thigh—'why don't he ask for it like a man instead of coming by there and looking'?"

"I did not."

"Do you deny that?"

"I deny it."

"Did Mrs. Wages finish her search of you?"

"She did."

"Is it not a fact that she was so embarrassed that she walked out of there when you uttered these words?"

"No, she did not walk out. They carried me out—"

"You are sure that the handcuffs weren't taken off while you were in the booking room?"

"I am positive that they wasn't."

"Who opened the door and put you in the cell?"

"Deputy Miller."

"And at that time were you offered food by the sheriff?"

"No, I wasn't."

"Do you deny that?"

"I deny it."

"What did you do after you got in the cell?"

"I was handcuffed. They told me to back up to that window where they put the food in there, and then he unlocked the handcuffs and taken them through the window from my back."

"Is it not a fact that the sheriff told you that you could make bond and get out of jail?"

"No, he did not."

"And isn't it a fact that when he told you that, you said, 'I don't care if I stay here and rot'?"

"No, I did not."

"While they were there and after they had locked the cell door behind you, what did you do?"

"What did I do? I sat down on the bed."

"Is it not a fact that you got on the bunk and pulled your dress up to your waist?"

"I did not."

Mrs. Wright was fighting back. Her body was alive. She no longer slumped on the chair with her head down. She sat up, eyes blazing. Her large arms, which had hung lifelessly at her sides, were now folded in her lap. "This is terrific," Jim whispered to me as the morning wore on and it became apparent that Leith meant to continue.

A white man trying to abuse her—this Mrs. Wright could

contend with; this was all too familiar. She was aware of all that was happening, saw the implications of questions before they were asked, and gave Leith all the answers she wanted to give and those I wanted to hear.

In the first few minutes I had made several objections to give Mrs. Wright time to think out her answers, but I soon stopped. She no longer needed help. The further Leith went, the more she buried him. She began to recall all the details of the arrest, remembered each time the men had touched her, each indignity suffered at the jail. Outrage, humiliation, anger, poured forth. Each question tapped a deeper well of feeling. Leith's attempts to control her—to make her give "yes" or "no" answers, to get her to stop her long, emotional sentences—failed. The jury and Judge Keady were anxious to hear her testimony.

"Did you see them any more on the night of the twenty-sixth?"

"I did."

"When, and who did you see?"

"I saw Sheriff Wages and Sheriff Miller."

"What time was that?"

"Just as soon as they put me in there, after they slammed the door and went on around. They left the booking-room door open and I could see them, and they had hurt me so bad, and I called them to get a doctor. I called Sheriff Wages and he ignored me."

"How long did they stay in the booking room?"

"Well, I don't know, but I called Sheriff Wages and he ignored me, and about, I reckon, ten minutes later, Deputy Miller came to the cell door and I said, 'I wants a doctor, you all have hurt me.' He laughed and said, 'All the doctors are out of town.' And he slammed the door between my cell and the booking room and I didn't see any more of them until the next day."

"Did you see Sheriff Wages around ten o'clock that night, when the lights were turned off in the cell block?"

"No, I did not."

"Isn't it a fact that most of the night you cursed in a loud voice in that cell?"

"No, I did not."

"Now, let me direct your attention to August 27, the next day. Did you see Sheriff Wages at eight-thirty that morning, or approximately eight-thirty?"

"I did not."

"Now, you testified yesterday that sometime that morning Wages and a person that he told you his name was Grant attacked you in the cell, is that correct?"

"They did."

"Now, where were you in the cell when Wages and this other man came in?"

"In the bed."

"What was the condition and position of your clothes at this time? Of your dress and your skirt?"

"Well, it was down. I was just laying flat on my back."

"Did Wages come inside the cell?"

"He most certainly did."

"And there was some other man with him?"

"There was."

"What, if anything, was said to you by Wages at that time?"

"He says, 'You not going to see no doctor. You not going to see no doctor in my jail.' "

"Didn't they ask you to go back with them? Didn't Wages ask you to go with them up to the courthouse?"

"They did not."

"Then he started handcuffing you?"

"He says, 'I'm going to get you out of here if I have to drag you out.' "

"Did he tell you where he was going to take you?"

"He did not."

"Did he ask you to go anywhere with him?"

"He did not."

"Now, you testified that he put a handcuff on your right arm?"

"Right arm."

"Was he able to put it on your left arm?"

"No, he was not able to put it on the left arm."

"Why?"

"I was lying in the bed and he didn't get a chance to put it on the other arm, and that's when he dragged me off the bed."

"Well, why didn't he have a chance? Were you resisting him?"

"Sure, I resisted him."

"All right. Now, did you tell the jury yesterday in your testimony that he and this trusty climbed up in the bunk and got on top of you?"

"I—I did."

"When did you start resisting, as soon as they put the handcuff on your right arm?"

"No, when they got in the bed to drag me, to get the other arm, say, 'We gonna take you out of here.' But he didn't say where."

"But you didn't resist until he put the handcuff on the right arm?"

"That's right."

"And he wasn't in the bed with you when he put the handcuff on your right arm?"

"He was."

"He was up on top of you in the bed?"

"He was in the bed with me."

"How much room is there between these two bunks? You were on the lower bunk?"

"I was on the lower bunk."

"How were they holding you?"

"By getting up into my stomach, holding me down, just holding me up against the wall, any way they could hold me."

"How high were they holding your arms above your head?"

"They was twisting 'um back like this."

"They were unable to put the handcuff onto your left arm?"

"Yes, sir, they were."

"They were unable to fasten the other handcuff onto your left arm because you were resisting them?"

"Sure I was resisting them, if that's what you call it. I was trying to keep 'um from putting it on that other arm."

The hot Mississippi Wednesday in May wore on, with Mrs. Wright on the stand. We took our one-hour lunch break. Mrs. Wright couldn't wait to get back on the stand. I returned to court at 1:30 feeling as though I hadn't left it. I was euphoric.

The cross-examination continued:

"How much did you weigh on August 27, 1965?"

"I just really don't know. About 200, I would say."

"How much did Wages weigh, if you know, on that date?"

"Well, I really wouldn't know."

"How big was this man in there with him?"

"Just about the same size E. W. Wages was."

"Now, in truth and in fact, after Wages put the handcuffs on your right arm, then you pushed yourself out of the bed with your feet, did you not?"

"I did not."

"Now, after you got onto the floor of the cell, regardless of whether you were pulled down there or whether you pushed yourself down there, what did they do to you?"

"They jumped in my stomach and started pounding me with their knees and still twisting my arms and beating me against the floor, backward and forward on the floor."

"Did they beat you about your arms and legs?"

"They did."

"Now, you said yesterday that your wrist was torn?"

"That's right."

"On your right hand?"

"On both hands."

"And would you explain again to me, please, how your wrist looked after they got through with you that time?"

"The flesh was torn, bruises, the print of their fingers where they hit me, you see, it's swollen right now. They held me so tight, they twisted, they torned, they gripped, they brought the grip down, they print their fingers into my flesh."

"They actually tore your skin?"

"Tore my skin."

"It wasn't a matter of just being bruised, but it was—"

"On the wrists, it was on the wrists, but here I have bumps and knots right now. It's blood clots or whatever you might call it here and all up in here. I'm not even able to put my shoes on; my husband have to tie my shoes for me."

"Now, you mentioned your teeth, that they knocked out two front teeth?"

"Right. They are here, right here."

"Those two right there?"

"Right here."

"They did that that morning—"

"That morning."

"Now, these teeth that you claim were knocked out was a bridge, was it not?"

"It wasn't a bridge, what I'm talking about. They was welded to my real teeth. They was welded in there with gold into my other teeth."

"Were they fastened to such an extent that if someone pushed them out it would cause injury to your mouth?"

"That's right."

"Did your gums bleed?"

"Yes."

"They are still bruised?"

"They are still black bruises, at times they are bleeding from it right now—"

"The next people you saw was when all of them came in with the doctors?"

"Came together."

"How long was it after Wages and this other man left that these other people came in?"

"I would say exactly about—I would say twenty minutes."

"Do you recall any time that morning Wayne Miller serving you with a warrant to appear at a lunacy hearing?"

"I do not."

"Do you ever remember seeing any type of paper?"

"Not from Wayne Miller."

"Did you see any paper?"

"After the doctors came they threw a paper in there to me when I was laying on the floor."

"Now, did you stay on the floor from the time that Wages and this man left until the time that the doctors came in?"

"I did."

"Lying in the same position in relation to the door?"

"I did."

"Now, about twenty minutes later, who came in?"

"Deputy Sheriff—Sheriff Wages, Deputy Miller, Deputy Cross, Dr. Howard, Dr. Middleton and Highway Patrolman Morgan, and the little man that he said was Deputy Grant, whoever he was."

"Did you testify yesterday that before August 27, 1965, you knew both Dr. Middleton and Dr. Howard?"

"I knew Dr. Howard."

"But you didn't know Dr. Middleton?"

"I did not."

"Isn't it a fact that one of the doctors came to the door and asked you were you hurt, what was wrong with you?"

"They was all standing there when he asked me that. I could hear them talking but I couldn't see who was standing there. Yes—"

"Did you answer him?"

"I told him I was hurt. I said, 'The laws have hurt me.' And he says, whichever doctor it was says, 'If you was acting right they wouldn't have to manhandle you.' That's when he threw that paper in there to me."

"Oh, so the doctor threw the paper in?"

"I guess it was. I don't know who threw it, whether it was the doctor or who threw it in there."

"Now, were you still lying in there on the floor?"

"I was lying on the floor."

"Were you able to get up?"

"No, I wasn't."

"Is it not a fact that when the first doctor started talking to you, and asked you how you were and said that he wanted to examine you, that you told him words to this effect, that 'No goddamned doctor is going to examine my black ass'?"

"They didn't even offer to examine me."

"You did not say those words?"

"I did not say that."

"So seven people came into the cell?"

"Seven peoples."

"Did you see anyone else there?"

"Well, I didn't see anyone, because I was lying on the floor. That's all I seen, was the ones that came in the cell."

"Is it not a fact that as they entered the cell you wheeled around and backed up into a corner and threatened them with the loose handcuff on your right arm?"

"No, I did not. I couldn't get up."

"You did not swing that at Dr. Howard?"

"No, I did not."

"Or at any other of these people?"

"No, I didn't."

"Now, how did they hold you?"

"Well, they just grabbed me and all of them got on me, and Deputy Miller kicked me on my right ankle."

"Did that leave any bruises?"

"It's a bruise now. A big knot sets on it right now."

"Well, were they able to sit you up?"

"Well, then after I said, 'I don't need no shot,' they threw me back on the floor. They slammed me around and drug my head against the wall, and as they went to slam back, my head hit the wall."

"Now, who all was holding you?"

"Six peoples was holding me in my stomach. They had me covered up and they was just holding me any way they could, twisting my arm."

"How high did they have the left arm?"

"Just about as high as I got it. I was laying on the floor, high enough for them to stick the needle right here. That was the onliest part of me that was out."

"Now, you testified yesterday, I believe, that these six people laid you down on the floor and sat on top of you while they gave you the shot."

"I know they did. They was on top of me, that's what I said. I was flat on my back on the floor. They slammed me back against that wall on the floor."

"And all six of these people were sitting on you?"

"Yes, any way they could get a place to hold or sit."

"Now, did anyone strike you while they were holding you, or were they just holding you?"

"Miller kicked me. I told you he kicked me."

"Other than Miller, did anybody strike you at this time?"

"No more than they slammed me against the wall, that's the onliest thing. And it hit my head right here, and I still have headaches from that. When they slammed me back, they was forcing me more than they thought they was, and they hit my head up against that—those bricks."

"Were you resisting them at this time that they were trying to hold you?"

"I was. My arms, sure—yes, I was."

"And they gave you a shot?"

"They said, 'Get her,' and they did. All of them grabbed me, and they did give me a shot."

"Who said 'Grab her'?"

"One of the officers. I don't know which one it was 'cause I couldn't see."

"Did they turn you loose after they gave you the shot?"

"When they give me the shot, they handcuffed me, see?"

"Isn't it a fact that they turned you loose and the doctor got out and you struck Deputy Cross with that loose handcuff?"

"No, they carried me out."

"They didn't carry you out as soon as they gave you the shot, did they?"

"They did. They did, they carried me out."

"Now, at this time, if I am correct, you had been hurt in the mouth, the bridge had been knocked out?"

"Right."

"Your lips were bruised and bleeding, along with your upper gums?"

"Yes, they had been bruised and bleeding just like you—it would stop for a little while; it wasn't dripping blood."

"And that was the condition you were in when you got to the Mississippi State Hospital at Whitfield?"

"That's right. That's right."

"How long did you stay at Whitfield?"

"Almost two months. I don't know exactly the date. I think from August the 27th to about October the 19th, somewhere like that. I'm not for sure."

"They discharged you sometime around October 19?"

"In October, yes, they did."

"When you went to Whitfield that day, you had a conversation with Dr. Modina Petersen, I believe. At that time at Whitfield did you tell Dr. Petersen that officers had arrested you on August 26 and that you had resisted arrest?"

"I didn't tell her I had resisted arrest. I told her they had arrested me and what the charges was."

"Did you tell her that you had resisted arrest?"

"It wasn't resisting arrest. It was running a stop sign."

Leith kept going. Judge Keady looked at him, astonished that he would keep on. I was surprised that the three other defense lawyers had not succeeded in stopping Leith.

The afternoon passed as had the morning, with Leith going back and forth over answers in an attempt to contradict Mrs. Wright. Though occasionally confused, Mrs. Wright often remembered detailed facts with precision. Leith finished his questioning at a few minutes after four. Mrs. Wright left the stand victorious.

Court time is strange for me. After I've been on trial in a new courtroom for more than a day, I always feel as if I've been in that courtroom for months. This case required a total absorption in a constantly changing situation for eight hours a day, in addition to two or three hours of preparation for that day, and five hours for the next. I had often before been in complicated six-week anti-trust trials, or long murder trials, but those cases are prepared gradually over months. Each day that we were on trial in Oxford we'd be at work shortly before 6:00 A.M., writing out the direct and cross-examinations of the witnesses to be called that day. We had to think about the facts we wanted to prove and determine how to present them to the jury, and which facts, if any, we did not want to call to the jury's attention.

Each evening we would try to find and then prepare the next day's witnesses. We would go over that day's testimony to make sure we had introduced all the facts (or had kept out those that might hurt us). Occasionally, when an important witness testified or when there was a complex legal argument, we ordered the daily transcript. I learned long ago not to rely on my memory about the exact wording of a sentence drawn out in an intensive examination. Often a witness will make a critical statement in an offhand manner, perhaps as part of another statement, and it will not be pursued immediately. I look at the testimony on the printed page in the evening, and if my client has been hurt, I try to devise a plan to minimize the damage. It may mean calling new witnesses. It may mean exploring that phase further with the witnesses after I have carefully laid out a cross-examination plan. Or it may mean leaving the answer alone until my summation, when it is too late for my opponent to explore the answer further.

The daily transcript is important for other reasons. It is difficult, at the end of a long trial, for the jury to remember many of the facts. In summing up, I always tell a jury to rely on their recollection of the facts. However, if I can read critical testimony from the daily transcript, they will not only take as true what the transcript says but will appreciate my efforts to get an accurate account of the testimony for them.

I knew that the defendants in this case were ordering daily transcripts. I did not want them to have Mrs. Wright's testimony before them as they examined her husband. They could easily make it appear that he was contradicting portions of his wife's testimony. I wanted him to testify today.

Judge Keady said, "It's near the end of the day. Shall we adjourn now?"

"I have a witness," I replied. "He will be finished, I'm sure, before the end of the day, and I thought we might use the remaining time for him."

"Fine. I'd like to use all the available time. Call your witness, Mr. Garbus."

I called Mr. Wright to the stand. Now that Mrs. Wright had testified fully, there was no need to keep Mr. Wright on the stand too long and expose him to days of cross-examination.

I asked Mr. Wright only three questions: whether his wife was in any way violent or abusive before or after the arrest; what her condition was when he saw her sitting in the car on her way to Whitfield; and what conversations he had had with her in Whitfield. I wanted to show that there was no reason for her to have been kept in a mental institution for two months. He gave the answers I wanted. The direct examination took less than three minutes.

Grover Harris began the cross-examination.

"Mr. Wright, didn't your wife once shoot you?"

I objected. "This is not proper cross-examination. He is limited by the scope of my direct examination and can't go to new areas."

"No, I'll allow it. It may go to the reasonableness of having Mrs. Wright put in Whitfield and keeping her there. Objection overruled," Judge Keady said. Mr. Wright answered the question "no."

Harris looked at a sheaf of official-looking papers as he continued. "Didn't your wife once take a shotgun and try to kill you?"

"No."

Harris looked at the papers before him once more. He looked at Mr. Wright as if the witness were lying. He tried to make it seem to the jury that he was reading from the papers before him.

"Weren't you, in 1961, admitted to a hospital with a bullet in your thigh?"

"Yes."

The jury believed that Harris had been reading from the hospital record and that Mr. Wright had been trapped into admitting what it seemed he was trying to deny.

"Would you mind telling the judge and jury if that bullet came from a shotgun?"

"Yes."

"And was that shotgun then being handled by your wife?"

"Not exactly."

"What do you mean, 'not exactly'? Did she or didn't she have her hands on the gun when you were shot?"

"Yes."

Harris should have stopped there, but the temptation to show the jury that Mr. Wright was a liar was irresistible. We had discussed this with Mr. Wright the evening before and prepared him to answer quickly to get in the true version of what had happened. Technically, Harris could stop him after a "yes" or "no" answer, but Harris had to be quicker than Wright to do that.

"So you were lying before when you said your wife hadn't tried to shoot you?"

"No, I wasn't." Wright continued, "My wife doesn't know how to shoot a gun. She picked up my shotgun, was moving it when it accidentally went off, putting a bullet in my leg." The answer came out too quickly for the lawyer to shut it off.

Harris, with the hospital record in front of him, knew these were the facts as given back in 1962 when Mr. Wright was taken to the hospital. Harris turned to the jury, his face changing from a scowl of anger to a smile of condescension, as if to say, "That is what black people do to one another—and *they're* suing *us*." He then said, "No further questions."

Leith, Hobbs, and Naughton told the judge they had no questions. Mr. Wright was excused, and Judge Keady adjourned court for the day.

That evening Jim Lewis and I drove out to Winona to get other witnesses to testify about other beatings Wages had been involved in and about the state of Mrs. Wright's health prior to the beatings. We went to the home of Mrs. Hopkins, Mrs. Wright's neighbor, a courageous woman who was a leader of the black community. Her children had been the first to go to schools attended by white children. For this, they and their mother had often been beaten. Her dingy wooden frame home, set in the middle of a soaking clay field, housed ten people, most of whom were related to her.

We arrived at dinnertime. The house, heated by a gas heater in nearly every room, was intensely hot and smelled of gas and house-cleaning materials. Plates of food were in the various rooms—on radiators, beds, and chairs—as the people in the house were eating. Mrs. Hopkins was a small, sixty-year-old woman, who looked as if she might have been taller at one time but was now hunched over, not from age but from her beatings.

Mrs. Hopkins, her voice barely audible, told us about a visit she'd had from Sheriff Wages. He and Deputy Sheriff Miller drove up one black, moonless evening with shotguns drawn and got out of the car with their guns pointed. The Hopkinses looked out the windows, saw Wages, and knew there would be trouble. Mrs. Hopkins went out to meet them. Wages, in a rage, said he was looking for one of Mrs. Hopkins's sons who had written a bad check.

Mrs. Hopkins, standing in the door, told them her son wasn't in the house. They grabbed her by the arm and threw her away from the doorway, and they kept her and her husband outside in the yard while they ransacked the house. They did not have a warrant, did not have the "right" to manhandle Mr. and Mrs. Hopkins, and did not have a right to enter, let alone destroy, the house. Mrs. Hopkins knew there was no bad check. It was just an excuse. They drove off when their rage was spent.

I decided not to call Mrs. Hopkins as a witness. The jury would not find Wages's behavior too disturbing. Perhaps more significant was her long record of civil-rights arrests, which would be brought out if she testified. We saw some other potential witnesses that evening, but for similar reasons we decided not to call them.

The following day I called Dr. William L. Jaquith to the stand. A courtly, dignified gentleman, he had examined Mrs.

Wright several times at Whitfield. I wanted his testimony to show the jury that there was no reason to put Mrs. Wright in Whitfield.

Dr. Jaquith was defensive and would, I knew, try to equivocate, for he was partially responsible for keeping Mrs. Wright there after his examination showed that she should have been released. I had gone to Whitfield and met with him before he took the stand. He was going to be as truthful as he could without casting blame on the defendants or on Dr. Modina Petersen, who, as the first to examine Mrs. Wright, was primarily responsible for keeping her at Whitfield.

Dr. Jaquith's qualifications were brought out. A 1940 graduate of the St. Louis University School of Medicine, he interned at Charity Hospital in New Orleans, Louisiana, and then, from 1941 to 1947, served in the United States Navy. He became Director of Whitfield in July 1949, and this was the position he held when I examined him.

Dr. Jaquith testified that the Whitfield hospital record showed Mrs. Wright was quiet on admission and cooperative, not violent and not depressed while in the hospital. I then asked him: "Dr. Jaquith, based upon the history that was given, the admission notes, patient's course of behavior as reported in the hospital record—all of which you have examined—the reports of the examining psychiatrist, and your own examination of the patient, do you have an opinion, based upon a reasonable degree of medical certainty, as to whether or not this patient was psychotic on October 14, 1965, when you saw her?"

"She was not psychotic, and I so certified in the record. My medical opinion was that she was mentally alert."

"Do you have an opinion, based upon a reasonable degree of medical certainty, as to whether or not this patient was psychotic upon admission on August 27?"

"I could only say, from reading the record, that Dr. Petersen, who is a very capable physician, found her to be not mentally ill at that time. That is all I could go by."

out calmly and smoothly. He said he had driven up to the Las Chance Café and assisted in the arrest. He had pulled up afte Wages, had heard Wages tell Mrs. Wright she was under ar rest, and had heard her say she was going inside to get a gun Mrs. Wright had stomped into the restaurant yelling an shouting. Wages had drawn his gun and gotten her out of th café. Miller said Wages had told him the woman had waved th gun around inside and threatened him.

Mrs. Wright was violent when Wages brought her out o the café, according to Miller. She cursed and tried to hi Wages and Miller, so that, in order to protect themselves, the had to put handcuffs on her. Her abusiveness, intemperate be havior, and cursing, and the fact that she had shot her husband a few years before, Miller testified, convinced him that there was something wrong with her.

Miller added another fact. He had been present at Mrs. Wright's disorderly-conduct arrest. He testified to her loud, angry manner. "She was yelling at the High Sheriff," he said, making it sound like one of the seven deadly sins. After she had paid her fine, she had walked out into the middle of the street for no apparent reason, Miller testified. "I thought it was ab- normal," he volunteered. The judge sustained my objection to the testimony, but the jury had already heard it.

Miller added the most important new element to the defense case, in response to his lawyer's questioning.

"Did you see C.W. at the jail the evening of the arrest?" Leith asked.

"Objection. His name is Mr. Wright."

"Reframe your question, sir. Objection sustained."

"Did you see Mr. Wright at the jail the evening of the ar- rest?"

"Yes."

"Did Mr. Wright talk to you that evening?"

"Yes."

"What did he say?"

"And the determination that you made was that she was not insane?"

"That's right, and we so certified back to the court—"

Leith began his cross-examination. He knew Jaquith's testi- mony had hurt his clients and he tried to show that Jaquith was wrong and that Mrs. Wright could be insane.

"Doctor, I refer you to Plaintiff's Exhibit 7, entitled 'Family History.' I believe you just testified that in your examination you try to get the family history and consider a lot of things in making your diagnosis. The family history shown on Plaintiff's Exhibit 7 indicates that plaintiff's grandmother, Jane Furnell, was in Whitfield, does it not?"

"Yes."

"What was the diagnosis of her condition?"

"Simple psychosis."

"Did you take that into consideration when you made your study of the individual?"

"No. This particular type of illness is one that is brought on by age, and hereditary factors are not in this one, such as they would be in a manic condition or schizophrenia. This is one of age and organic changes."

"But would it not be something that should be considered in examinations to determine whether or not a person was suffer- ing from psychosis—the family history?"

"The family history is important, that's true. But in this par- ticular instance it would not be pertinent to Henrietta Wright."

"You did not consider that in your study of the patient?"

"Not as a hereditary factor."

"Dr. Jaquith, are you not familiar with cases that have been diagnosed as being without psychosis and later have been found to be suffering from psychosis after discharge from Mis- sissippi State Hospital?"

"I don't claim any infallibility. We are subject to human error."

"And there have been cases?"

"There have been cases that I have had where I missed the diagnosis, that's correct."

"In other words, it's just a difficult field?"

"It's a difficult field—"

After Leith finished his cross-examination, I told the judge we rested our case. Before the defense lawyers could get up to present motions to dismiss, Judge Keady said, "Let's have the motions back in chambers. Court is adjourned for ten minutes." This was a critical moment. We had presented all the proof we had. Judge Keady, on defendants' motion to dismiss, would rule whether we had stated a claim against each defendant. If we had not, our case would be dismissed against that defendant.

We were required to show that each person we were suing had been involved in the beatings and hospitalization. Mrs. Wright had difficulty in telling exactly who it was that punched and beat her. The biggest problem, however, would be to resist the doctors' motions. The doctors' lawyers would claim that the doctors had no knowledge of the beatings, that they saw an angry, upset woman and ordered her committed on the basis of the history given by the sheriffs and patrolman.

We all filed into Judge Keady's chambers. Leith, Hobbs, and Naughton made motions to dismiss against their clients on the grounds of failure of proof.

Harris (representing the doctors) got up: "Your Honor, I want to submit a legal memorandum showing why the case against the doctors must be dismissed at this time." He handed the court and each of the lawyers a detailed brief.

It was getting dark outside, and as the briefs were being handed out, I looked out the window on the right side of the large room. I could see miles and miles of flat land, now darkening as evening approached. The Wrights, sitting in a courtroom where few blacks had sat before, would in a few days be having their dinner at about this time. What would they be feeling then, after the trial? Were we right even though we knew there was no chance of w we thought the case should be tried? Is there rea be gained by losing? What would Wages and Mil rest do to the Wrights after that?

Harris repeated his request for dismissal, pointi the doctors had been appointed by the court to investigation and had been acting as officers of the judge could not be held liable for making a mista course of his official duties; neither, therefore, could of the court. Before I could respond, Judge Keady s reserve decision on the motion until after the defe case." Harris was stunned. This meant the case would go jury with the doctors still as defendants. We left the j chambers and returned to the courtroom, and Judge K adjourned until the following day.

The defense began the next morning. Leith called Sheri Wayne Miller as his first witness. Through an oversight by ou lawyer in preparing the case, Wayne Miller had not been sued. The mistake had implications. Leith was going to show that Miller, an "objective" person (because he was not a party to the lawsuit), confirmed all the things his clients would say later.

It soon became clear that the defendants were not going to be content with denying the brutality. They were going to come up with a new reason for Mrs. Wright's incarceration in Whitfield for two months in 1965—a reason that had never once been mentioned in the four years between the arrest and the trial, one that would fit in nicely with the fact that Mr. Wright had a bullet in his leg in 1962, a reason that would rule out any liability on the part of the defendants for keeping Mrs. Wright in Whitfield for forty-nine days.

Sheriff Miller, a blond, crew-cut, well-built six-footer with square features, spoke directly to the jury. His answers came

"Old C.W. came to jail that evening, told us his wife was acting crazy, had once before shot him with a gun, and asked us to put her away. Said he was afraid of her and that Whitfield would be good for her."

"Did you tell the doctors that morning that Mr. Wright wanted her put away?"

"Yes."

I cross-examined the witness. I tried to show he was lying by contrasting his testimony in court with testimony given in his pretrial examination several years before. Surprisingly, he hadn't been shown that testimony before he went to the witness stand.

"Sheriff Miller, you previously testified that after you came up to the Last Chance Café and placed Mrs. Wright under arrest she became violent, is that right?"

"That's right."

"She started to become violent outside the café?"

"That's right."

"This was before you put her into the car, is that right?"

"That is right."

"And will you describe how she became violent?"

"She started cussing us and swinging her arms in order to strike us."

"Do you recall testifying in this case in the deposition back in Jackson?"

"I do."

"Were you under oath then as now?"

"Yes."

"Did you swear to tell the truth then before a notary public?"

"Yes."

"Were you represented by a lawyer then?"

"Yes."

"Did you go over your testimony then with your lawyers before you testified, as you did today?"

"Yes."

"I am now referring to page 26 of that deposition:

> Q. What did you do with her then?
> A. Put her in Sheriff Wages's patrol car.
> Q. And then what happened?
> A. We proceeded to the jail with Mrs. Wright and Mr. Cross in his car.
> Q. Had Mrs. Wright been violent at any time up to that point?
> A. Not violent.

"Do you recall those questions and answers?"

The witness did not answer.

I raised my voice: "Sheriff Miller, do you recall those questions and answers?"

"I recall the deposition."

"Were you telling the truth then back in Jackson or were you lying then back in Jackson?"

"It has been a long time since those depositions were given."

"I am sure it has been. Were you telling the truth back in Jackson—"

"I was."

". . . when you said she wasn't violent at any time prior to getting to jail?"

"I was."

"You previously testified that she walked out to the car and then she started to hit and strike you and Cross, and that after she did that you put handcuffs on her to protect yourselves—that she had started the trouble. Is that right?"

"That's right."

"It wasn't that first you put the cuffs on and then, in reaction to your roughing her up, she tried to defend herself?"

"No, sir."

"Do you recall the following questions and answers at your

examination before trial in 1966, six months after this happened?

> *Q.* Did she attempt to strike you and the sheriff or Mr. Cross at that time?
> *A.* Yes, she did.
> *Q.* How did she do that?
> *A.* When we were placing the handcuffs on her, she drew back and hit Mr. Cross.
> *Q.* Had she tried to hit you before?
> *A.* No.

"Do you recall saying that?"

"Yes, sir."

"Were you telling the truth in Jackson or were you lying in Jackson?"

"I was telling the truth in Jackson."

"Now, have you had any conversation with the lawyers or anybody since 1966 to make you change your testimony about the time you placed the handcuffs on her and whether or not she was violent when you took her out to the car?"

"No, sir, I have not."

"Prior to the time you came here to testify in the last few days, did you discuss this case or your testimony with your lawyers?"

"I don't have a lawyer."

"You can, since you are not a party, talk to any of the lawyers in the case about what happened. Did you discuss your testimony with me or Mr. Lewis before you came here?"

"I did not."

"Did you discuss it with one of these four gentlemen sitting at the defense table?"

"All the lawyers."

"All the lawyers. And these are the lawyers that represent Sheriff Wages and Dr. Howard and Dr. Middleton, is that right?"

"That's right, sir."

"Were all four lawyers together?"

"That's right, sir."

"They went over your testimony with you?"

"Yes."

"Were the defendants there at the same time?"

"Yes."

"Did you hear their testimony?"

"Yes."

"And by the time you left the lawyers' office, was all the testimony nearly the same?"

"Yes."

"You testified on direct examination that you served papers on Mrs. Wright because that is what the statute requires. Do you know the requirements of the statute, Sheriff Miller?"

"Yes, sir, I do."

"Now, will you tell me how you served these papers on her?"

"I handed the lunacy warrant to the plaintiff."

"Where was she at that time?"

"She was in the jail cell at the county jail."

"Did she read that warrant?"

"I do not know."

"Was she lying on the floor?"

"Yes, sir, that's right."

"You either threw it in on the floor or you gave it to her while she was on the floor, but you don't know whether she read it or not, is that right?"

"I handed the warrant to her."

"You want this jury to believe she was lying on the floor and she reached up to take the warrant?"

The witness did not answer.

"Do you know whether she read it or not?"

"I do not know."

"Did you ever tell her that she had a right to have people testify at that hearing about the state of her sanity?"

Harris objected, but Judge Keady overruled him. I repeated the question.

"Did you tell her when you served her that she had a right to have people at the lunacy hearing to testify in her behalf?"

"I was not required to tell her anything."

"You previously stated you knew the 'requirements of the statute.' Do you know that the law with respect to lunacy hearings requires that the person be informed that she can have people testify in her behalf?"

"I was advised to hand her the warrant."

"That wasn't the question. Answer my question."

He glared at me but did not answer.

"I see. In other words, you know part of the statute perfectly and the other parts you don't know at all. Is that what you want the jury to believe?"

Again, he did not answer.

"You testified previously she had hit a lot of people. Did she ever hit you?"

"She did not."

"You also testified previously that she went in to get the gun when Wages approached her. Correct?"

"My testimony is that she said that she had a gun and she might use it, and she then went into the café."

"Then, as I understood your testimony, you stood out in the yard for ten or fifteen minutes while you waited for Sheriff Wages, is that right?"

"That's correct."

"How many feet from the window facing you did you stand and wait?"

"Twenty-five feet."

"Where were you standing?"

"Beside my car."

"Were you between the car and the window?"

"Yes."

"And was your car in the driveway?"

"That is right."

"Is the driveway about twenty-five feet from the front of the café?"

"That is right."

"Can the bullet from a .38 revolver travel twenty-five feet?"

"Yes."

"Didn't you think it was a little dangerous to allow this woman, whom you say you know is crazy and had previously shot her husband, to walk in to get a gun and for you to stand exposed in the yard twenty-five feet away for ten or fifteen minutes?"

"I stayed far enough back so that I was not in great danger."

"Is that what you want this jury to believe? That you left yourself exposed like that?"

"I felt that I was not in great danger at that time."

"Even though this very violent, very hostile woman went in to get a gun?"

"That's right."

"Now, this whole business about the violence and the fighting and the obscenity and Mr. Wright's story to take her away, that is all just made up. It's a lie, isn't it, Sheriff?"

"It is not."

"None of that ever happened. It was just made up in the lawyer's office?"

"No."

"Did you ever, in 1967, 1968, or 1969, tell Dr. Middleton that Mr. Wright had asked that his wife be put away?"

"I did not."

"Did you ever tell that to Dr. Howard prior to trial?"

"I did not."

"Did you ever tell that to the admitting physician at Whitfield?"

"I did not."

"The first time you said it was when you testified in this court, is that right?"

"It was not."

"Did you ever say it at your deposition back in Jackson, in 1966?"

"Yes, I believe I did."

"You believe you did. Would you care to show me where in your deposition of some seventy-five pages you ever said that you told any of the doctors Mr. Wright had ever requested that this woman be put in an institution?"

I handed Miller the transcript of the deposition. He read it and could not find any place in it where he had told of Mr. Wright's asking for the confinement of Mrs. Wright. Miller glared at me.

I put the question again: "All right now, let's go back. Is there anything in your deposition—given six months after the arrest, when you were asked by plaintiff's lawyers and these four lawyers sitting here today to tell all that had happened—is there anything in your deposition about telling Dr. Howard, Dr. Middleton, or Dr. Petersen about C. W. Wright having asked to have his wife committed?"

"No sir."

"Your previous answer was false?"

The jury, realizing he was lying, leaned forward to hear the answer. Miller, teeth pressed together, body thrust forward as if he were going to leap at me, did not answer the question. After a few seconds, when it was clear to everyone in the courtroom that Miller was so livid with anger that he would not answer unless the judge directed him to do so, I turned toward my seat and said, "No more questions."

Donald Cross, a lean man with a large Adam's apple under a thin face, was the next witness. His testimony, under direct examination, was the same as Miller's. I knew now that I must go tortuously over each bit of testimony to show that the witness was lying. On my cross-examination of Cross, I tried to show that, because Mrs. Wright had been beaten, the law officers ignored the usual procedure of taking the accused before a judge. Then I used Cross's previous testimony, given at the examination before trial, to demonstrate that the testimony he was now giving was false. He clutched the arms of the witness chair as I started.

"Did you at any time make a call to contact any judge with respect to the criminal proceedings that were then lodged against Mrs. Wright?"

"I did not."

"Did you make any attempt to bring her before any judge that day?"

"I did not."

"Was any attempt made by anyone, to your knowledge, to bring her before the judge on Friday?"

"No."

"Was she brought before any judge before about October 20, some two months after this happened?"

"I don't recall."

"In other words, you brought her into jail and she was never brought before a judge for some two months as a result of her criminal arrest, is that right?"

"I believe she was confined at Whitfield at that time."

"Will you give me a 'yes' or 'no' answer?"

"No. We never took her to a judge."

"Now, Mr. Cross, as I recollect your direct testimony, you said she called you a 'white son-of-a-bitch.' "

"Right."

"You remember that clearly today, don't you, because you're not called that too often and it would stick in your mind?"

"Right."

"Have you ever testified in any other proceeding against Mrs. Wright?"

"I believe I testified in circuit court in a case involving Mrs. Wright at one time, yes."

"That was the criminal proceeding that arose out of this incident, where she was charged with reckless driving after she registered to vote, is that right?"

"Yes, sir."

Cross, having spoken a few words with Miller before he took the stand, knew I was going to use that testimony to bring out whatever inconsistencies there were. His disgust for me increased as the noose was slowly drawn. Through my questioning I tried to build a bit of suspense for the answer to come. Cross gave the time and date of his testimony in the criminal court, admitted that he was under oath and that he had spoken to a lawyer before he testified.

"When you were asked this question—at her criminal trial— did you give this answer? I am now refering to page 33:

> *Q.* But she didn't call you 'White son-of-a-bitch,' did she?
> *A.* No.

"Do you remember giving that answer?"

"I don't remember it, no. I would have to read the statement."

"Well, you take a look at the record and see if that is your testimony in the criminal court."

He looked at the testimony. "If it is in the record, I must have said it."

"Were you telling the truth then when you testified in the criminal court, or are you telling the truth now?"

"I guess I was mistaken now."

"Now, Mr. Cross, is it your testimony that she started to strike you when you were leaving the Last Chance Café and then you put the handcuffs on her?"

"Yes."

"Do you recall giving these answers in the criminal court:

> *Q.* And on this striking you testified about, I believe you said she struck with the left arm, you had her right arm handcuffed and she struck with her left arm?
>
> *A.* I don't remember exactly which arm the cuffs were on, the free arm is the one she struck with. Now, whether it was the left or the right, I don't remember.
>
> *Q.* And this striking was after she had the cuffs on one of her two arms, is that correct?
>
> *A.* That's right.

"Do you recall giving those answers in the criminal court?"

"There is a possibility that—"

"There is a possibility? Mr. Marshall, will you show the witness the transcript? Take a look at the transcript and see if those were your answers, Mr. Cross."

"Well, I did."

"You were telling the truth when you testified in the criminal court?"

"Sure."

"The striking was after you put the handcuffs on her, is that right?"

He refused to admit he had lied, but it was apparent to everyone in the courtroom. I left that point and continued. I tried to show that every aspect of the defense was false and that part of it had been manufactured in the lawyer's office. I wanted the jury to feel, if not a sense of rage, at least that the defendants and their lawyers were now lying.

"The striking was after you put the handcuffs on?"

"Yes."

"Did Miller tell you when you got there she had a gun?"

"He told me that, yes, he surely did."

"Did you find any gun in there on Thursday night?"

"We didn't have authority to—"

"I asked you whether or not you found the gun on Thursday night, Mr. Cross."

"Without a search warrant we didn't search for one."

"Mr. Cross, do you know how to answer a question with a 'yes' or 'no'?"

"Yes."

"Did you find the gun?"

"No."

"You say you can't search before you have a search warrant?"

"Right."

"Were you in jail when Mrs. Wright was searched by Mrs. Wages?"

"Right."

"Did she have a search warrant?"

"She didn't have to."

"She didn't need one to make a personal search over the witness's body?"

"She was under arrest."

I wanted Miller to admit that it was not uncommon for black women of Oxford to suffer the indignities Mrs. Wright had been subjected to at the hands of the High Sheriff. In the question, I changed the sex of the person conducting Mrs. Wright's examination. I knew the question could be stopped by an objection, but I asked it anyway, walking toward my seat at the counsel table in order to encourage the defense lawyers to relax, thinking my last question was a throwaway. I wanted the image that the answer would elicit to remain with the jury.

"And that permits a male officer to place his hands all over a black lady's body, her breast, her thighs, and her buttocks?"

"That's right."

"I have no further questions."

Highway Patrolman Billy Morgan, another powerfully built

young man, testified that he had come to the scene as Wages entered the café to make the arrest. He drove back to the jail with Mrs. Wright in the car. Although his direct testimony was full and detailed, there was one question his lawyers did not ask him: Did Mrs. Wright have a gun when arrested?

I began my cross-examination.

"Now, on Thursday evening, when you were called to her house, did Deputy Sheriff Miller tell you that Mrs. Wright said she had a gun?"

"No, sir."

"You didn't hear anything about a gun that evening?"

"No, sir, I didn't."

"No one on Thursday evening, August 26, said that Mrs. Wright had a gun, is that right?"

"That's correct, sir."

"When was the first time you heard anything about Mrs. Wright having a gun on that evening?"

"The first I knew of her having a gun was in court."

"You never knew about her having a gun that evening—"

"No, sir."

"—until you came to court three days ago?"

"That's correct, sir."

"I have no other questions."

Dr. Howard was called next. A middle-aged man with eyes like colorless lenses, he bounded to the witness stand and said, on direct examination, that he had been called to the jail by the chancery clerk, made an examination of Mrs. Wright, and determined she should be placed in Whitfield. He had given Mrs. Wright an "official examination." "There were no physical signs indicating she had been beaten, nor were there any teeth missing," he said. "There were some minor bruises on her," but, according to Dr. Howard, Sheriff Wages told him, "She did it to herself when she was thrashing about."

I cross-examined him.

"Dr. Howard, you testified, on your direct examination, that you gave an official examination to Mrs. Wright and none of her teeth were missing, is that right?"

"Apparent to me."

"It wasn't apparent to you. That wasn't what you said before. How close were you to her face?"

"I was about a yard from her."

"From three feet away you didn't see any teeth missing?"

"No."

"Her mouth wasn't closed the whole time she was there, was it?"

"No."

"How good is your eyesight, sir?"

"Very good, sir."

"Very good. From that distance you should have been able to see if her mouth was bloody and if any teeth were missing, shouldn't you?"

"I believe that's right."

"Did you know that the dentist who examined Mrs. Wright at Whitfield on Friday, two hours after your examination, found two teeth missing?"

"If I had made the same examination the dentist did I might have seen things, but I didn't see anything. I don't know anything about that, no, sir."

The doctor considered himself a cut above the officers and patrolman. It was more important to show that he was not being truthful than to show how unprofessional he had been. Because of his standing in the community and because of the glances we had exchanged when passing one another in the courtroom, he expected me to treat him with the deference of one professional to another. He knew now that his expectations were wrong.

"Now, Doctor, that Friday morning you took the history of the arrest and the lady's background from Mr. Wages?"

"Yes."

"And he told you, as I recall, that she was cursing and she had been speeding and she had been resisting arrest?"

"Right."

"Did Mr. Wages ever tell you that Mrs. Wright's husband wanted her committed?"

"No, sir."

"He never said a word about it?"

"No, sir."

"Did Mr. Wages ever tell you that Mr. Wright said, 'Well, she has been acting a little crazy lately'?"

"No, sir."

"Did Deputy Miller ever tell you Mr. Wright said he wanted Mrs. Wright committed?"

"No, sir."

"Doctor, it would be perhaps the most important fact in the woman's history to tell a physician who was going to put a woman in an institution that her husband wanted her put away and the reasons for it?"

"It would be an important fact."

"The most important fact, because he has been living with her. He really knows what she's about."

"Very important."

"Thank you. Were you, that morning, told by anyone that Mrs. Wright had a gun the night before?"

"No, sir."

"Never told about her threatening to get a gun?"

"No, sir."

"That was also never mentioned to you?"

"No, sir."

"The first time you have heard this story about a gun, and the first time you have heard this story about Mr. Wright saying 'Take my wife away,' that was probably in court Tuesday or Wednesday during the cross-examination, when the defense lawyers were putting those questions to Mrs. Wright, is that right?"

"That's right."

"You never heard it before?"

"No, sir."

"Now, you testified on direct examination, as I recall, that the shot was given into her right arm. Is that right?"

"Right."

"That is important in this case because Mrs. Wright claims the shot was in her left arm, and it was her left arm that has been, for the past four years, giving her pain. You heard her testify to that on Tuesday and Wednesday?"

"I did."

"And you testify today the shot was in the right arm?"

"I do."

"You say she's wrong about her testimony?"

"Yes."

"You say she's lying?"

"Well, she's wrong."

"Okay. How far away were you when that shot was put into her right arm?"

"I was standing by the cell door."

"How far is that?"

"That would be about six or seven feet from where the patient was."

"From seven feet away you could certainly see into which arm she was getting the shot."

"Yes, sir."

"You have good eyesight?"

"Yes, sir."

"You may not have been able to see her teeth from three feet, but you could certainly see her arm?"

"Yes, sir."

"Her arms are bigger than her teeth?"

"Right."

"Now, at your examination in Jackson, do you recall this question and answer:

> *Q.* Do you know in which arm Dr. Middleton gave
> her the injection?
> *A.* No, sir.

"Do you remember that, Doctor?"

"Well, no, I don't remember exactly that question."

"Well, here, take a look at your testimony. It's at page 16."

The witness reluctantly looked at the transcript and answered: "I still believe it was given in her right arm, because that was the one that the handcuff was on."

"The only question is, was that your testimony given three months after the incident?"

"That was my testimony there."

"Now, you are the third witness today I will ask this same question. Were you telling the truth or lying in Jackson?"

"At that time I think I was telling the truth, yes."

"You *think* you were telling the truth. Is that something you have to think about?"

The witness did not respond. I waited while he groped for an answer. When no answer came, I went to the next question.

"Did you have any discussion with Mr. Harris about your testimony about which of Mrs. Wright's arms was involved?"

"No, sir."

"You didn't discuss this point at all, never went over it in your preparation? Is that what you want Judge Keady and the jury to believe?"

"Oh, yes, I think we did. We've had some discussion about which arm, yes, sir."

"Sure you did. When did you have that discussion?"

"Oh, I reckon since we've had this—"

"You probably had some discussion today, right before you testified?"

"I don't know about today, but we've had it in the past few days."

I knew the answer to my last question before I placed it: "Have you ever committed one of your private patients to Whitfield based on the kind of examination you gave Mrs. Wright?"

Dr. Howard gave an honest answer: "No."

The next witness was Dr. Middleton, the junior of the examining team. His direct testimony was the same as Dr. Howard's. I wanted to show again that Wages's testimony that Mrs. Wright had a gun was false. Dr. Middleton had no illusions about how the cross-examination would go. He was antagonistic as I began to question him.

"Now, Dr. Middleton, you saw Sheriff Wages that morning and he gave you a history about Mrs. Wright, is that right?"

"Yes."

"Did he ever tell you that her husband wanted her to be put away?"

"I don't recall."

"That would be pretty important, wouldn't it, with respect to whether or not a woman is sick, if her husband says she has been acting 'crazy' for the last few weeks?"

"Are you asking a question?"

"Doctor, can't you tell I'm asking you a question?"

"Yes."

"Then answer it. Would that be a very significant factor in helping you make a diagnosis?"

"Yes, it would be."

"But you don't recall Sheriff Wages telling you that her husband wanted to have her put away?"

"No, I don't recall that conversation with him."

"Do you recall any conversation with Sheriff Wages about whether or not the woman had been running around with a gun or threatening to use a gun on Thursday?"

"Yes, sir, he mentioned that."

"He mentioned a gun?"

"Yes."

"Did you take notes of the woman's behavior that day and did you put in your notes everything that was important?"

"Yes."

His notes had been shown to Mrs. Wright's lawyers in Jackson in 1966 during his pretrial examination. A copy had been made for our files and I had read it before Middleton took the stand. I knew there was nothing in the notes about a gun.

"May I see your notes?" I asked. The doctor did not move, and his lawyers did not make any gesture toward him. Judge Keady and the jury by this time were waiting for me to bring out the witness's contradictions. For a while, the jurors forgot the racial issues that had brought us together in Oxford this warm May day, and became involved in the age-old drama of the lying witness being caught by the cross-examiner.

There was silence in the courtroom. It was broken by Judge Keady's sharp direction to the doctor. "Give them to Mr. Garbus." As Dr. Middleton took the notes out of his file and began to hand them to me, I said: "Look in your notes. Read them carefully. Is there anything in your notes about the woman using a gun or threatening to use a gun?"

"No, sir. Ask the question again."

"Do you recall specifically—specifically, now—whether Sheriff Wages told you that that woman had a gun on Thursday."

"No, sir, he didn't tell me that he had seen any gun in her possession, no."

"Did he ever tell you that any of his deputy sheriffs had ever been threatened with a gun that she had?"

"No, sir."

"Do you recall at any time on Friday, the day of the lunacy hearing, having any of the deputy sheriffs, whether it be Miller, Wages, or Highway Patrolman Morgan, or Cross, tell you about this woman having a gun Thursday night?"

"No, sir."

"Now, after you gave her the shot, did she calm down?"

"Yes, sir, she was relatively calm."

"She was then responsive to your questions?"

"Yes, sir."

"Was she hallucinated at that time? Did she make up wild stories?"

"She wouldn't talk to me. No."

"Did you ever try and determine, by physical examination or by asking questions, if anyone had been beating her on her arms and legs?"

"No."

"Now, you stated before that you made an examination of her and you checked for contusions and abrasions, and also, I suppose, whether or not she had had any teeth knocked out, is that right?"

"I didn't specifically look in her mouth for teeth, probably, but I did check for bruises, contusions, on her arms and legs and face and lips."

"Were any teeth knocked out?"

"I am not sure."

"Now, with respect to bruises and contusions, do you believe that if a person of the black race is badly beaten, there is not necessarily the same discoloration of the skin as when the victim is white?"

"Well, it would have to be a mighty deep blow for a bruise not to show up on the skin, even in the black race."

"Right, it would have to be a deep blow so that you couldn't see the bruise. It would have to be a deep-seated injury."

"Well, I would have to answer that 'Yes.'"

"You would have to answer yes. You'd rather not answer yes, if you could. Is that right, Doctor?"

The doctor did not answer immediately. I wanted to end the examination on this note and said, as I went back to my seat, "I have no further questions."

Each of the defendants testified and, after the defendants rested their case, we gave our summation to the jury. The judge instructed the jury on the law and, although it was now well into the evening, he decided to let them start deliberating. Judge Keady had another trial set for the next day and wanted the courtroom free so he could begin first thing in the morning.

The jury went out at 9 P.M. Jim and I stood at the counsel table waiting for a quick verdict, expecting the jury back within ten minutes. I was told there had been five previous jury cases in Mississippi in which a black plaintiff sought to get a money judgment against a white person. Four of the juries had deliberated less than seven minutes before they announced the judgment for the white person. In the fifth case, the jury became confused. Thinking it was a criminal case and wanting to come back with a verdict against the black person, they thought they had to say "not guilty." But no one knew how to spell "guilty." They finally came back in twelve minutes with a verdict slip reading "Not G."

A large crowd had gathered in the corridors outside the courtroom and in front of the building. There isn't much to do in Oxford in the evening. The stores had all been closed. The only light around the town square was that cast from the courthouse. People milled around, for the trial was the best (and only) event in town that week.

As soon as the jury retired to the jury room, I spoke to Mrs. Wright. She was exhausted but relaxed. The tension of the trial had left her. She had testified, had told her story, and was now waiting for a jury verdict. A pleased, peaceful smile was on her face. I said to the Wrights: "There's no hope of winning. You understand that?"

"We do."

"Mr. Wright, no matter what happened today, the jury will not return a verdict in Mrs. Wright's favor."

He was smiling deeply and broadly. "I understand that. I want to thank you. You've been wonderful. We've never had anybody say the things you said about the sheriffs. Sheriff Wages has been stood up to. The folks know about it."

Jim Lewis, with a sense of relief now that the case was over, sat in the witness chair by the judge's bench. "We did all we could. The case went in well. We gave them as clear an issue as they could have. There's no one in the jury who really can believe that Mrs. Wright wasn't beaten and that the sheriffs weren't all lying. Keady knows it."

At 9:12 the jury had not yet returned. Jim and I both knew we'd broken the record. The big-faced clock at the back of the courtroom showed 9:20, then 9:25, and still the jury was out.

I asked Jim whether he thought that, when the jury came in against us, we should move to set aside the verdict as contrary to the evidence and ask the judge to direct a verdict in our favor. This motion is aimed at the judge's discretion. The request is standard in trial procedure but rarely succeeds. There was no chance of its winning here. If Keady were to grant it, he could be virtually ostracized in the community. However, there would be psychological value in making the motion. It would show the jury that their word wasn't the last and that we were still fighting. It would also indicate that we might appeal to a higher court (though we knew we wouldn't). There was no chance, we felt, of getting a Mississippi Appellate Court to reverse a Mississippi jury on the basis of this record. I decided to make the motion.

Mr. Harris, sitting at the counsel table, looked concerned. He was amazed that the doctors were still in the case. At various points during the trial, he had promised the doctors that the charges against them would be dismissed. He never expected to be sitting in an Oxford courtroom waiting for a jury verdict and certainly never expected to be waiting a half hour for it.

No doctor likes to be sued. Harris, representing the insurance company, had probably defended under a malpractice policy. Whatever the outcome, the doctors in this case were sure to pay more for their insurance in future and might have to pay part of the lawyer's fees. They would be more careful the next time they were asked to put anyone into a mental institution and more careful the next time they saw a black woman in Mrs. Wright's situation in jail. They would also rely less on stories given to them by Mississippi law-enforcement people.

Naughton, the assistant attorney for the state of Mississippi, a well-built six-footer with Rudy Vallee hair, had not said much during the trial. He walked over to me now.

"Are you going to try the Ben Brown case? That's the student killed on the college campus, Mr. Garbus. Can you imagine, his parents are suing us for killing him. Well, it was his fault. He walked in front of a bullet. We should have charged him with reckless walking." He laughed and looked at me to see if he and I didn't really believe in the same things. He expected me to join in the laughter, the laughter of two white men who, although they fight in court, really know where the blacks belong. He thought I would at least think he was funny. I smiled and said, "Fuck you," and walked away.

It was 9:35, then 9:40. I went out to the high-ceilinged, olive-green corridors to get a breath of fresh air. Some highway patrolmen had congregated on the far side of the courtroom, and when they saw me in the hallway, they started to move toward me.

"Slick, think you did a pretty good job? Think you're going to win?" I looked at them, smiled, and continued to walk down the hall. They followed me.

"Well, Slick, came down from New York? What do you think of our hospitality? Think there's any chance of winning? I hope not, for your sake."

I went back into the courtroom. The Wrights began to believe we could win. I again told Mrs. Wright that the fact that the jury was out this long did not mean anything. Leith, the lawyer for Sheriff Wages, said, with an edge of uncertainty in his voice: "The reason they're out so long is that they can't agree on a foreman. They've probably been arguing about that for a half hour. There's nothing else to argue about."

And still the jury did not return.

There had been a few Negroes and some college students in court during most of the trial. Now there were about sixty people quietly milling about the courtroom. They were the white residents of Oxford and Winona. Each time I walked over to the Wrights, talked and joked with them, I saw the people in the courtroom stiffen as they saw the good feeling between us.

I again walked out into the hall. We'd been in that courtroom since 8:30 A.M. It was the longest trial day I'd ever put in, one of the most exhausting trial weeks I'd ever known. Jim and I had gotten up each morning at six and had worked past midnight every day. Quite apart from all the other pressures, trying a case in a different state with different practices and procedures is difficult. Much of the magical, nonsensical language of the law uttered in the Mississippi courtroom was new to me, and often it wasn't until I had reacted that I fully understood the significance of many of the words. Trying a case against four other lawyers also adds to the tension.

A squat, hydrant-shaped, thick-necked trooper in tinted glasses bumped me as I left the courtroom. "Getting cocky, Slick? Think you've put one over on us? You really do think you're going to win, don't you? Where are you sleeping tonight? Need any help getting out of town?"

The sheriffs' lawyers saw what was going on, laughed, and walked away. The people in the courtroom were getting more and more restless the longer the jury stayed out. Those of the defendants' friends and relatives who had been laughing and joking when the jury first went out now turned hateful stares at the Wrights, Jim, and me. I ignored the patrolman, walked out to the corridor and into the large open area above the stairwell. There were now about a hundred people on the street and on the first floor of the courthouse. More of the sheriffs' friends, the highway patrolman's friends, and people from Winona had come around.

As I was standing at the top of the stairs looking through the circular window into the courtyard, a burly, flower-shirted man in his early thirties knocked into me. "Hey, Slick, are you enjoying Oxford? Think you're gonna win? Go to hell!"

I turned around and walked inside. The jurors were seated in a room directly across the corridor from the courtroom. The marshal stood outside the door, guarding it, allowing no one to enter or exit. At about ten, there was a knock and the marshal went into the jury room. We felt the jury would be right out. But, after a minute, the marshal resumed his place. The defendants' concern became more apparent, for it seemed the jury was locked in serious debate.

Ten-ten, ten-fifteen. At 10:29, one hour and twenty-nine minutes after they began their deliberation, the jury knocked again, came out, told the marshal they had reached a verdict, and filed back into the courtroom. After they were seated, the clerk summoned Judge Keady from his chambers. The judge mounted the bench and asked the jurors if they had reached a verdict. They told him they had.

The foreman, at 10:31, said: "We find a verdict for all defendants against Mrs. Wright." The spectators breathed a sigh of relief.

Judge Keady received the verdict without emotion. "Mr. Garbus, do you have any motions?"

"I move to set aside the jury verdict on the grounds that it is against the weight and is contrary to the evidence; it is based on facts that were not presented in this court. And I ask that

Your Honor direct a verdict against each of the defendants."
The doctors looked anxiously at their lawyers.

The judge acted quickly. "Motion denied. Court is adjourned."

Harris got up and left the courtroom. The jurors, for the first time in four days, left the jury box without the escort of the marshal. Mr. Hall, the foreman, started to come over to me, changed his mind, and walked out of the courtroom. I went through the entrance to Judge Keady's chambers and told Mr. Fitzpatrick, his law clerk, that I wished to talk to the judge.

The heat had been shut off in the courtroom and it was getting chilly. The judge, standing behind his desk, was putting on his coat. When he saw me, he walked over.

"Judge Keady, thank you. I've never been treated more fairly in any court."

"Mr. Garbus, this has been a very painful case for all of us. You've done a lot of good by coming down here. Come back again."

The foreman of the jury was waiting for me outside the courtroom. "Three of the jurors were very angry. They believed the sheriff and the others lied. Some of the others agreed. But we felt she wasn't hurt as bad as she said she was." He turned and went down the stairs.

We walked outside into the dark clear night. The ominous Mississippi night—which had so often harbored black men hanging from their necks, the burning cross, the vicious beating—had lost some of its threat for Mr. and Mrs. Wright. Jim and I stood by a rented car and said good night to the Wrights. "It was wonderful," said Mr. Wright.

They went their way; we ours.

Twelve days later Mrs. Wright began serving her ninety-day sentence for reckless driving.

# Two

*The People against Lenny Bruce*

"I'M DOING MY ACT and a guy comes in. I know he's a cop—I've had plenty of experience with them. He starts taking down as much of my act as he can. He doesn't miss a dirty word; he doesn't get too much of the rest. He arrests me. We go to court. Me and my lawyers have to defend the act he says I gave. All he says are the dirty words. *His* act *is* obscene. I'm convicted and have to hire lawyers, maybe go to jail—because of *his* act. There's something screwy about the whole thing."

That was Lenny Bruce, comic, talking.

Leonard Bruce, formerly Leonard Schneider, died August 3, 1966, at the age of forty-two, during the appeal of his New York obscenity conviction. Vincent Cuccia, one of the district attorneys who helped try the case against him, said, "I feel terrible about Bruce. We drove him into poverty and bankruptcy and then murdered him. I watched him gradually fall apart. It's the only thing I did in Hogan's office that I'm really ashamed of. We all knew what we were doing. We used the law to kill him."

My own contact with Bruce began one Sunday night in April 1964. Ephraim London—one of the country's leading experts on constitutional law—called me at my home to say, "Lenny Bruce is sitting in my office. He has to be in court tomorrow. He has just been arrested for a performance he gave in Greenwich Village and I have agreed to represent him. I'd like to have you try the case with me. If you're free tomorrow morning, perhaps you can appear at the arraignment in criminal court. The charge is obscenity."

I had seen Bruce perform many times and knew of his previous arrests. It had always seemed to me that the charges brought against Bruce were public exercises in hypocrisy—he was being arrested because of his attacks on religion and public figures, rather than because of his use of dirty words.

I have always been opposed to censorship in sexual matters. Inevitably, it leads to the censorship of political and social thought. Allowing judges or juries, literary critics or policemen to decide what others shall read provides them with an inordinate sense of power. One of the rationales for obscenity laws is that reading or listening to obscene material leads to antisocial behavior. Having seen Bruce on stage years before, I was looking forward to any proof the state could produce to show that Bruce's performance could lead to anything more dangerous than a critical view of our society.

At his arraignment in Manhattan Criminal Court he wore a denim suit without a shirt. The suit jacket was open, exposing the hair on his chest. He was surrounded by a coterie of admirers, including some very pretty women, many of whom were later to be present throughout his trial.

Bruce was rather short, perhaps five feet eight inches, and inclined to chubbiness. I introduced myself and told him I would try to have the arraignment adjourned for about a month in order to give us time to locate witnesses and prepare our defense.

The case was in the middle of a crowded calendar. Normally, the district attorney assigned to the arraignment part handles all the cases on the calendar. When the case was called in its normal sequence, I was informed of a delay; we would be waiting for Mr. Richard Kuh, a district attorney specially assigned to the case. Bruce's comment: "Oh oh, the fix is on."

When Kuh finally appeared, he advised the judge that we ought not to be granted an adjournment since the case was not substantial enough to warrant it. He said if we were not ready to go by Monday, then we certainly ought to be ready for trial by Wednesday. "Mr. Garbus is the third attorney and the case hasn't even started," he said. Furthermore, a subpoena had been served on Bruce requiring him to produce tapes of his performance. His former lawyer (who was not in court) had promised to have the tapes there that morning.

Kuh and I argued bitterly over the question of when the trial should start.

"Judge," I said, "I never even met my client until this morning. This is a serious charge and we require time to prepare a proper defense."

Kuh came back with, "It's a standard obscenity case. The entire trial should not take more than two days. They are just trying to delay the case."

"Not at all, Your Honor. We intend to show that Bruce is a serious social critic and that the words he used were necessary for his performances. We also intend to show that the obscenity law is simply a way of limiting the scope of a serious political and social satirist."

At this, Kuh laughed. The judge joined him when I went on to say I thought our case would take not less than two weeks.

After further wrangling, the judge at last granted an adjournment but then demanded that I produce the tapes. I asked for ten minutes to speak to my client and took him outside the room.

"Lenny, where are the tapes?"

"Martin, it's better if you don't know." His reluctance was based on the feeling that he could be prosecuted on the evidence of his own tapes.

"Just tell me where the tapes are. I won't hand them over. I'll find some way of avoiding it. We can claim that, since it's your own voice on your tapes, it would be like a confession and would violate the Fifth Amendment—that it can be used against you. But I have to know where they are. At least give me the facts, so that I can answer the judge's questions."

"You're an officer of the court, Martin. If I tell you where the tapes are, you have to tell the court."

I shook my head. "I'm your lawyer."

"But you're an officer of the court first. You were that yesterday. You're my lawyer today."

"I promise you I won't hand over the tapes. Just tell me where they are."

"I can't tell you. If they get the tapes, they will convict me and won't let me do my act. I've been through this before. It's the same thing that happened to me in Chicago." He pleaded with me not to ask him any more about the tapes.

"Lenny, if the judge asks me questions, I have to give some reason for not turning them over. I can't tell him I don't know anything about them when you've already been served with a subpoena. Kuh claims your lawyer promised to bring the tapes."

"Kuh is wrong. The subpoena is defective."

I never found out where the tapes were. He seemed to be playing cat and mouse with all of us, and there was some doubt on my part that the tapes ever existed. There was no point in wrangling about it any further, and with the consent of the judge the issue of the tapes was reserved for our next court appearance.

I studied the complaint again on my way back to the office. He was charged with having participated in an "obscene, indecent, immoral and impure drama, play, exhibition, show and entertainment and an obscene, indecent, immoral and impure scene, tableau, play, exhibition, show and entertainment which would tend to the corruption of the morals of youths and others." The complaint said he had done this three times at the Café Au Go Go, and he and the owners of the café, Howard and Ella Solomon, were therefore charged with three separate crimes. This could result in a three-year jail sentence and a substantial fine for each.

The trial began two months later, on June 16, 1964, and dragged out over six weeks. While we were going through the many preliminary motions necessary to the defense, I got to know Lenny. He was understandably suspicious of lawyers, since many he had known had used his legal problems to get publicity for themselves. In addition he had other, more serious doubts about the legal process. He felt trapped in a jungle of courtrooms, hearings, prosecutors, and judges, with no way to make people understand who he was and what he was trying to say. The rules of evidence and the legal atmosphere, with its strange language, muffled individuality. A court can be impersonal almost to the point of hostility. A defendant rarely "knows" his own lawyer and can hardly ever really communicate with his judge and prosecutor.

Even before the case went to trial, Lenny had nine separate days of pretrial hearings. He confronted five different judges and three different prosecutors. In order to maintain his sanity, he had to believe that the best possible job was being done for him. But he was unable to bring himself to trust anyone. He read every case dealing with obscenity laws and believed he understood them all. His do-it-yourself approach was a serious obstacle to the conduct of his defense.

For Lenny Bruce and many like him, the legal process was torture. Many of the legal problems in the case were uniquely shaped, to add to the strain. When a painting, film, or book is prosecuted, there is little doubt about the artist's actual words or pictures, although there will still be differences of opinion about what the words or pictures mean. But in Bruce's case we had the prosecution of a live performance, one that varied from night to night. Each of Lenny's one-hour performances was assembled differently. He would put sketches together and then highlight different themes by emphasizing different parts of the sketches. Since there were no movies of the performance in question, it was impossible for the court to have Bruce's objectionable act before it as it tried to judge his performance.

Bruce's arrest was only the beginning of the prosecution of some of the new art forms. "Happenings" and free-form theater were emerging from the lofts and university theaters and finding their way to Broadway. The legal problem of prosecuting an art form when no one knew exactly what had been said or shown would be significant in later trials. There were other unique aspects to Lenny's trial. The creator of the work is not usually the defendant in an obscenity trial. I have defended works as different in character and context as those of Pierre Louÿs, Aubrey Beardsley, and Terry Southern. The defendants were either booksellers, distributors, or motion-picture projectionists. They seldom experienced the anxiety of the courtroom. Lenny, on the other hand, was in court every day and had definite opinions about every step of the litigation. He saw churchmen, district attorneys, police, judges, and private citizens constantly judging him and coming to the conclusion that he was a nasty, dangerous little man. His inability to communicate with those who condemned him was as painful to him as being stretched on the rack.

Before the trial, he had been performing in New York and elsewhere for years and had sold hundreds of thousands of records. He had been arrested elsewhere but never before in New York. New York, in early 1964, was in the midst of a "pornography scare." Father Morton Hill, a Jesuit priest, formed an unholy alliance with Rabbi Moshe Neumann to create Operation Yorkville, dedicated to forcing newsdealers, bookstore owners, and film exhibitors to remove material the clergymen found objectionable. When a storeowner refused, a call to District Attorney Frank Hogan often resulted in a visit from the police. Father Hill's newsletter, luxuriating in statistical analysis, proclaimed that there were enough filthy books in New York for each man, woman, and child to have seven pounds' worth. During this period, I often debated the two clergymen on radio and television and before community groups, and found audiences generally on their side.

Arresting Bruce meant not only getting rid of a dirty-mouthed comedian and appeasing the Father Hills but also attacking a favorite of a New York intellectual group that Hogan felt was nearly always critical of law enforcement. It was a chance to show the power of the law. Hogan's assistant, Richard Kuh, was a stocky man in his late thirties who looked and moved like a retired middleweight fighter. I had encountered him before and knew he was an excellent trial lawyer who believed that the country would be safer if people like Bruce were put in jail.

Neither Kuh nor Hogan had ever seen Bruce perform. The Commissioner of Licenses was asked to send a man to cover Bruce's performance and report back to the district attorney's office. Armed with a notebook and lapel mike (and seemingly devoid of any sense of humor), Inspector Herbert S. Ruhe, a former C.I.A. man, subjected himself to Bruce's performance at the Café Au Go Go. In his testimony he said, "I was there to witness a performance of the performer Lenny Bruce, to note vulgar, objectionable, and lewd materials which he might produce."

That was what he went to hear and that was all he did hear. He returned with notes containing more "dirty words" per minute than Bruce would ordinarily come up with in twenty-five performances. In addition, he included his own estimate of the satirical value of what he was hearing ("philosophical clap-trap on human nature"). It was not much, but it was enough for Hogan and Kuh to go ahead with the prosecution.

Bruce's arrest created a furor. Kuh and Hogan were criticized sharply by prominent members of the community. A petition signed by one hundred well-known artists and writers who protested the arrest included Lionel Trilling, Norman Mailer, Theodor Reik, James Baldwin, and William Styron. To Hogan's further surprise, he found that most of the young lawyers in his office were opposed to the prosecution. Jerry Harris, in charge of obscenity prosecutions in Manhattan, was assigned to try the case. He had never seen Bruce perform, but after listening to Inspector Ruhe's tapes of Bruce he said, "Bruce was very funny. I don't think we ought to prosecute him. The tapes were so funny I nearly burst out laughing several times. Finally, I had to decide whether I could, in good conscience, be the district attorney on the case. I told Hogan I could not. I saw Lenny a few times during the trial and he always gave me his sad smile. He knew I had refused."

Hogan found himself in the unusual position of looking for a lawyer to try the case. Several lawyers in the Rackets and Homicide Bureaus were asked, but they all refused. Kuh then agreed to take it, and the district attorney's office decided to submit the case to the grand jury, although they could have prosecuted on Kuh's complaint alone. Hogan needed the grand jury to back him up if the prosecution fell on its face (as, in fact, it did). He could then say that the people of New York, as represented by the grand jury, had decided that charges should be pressed. In practice, a grand jury will almost always bring an indictment when the district attorney is determined to make the defendant stand trial.

Today, in many states, before an arrest is made because of an obscene book or film, a judge makes an initial determination that there are reasonable grounds to find the work objectionable. This is a far better procedure and is what the Constitution requires. Had this procedure existed in 1964, Bruce might be alive today. But in the Bruce case the district attorney alone made the decision.

One factor that should discourage the fair-minded prosecutor or grand jury from beginning a criminal procedure is the certainty of reversal. Most of the appellate lawyers in Hogan's

office said a conviction of Bruce would not stand up on appeal;
yet they could not convince Kuh and Hogan. Kuh said the key
question in deciding whether to prosecute an obscenity
offender was the possibility (not the probability) that the conviction would be upheld. This test allows the state to subject
people like Lenny Bruce to harassment, arrests, and enormous
legal fees. The combination can break the strongest of men—
and Bruce was not that.

The state of obscenity law was in its usual flux. Often a
grand jury will have case law read to it to determine whether a
crime was committed. The Bruce grand jury, after the words
of the United States Supreme Court concerning definitions of
obscenity were read to it, knew no more than before about
whether Bruce had violated any law.

Before the Bruce trial started, the United States Supreme
Court had heard arguments from Ephraim London in a case he
and I were involved in, entitled *Jacobellis v. Ohio.* The unre-
solved legal principles argued in the Jacobellis case were to be
key issues in the Bruce case. As we tried Lenny's case, we constantly looked over our shoulders to see if the Supreme Court
had rendered a decision in the Jacobellis case. And, as it turned
out, that decision came down during the middle of the trial
and affected the course of Lenny's case.

The legal test for obscenity when the Bruce trial began had
been laid down by Mr. Justice Brennan in *Roth v. United
States,* a case decided in 1957 by the Supreme Court. In his
ruling, Justice Brennan rejected the early standard of judging
obscenity by the effect of isolated passages upon the most sus-
ceptible persons. He said the test was whether, applying contemporary community standards, the dominant theme of the
material taken as a whole appeals to the prurient interest of the
average person and is without redeeming social importance.
Unfortunately, the new test raised as many questions as it answered. The Bruce trial, although dealing with every aspect of
the Roth test, was to put special emphasis on the phrases

"without redeeming social importance" and "contemporary community standards." These phrases, and what they meant, were the subject of the argument in the Jacobellis case.

Lower courts, aware of the necessity of defining "community standards," knew that the determination as to whether a work is obscene might vary from community to community, depending on the prevailing standard in each area. As a result, a questionable film might be shown in one city but not in a neighboring one. This had particular relevance to Bruce since he had already been acquitted on obscenity charges in other states. Was he required to defend himself in every state in which he performed?

There were other issues as well. Courts throughout the country were evaluating the degree of social importance which might be present in the work in question. They would weigh the social value against the other elements to arrive at a decision, rather than hold that if the work had any social value at all it could not be banned. In the case of Bruce, it was our contention that if a work had *any* value at all, it could not be considered obscene. If the courts were allowed to balance one element against another, it would make an already vague test meaningless.

In the years following the Roth decision, books like *Tropic of Cancer* and *Fanny Hill* were being found obscene in some states and not in others. States like Mississippi were ready to ban works dealing with racial matters on the grounds that they were obscene. Southern courts could find a film or a book dealing with intermarriage "without redeeming social value" and therefore ripe for suppression.

All these issues would again be brought to the fore in the Bruce case and further complicate the already enormously involved testimony that was to be heard on both sides.

The Bruce case was tried before three judges of the criminal court: John M. Murtagh, Kenneth Phipps, and J. Randall Creel. Murtagh, the presiding judge, had coauthored a book about prostitution, *Cast the First Stone*, and had earned, I thought, an undeserved reputation as a sympathetic and liberal judge. As chief justice of the criminal court, he dominated his two colleagues and ran the trial as if they were not there. Judges are supposed to be assigned by chance to the cases they will preside over, but it had been my experience that in *causes célèbres*, where the district attorney's office desperately wants a conviction, Murtagh is apt to be assigned to the case—not only because he is conviction-prone but also because he is one of the better judges and there would be a smaller chance of reversal for technical errors.

Due to the number of spectators, the case had been transferred from a small courtroom on the lower floor of the Criminal Courts Building to one of the larger courtrooms usually reserved for more serious crimes. This large courtroom, with its lofty ceilings, twenty-foot-high windows, and unusual number of attendants, bailiffs, and police, seemed only to emphasize the prosecution's sense that Lenny had committed a monstrous crime.

Inspector Ruhe took the stand and told of his visit to the Café Au Go Go and what he had seen and heard there. He had come armed with his notes and prepared to give his own version of Bruce's performance, but he was clearly uncomfortable with his material. He perspired, fidgeted, and became embarrassed every time he had to repeat a "dirty" word.

The state had hoped that Ruhe's notes would go into the evidence as an accurate transcript of the performance, but the notes were so confused that the court would not admit them. Kuh told Ruhe to use the notes to refresh his memory. This meant that Ruhe had to repeat nearly every word he had taken down. He was loud and clear when he spoke unobjectionable

words and almost inaudible when he came to those which embarrassed him. Thus, he was changing not only Bruce's language but his meaning. It was as if Ruhe's version of *Ulysses*
were being tried rather than the work itself. Bruce, like any
performer, was in agony as he was forced to watch his material
being butchered:

> Now, I wonder how many of you in the audience
> have ever performed an unnatural act . . . like pissing
> in the sink . . . One time in your life have you ever
> pissed in the sink? [Here follows a monologue skit on
> a man who wants to urinate into a washbasin and gets
> his roommate angry.] What are you doing? . . . I am
> washing my leg . . . Bullshit, you were jerking off
> into the sink . . . No, really, I am washing my leg
> . . . Well, if you have to do it go out on the ledge
> . . . The fellow goes out on the window ledge . . .
> People think he wants to commit suicide . . . All he
> wants to do is urinate . . . A priest talks to him . . .
> fire trucks appear . . . nets and ladders . . . Finally
> the guy's mother . . . Mamma, all I want to do is take
> a piss . . . Go ahead, son, piss . . . I can't, Mamma,
> there are too many people looking . . . I can't piss
> when all these people are looking . . . So run some
> water, you down there . . . Turn on the hoses . . .
> Can't you see the boy wants to pee-pee . . .

Through all this the court maintained its air of intense gravity.
Judge Murtagh, tall and courtly, with his powdered cheeks and
flat hair parted in the middle, looked perplexed because the
act sounded like nonsense. The judges, unfamiliar with many
of the Yiddish expressions which were scattered throughout
Bruce's material, would often halt the performance to ask
Ruhe to speak louder or to clarify a word. The court reporter,
faced with words such as "shtup," "schmuck," and "tuchus,"
was having as much difficulty as if he had been forced to take

down testimony in Sanskrit. At times, there would be a pause of three to five minutes while the spelling and epistemology of "putz" or "mezuzah" were discussed.

Ruhe slowly warmed to his task, saying the words more distinctly as he gained confidence. And still the judges and court reporter kept asking for repetition. Lenny leaned over to me and whispered, "Look at their faces when they say those words. They're enjoying it. They've never been able to say those words before and here they are in a public place yelling it out. It's too much. Look at Murtagh's face. Every time he says the word his face looks like he's just come back from the bathroom."

Ruhe (referring to his notes) went on with the farce:

> . . . There is this Masked Man. Masked Man . . . the do-gooder . . . Something needs doing, I'll do it for you . . . What's in it for you, Masked Man . . . Nothing . . . You're talking shit, buddy, take something . . . Okay, okay, see that Indian over there . . . You mean Tonto . . . Yes, I mean Tonto . . . I want Tonto . . . What do you want him for? . . . I want him to perform an unnatural act . . . Oh, my God, an unnatural act . . . Masked Man is a fag . . . a damn queer . . . Fag Man, that's what you are . . . Look, I want the horse too . . . The horse? What do you want the horse for . . . For the act . . . Masked Man is a stone freak . . .

Ruhe was enjoying himself now, his description becoming a performance in its own right. As one reporter later noted, the proceedings began "to resemble the audition of a Lenny Bruce impersonator for amateur night on the Ed Sullivan show."

Lenny was almost beside himself. "Listen to him. All he wants is to be an actor. This trial is his chance. Listening to him is like listening to Ezra Pound reading the Bible. He loves doing my act. He's looking to see if there are any talent scouts in the courtroom. And he'll look at tomorrow's papers for his reviews."

Before he left the stand, Ruhe said he saw Bruce slide his hands up and down the microphone as part of a "masturbatory gesture." He said Bruce also touched his "crotch." Lenny's face went pale. "That's it. That's the trick. That's how they're going to get me. Martin, I would never do anything like that— I know better. It's one thing to talk about tits and asses. But to show how to jerk off—they'd put me away for life."

The next witness, Patrolman Robert Lane, also testified that Bruce had made gestures that originated in the area of his crotch. Lenny, hearing Lane confirm Ruhe's testimony, hit a level of depression from which he was not able to rise throughout most of the trial. He knew enough obscenity law to know that he could be convicted more easily for what he did than for what he said.

I was furious at the state's testimony. I believed it to be false, and I was convinced the district attorney and the judges did also. All the same, there it was, and it had hurt us badly.

After three days of testimony, the state rested. All their witnesses had substantiated Ruhe's testimony that dirty words had been used. No one had been able to prove that Bruce had exceeded contemporary community standards or, for that matter, exactly what the community's standards were. No one claimed that Bruce's work had aroused prurient interest. The case should have ended there. Our motions to dismiss should have been granted without extended argument. They were, instead, denied without extended argument.

All that long third day Lenny complained about stomach pains. He looked drawn and defeated. During the first two days of testimony, he had reacted to each question and answer with a comment or note; now he sat silent, slumped in his chair. During recess, his vibrancy usually made him the center of a group as he analyzed, lectured, and joked about the previous court session. But that day, sick and disheartened, he neglected his audience.

I called Lenny the next morning and was informed that he was ill with pleurisy and had been taken to the hospital. The prognosis was that he would be there for ten days. We asked for an adjournment and it was granted. Two evenings later I went to visit him in the hospital.

His room was dark, with just a small light in one corner. Flowers sent by admirers overflowed into the hall. He was unshaven and looked terrible, but scattered over the bed and floor were at least two dozen law books. He had read our preliminary brief and said, in an apologetic but still faintly accusing voice, "There was an amendment to Section 1140 back in 1930 and it changes the meaning of the section. The amendment excluded actors. I just came across the case of a rabbi who was arrested for not having a license to run a butcher shop, and that case, because of the amendment, is the same as mine. He was acquitted because he was not the principal. You didn't cite the case in your brief."

I tried to explain to him that the case of the rabbi had no bearing on his own case, but it was impossible to get through to him. I could not tell him what he really wanted to hear—that his research was brilliant. Most of the lawbooks he had pored over were deadly dull, but he had read them thoroughly and with obvious enjoyment. "I read four of these from cover to cover," he said. Meanwhile, nurses kept coming and going through the room. He was their favorite patient—gentle, amusing, and uncomplaining.

While he was in the hospital, we spent our time interviewing and preparing witnesses. In Bruce's case, as in most obscenity prosecutions, we would have to rely heavily on expert witnesses. Psychiatrists testify the work is not arousing. Knowledgeable people in the communications media testify the work does not exceed contemporary community standards. Reviewers acclaim the literary qualities.

In selecting our witnesses, we tried to produce experts who could testify on every fragment of the Supreme Court definition of obscenity. We wanted expert testimony on the use of language in our society, and on the standards of acceptance of the language used by Bruce to show that his comments were substantially similar to those of many other writers and performers in present and past society. The judges, accustomed to traditional art forms, would have trouble understanding Bruce's act; so we must give the court the necessary background to evaluate what would appear to them to be a disorganized performance.

Ephraim London and I spoke to dozens of witnesses and picked those that would give the case the substance we needed. Yet we knew that after all the expert testimony was given and all the learned literary, psychiatric, and sociological articles were discussed, it would still come down to the decisions of judges who would be affected strongly by their own taboos. And with the court we had, there would almost certainly be a decision to convict. Even Chief Justice Warren, hearing obscenity cases in the rarefied atmosphere of the Supreme Court, seemed to apply as a test: Would I want my daughters to read this?

Thurman Arnold, a former federal appellate judge, had said, at a time when the test of obscenity seemed to be whether the female pubic hairs were visible, "It's ridiculous and unseemly to imagine the Justices of the Supreme Court poring over 'dirty' books and pictures and then coolly confining themselves to consideration of abstract legal doctrine."

Our first witness was Richard Gilman, then the literary and drama critic for *Newsweek*. His testimony that Bruce's monologues had artistic merit and indicated serious social concerns was treated by the judges with a mixture of indifference and disrespect. They were so outraged by Bruce's words that they could not believe there were ideas behind them.

Our next witness was one the judges could not easily ignore.

Her very presence jarred them. Dorothy Kilgallen, the long-time Hearst newspaper feature writer and columnist, had written warmly of Bruce's talent years before. I called her a few days before the trial and she said, "He's a brilliant man and I don't think his language is obscene, whatever that means. He is trying to stimulate his audience and make them think."

I met her a few days before she was to testify. She was as she appeared on television—prim, deliberate, thoughtful, and acerbic. She could hardly, as could some of our other witnesses, be accused of being committed to Bruce as a cause. It had become nearly traditional in defending against obscenity charges to bring forth the same people again and again as witnesses. Many of our witnesses had testified before and would testify again against any form of censorship. But the fact that Dorothy Kilgallen, who was considered by many to be a spokesman for the more prudish elements in the entertainment world, testified voluntarily for the defense showed that Bruce was not only the darling of the avant-garde. Dorothy disagreed with much of Bruce's criticism, was in favor of obscenity laws, and did not like the indiscriminate use of dirty language. But she knew, as much as one could in the muddled area of obscenity, that Bruce was innocent of the charge. She was determined to convey her feelings to the court.

I first asked for her qualifications as an expert on the standards of entertainment.

"Miss Kilgallen, what kind of work do you do?"

"I'm a writer and I appear on television."

"By whom are you employed?"

"The *New York Journal American,* 220 South Street."

"How long have you been employed by the *New York Journal American?*"

"Since 1931."

"In what capacity are you employed by the *Journal American?*"

"As a Broadway columnist."

"What does that involve?"

"It involves motion pictures, theater criticism, notes about famous people, occasionally politics. Mostly show business, nightclubs, theaters, and movies."

"Do you write a daily column for the *Journal American?*"

"Six days a week."

"Is that column syndicated?"

"It's syndicated by King Features Syndicate."

"And where does that column appear as a result of the syndication?"

"It appears in newspapers throughout the country, in various cities from Maine to Texas, and in Canada and in Australia and other places."

"And is it part of your duties to attend nightclubs, theaters, and movie openings?"

"Yes, it is."

"Is it fair to say that during the course of your employment by the *Journal American* you have seen all of the major nightclub, theater, or movie openings during the last ten or fifteen years?"

"That is true."

"Have you had occasion to see the defendant, Lenny Bruce, perform?"

"Yes, I have."

"When was that?"

"I saw him first in Chicago. I was visiting friends there and he was just coming up, I guess, just becoming very popular, and they took me to see him. I was very much impressed."

"Miss Kilgallen, have you for the past several years had a radio program concerning itself with drama and theater criticism?"

"Yes, for seventeen years until a year ago last April."

"On what station?"

"WOR."

"Are you also a television performer?"

"Yes, but not in a critical sense."

I told the court that I felt she was qualified to testify as an expert. Kuh objected and desperately tried to have Miss Kilgallen excluded on the grounds that she was not qualified to testify about community standards. He failed, and I continued.

"Do you have an opinion, Miss Kilgallen, as to the artistic merit of the contents of the performances of Mr. Bruce, as set forth in People's Exhibits 4A and 5A?"

"Yes, I do."

"What is your opinion?"

"I think he's a brilliant satirist, perhaps the most brilliant that I have ever seen; and I think his social commentary, whether I agree with it or not, is extremely valid and important, and I have enjoyed his acts on several occasions. I did not see the one that is in question here, but I read it. Of course, it is impossible to judge completely without having heard his voice and seen his gestures, but I can say that on the occasions when I saw him I was very impressed with his intelligence, with his material, with his ability to comment on events of the day straight out of a newspaper, which was apparently ad-libbed."

"Can you describe for us whether there is any form or unity to the method of performance which Mr. Bruce has?"

"Yes. His unity, I believe, is social commentary. He goes from one subject to another, but there is always the thread of the world around us and what is happening today, what has happened, and what might happen tomorrow. Whether he's talking about war or peace or religion or Russia or New York, there is always a thread and a unity."

"Miss Kilgallen, I show you page 6 of People's Exhibit number 5A, which relates to the performance of April 7, 1964, and I ask you what social comment Mr. Bruce is making when he says that when blacks finally do sit on juries they will convict whites as unfairly as they themselves have been convicted for years."

Judge Murtagh interrupted: "Counselor, we will permit the

READY FOR THE DEFENSE

question, but may I observe that if it is necessary to call an expert witness to interpret language, that language probably is not the kind that will convey much to the audience. You are asking an expert witness, now, to interpret the English language to a court."

I replied: "No, I'm not. I'm asking her to discuss the comment that Mr. Bruce makes—the social comment in this particular part of the monologue." We argued a bit more before Murtagh finally agreed to hear her answer.

"I think that in this case," she said, "Mr. Bruce is hopeful that the Negroes will get a better break; that because of the civil-rights law being passed, they will sit on juries, where they have never sat before. And like all people, they will at first commit injustices. Bruce is a great performer. I have enormous respect for him."

Hearing this, Bruce put his head down and his hands in front of his face. I heard a muffled cry. Afterward, Lenny told me how touched he was by Kilgallen's testimony.

I next attempted to soften the shock the court felt at Bruce's taboo words (they collectively grimaced each time the words were said in the courtroom) by having Miss Kilgallen respond to questions with those words. I knew she would react well. The judges blanched as I began.

"Miss Kilgallen, in the transcripts the words 'motherfucker,' 'cocksucker,' 'fuck,' 'shit,' 'ass' are found, isn't that correct?"

"Yes."

"Is there an artistic purpose in the use of language as set forth in these transcripts in evidence?"

"In my opinion there is."

"In what way?"

"Well, I think that Lenny Bruce, as a nightclub performer, employs these words the way James Baldwin or Tennessee Williams or playwrights employ them on the Broadway stage —for emphasis or because that is the way that people in a given situation would talk. They would use those words."

"Are these words also used in *The Carpetbaggers,* a book by Harold Robbins, presently being sold?"

"Yes."

"Can you tell of any other books that are being distributed that have the same language?"

"Norman Mailer certainly used all of these in his books, which were best sellers. James Joyce and Henry Miller used them, as well as many other authors who are regarded as classical writers."

"Miss Kilgallen, I now refer you to part of Mr. Bruce's performance—a dialogue between Mr. Goldwater and a group of American Negroes, in which Mr. Goldwater can't seem to understand the words used by the Negroes—and I ask you what social comment is made by Mr. Bruce."

"I think this part of the transcript indicates that Mr. Bruce feels that Senator Goldwater does not have much rapport with the Negro, that he's apart from them, as are many people in Arizona, that he doesn't speak their language, and that they can't get through to him; but they do get through to Mr. Bruce and he is with them. He says it's a different language and a different culture, and I think that's one of the reasons that he employed the words he did, because that is part of a different culture. It's not Mr. Goldwater's culture."

"Have you heard the word 'motherfucker' before?"

"Yes."

"How is the word used?"

"Sometimes it is used as an epithet, a term of opprobrium, and sometimes I have heard it used among show-business people, who speak rather frankly and roughly, as a term of endearment."

Bruce's comments about Jackie Kennedy's actions immediately after the first bullet tore into President Kennedy were among the most disturbing to the court. He said Jackie Kennedy, hearing the shots, had tried to escape. He said she, like anyone else who felt she was being shot at, would "haul ass."

They could not see any story line in that part of the monologue. Perhaps they would be less shocked after Miss Kilgallen's calm appraisal. I resumed my questioning.

"Miss Kilgallen, now directing your attention to People's Exhibit 5A, which is the April 7, 1964 performance, I would like you to read the beginning of a reference to Mrs. Kennedy and tell us what social comment is being made."

"I get the impression that Mr. Bruce did not agree with the general press information about Mrs. Kennedy climbing aboard the car—aboard the rear of the car—to help the Service man aboard; that she was frightened and confused, and that the Secret Service man, if he did get a medal, did not really deserve it for heroism. I can't say that I agree with that. I wasn't there. I don't know what was in Mrs. Kennedy's mind or the Secret Service man's mind, but I think it was another of Mr. Bruce's social commentaries."

I concluded her direct examination on that note.


On cross-examination Kuh tried to show that Miss Kilgallen did not use the same language in her *Journal American* column that Bruce used in his performances. His questioning allowed her to answer that there are different standards for different media (a point later made by John Fischer, an editor of *Harper's Magazine* and a rebuttal witness for the state).

"You stated those words you don't use. Can you tell me if the prevailing portion of the community finds them repugnant, in terms of usage in mixed company, in the public performances?"

"I cannot speak for the majority of the community; I can only speak for myself. But I believe certain words are valid and are not objectionable if they are used in the proper context and if they seem right at the time and if they are said in the proper manner. Some people can be offensive without using what we would call a dirty word. Some people could use a dirty word and not be offensive."

"Can you tell me how words or the phrases on page 2, 'shit in your pants' and 'cocksucker,' are used in a way that blends artistic merit, that demonstrates Mr. Bruce's moral character, and that is inoffensive?"

"Mr. Bruce sometimes uses those words almost as a throw-away."

Judge Murtagh interrupted. "What does that mean?"

Miss Kilgallen resumed. "That's show-business parlance, I'm afraid, Your Honor. It's an offhand thing that you almost don't hear."

"How is the fact that words such as that are offhand, how does that make it proper if it is improper otherwise?"

"Well, Your Honor, to me words are just words, and if the intent and the effect is not offensive, the words in themselves are not offensive. A four-letter word that might be objection-able to my mother, if it is said ten times, might sound innocent; it's just a word. It depends on how it's done. I have seen enter-tainers, and I have criticized them, who didn't use these words but were offensive, nevertheless, and I can give you examples. I have criticized them—"

"Never mind that," Murtagh interrupted. "How about this. Why is this not offensive?"

"Because of the way Mr. Bruce delivers the lines and because they seem—"

"Did you hear him on these two occasions?"

"No, but knowing his performances, I can almost picture the way he said them."

Kuh switched to the Jackie Kennedy story, thinking he could prove to Miss Kilgallen that Bruce's performance was objec-tionable. Many witnesses in obscenity trials have what seem to be ambivalent attitudes, which a skillful cross-examiner can ex-ploit. The witness may not like the work he is testifying about, would not show it to his children, yet believes the police should not censor it. If pressed, he can be forced to articulate his distaste and concede that the flow of objectionable materials must be stopped. Often, a witness first begins to think about some of the deeper issues while he is on the stand. Thus, the fact that Dorothy Kilgallen said she believed in censorship of certain materials made her more effective as a witness.

As a result of the 1957 Roth decision, the law had for some years been clear in at least one area—that the work must be evaluated as a whole and that it is impermissible to declare a work obscene merely because one portion does not seem to be making a significant contribution. Dorothy Kilgallen, in response to Kuh's goading, often exhibited a better understanding of the law than the judge did.

"Can you tell us how the use of this language, not in Mr. Bruce's eyes but in your eyes, as a critic, as a person who was qualified here as an expert witness, will you tell us how the use of this sentence that I read is necessary to the artistic unity, if you will, of the Jackie Kennedy story?"

"I think that the necessity comes from the writer or the performer of the material. I believe Mr. Bruce is both his own writer and performer, and if he feels it's necessary, I do not object to that."

"Well, are you saying, then, that in your eyes Mr. Bruce can do no wrong?"

I objected.

"Objection overruled."

"No."

"We discussed before Lenny Bruce's use of the word 'motherfucker.' Can you tell me when James Joyce or Norman Mailer or Arthur Miller has called his audience 'motherfucker'?"

"I can't tell you anything verbatim from the books because I read them years ago. I would imagine, this would be my best guess, that they did not call their audiences anything. There's another book called *The Naked Lunch* which I couldn't even finish reading, but it's published, and I think the author should be in jail. And he used—"

"Unfortunately we can't do everything at once, Miss Kilgallen. Are you judging the non-obscene quality and the artistic quality of Bruce by the fact that *The Naked Lunch* is a book, as of this date, that is sold in the community?"

"No, I'm not. I just mentioned it because you asked me for some books."

"And *The Naked Lunch* is a book you found impossible to read, is that correct?"

"Yes, I found it revolting."

"What was revolting about it?"

"Just the way it was written. It seemed to use words for shock value, not for any valid reason, and I object to that."

"And when Lenny Bruce—I ask you to turn to the April 1 tape, page 4, starting at the bottom of page 4, and I ask you to read the portion starting, bottom line, 'the attraction in Las Vegas, tits and ass, I beg your pardon. Tits and ass, that's what is the attraction, is just tits and ass and tits and ass,' and going all through the page, 'tits and ass and my mother's titties' and so forth, and I ask you if you find some shock value in that?"

"No, I don't think it's particularly shocking. It's just a word."

"Just two words, in fact."

"Yes. If you said 'ass' and you meant a donkey, you could say it and you wouldn't blush."

"Do you find this constant reproduction—repetition, I was going to say—of the words 'tits and ass, tits and ass, tits and ass' at that point there for shock value?"

"No, I think there he's being critical of the monotony of what is on view in Las Vegas."

"And you find that the constant repetition of these words is necessary to express that monotony?"

"I think he felt that it was."

Dorothy Kilgallen left the witness stand as cool and as unruffled as when she began testifying. She and Lenny exchanged emotion-filled glances. Lenny leaned over to me. "I can say anything about violence, lead in your ass, torturing the prisoners, people living with garbage—no one bothers me. Just mention tits and asses—busted. In Sweden they censor violence all over the place. Western movies—censored; violence there is bad. The Swedes can't understand our violence. Sex—they don't touch it."

That evening I went to Lenny's hotel room. His bed was covered with disposable needles, hundreds of pictures of Marilyn Monroe ("I can tell by looking at her pictures what she was on"), and pieces of electronic equipment. Sitting wearily on the bed, Lenny pointed to all the junk and said wryly, "The All-American Boy's Bed."

He changed the conversation to an article in that day's paper accusing him of being a junkie. In earlier days, Bruce had been arrested and convicted for drug use. We both knew that each time he went into the bathroom in the courthouse a New York plainclothesman followed him, hoping to catch him with heroin. They peered into the cubicles but never found him with anything. "Martin, believe me, I've never used the stuff. They set me up. Detective White, the guy who arrested me, was the next year arrested and himself convicted for being an addict. While I was in the navy, I started to use goof balls. Then I was using too much and the doctors gave me shots to get me the other way. And I became addicted to the stuff the doctors prescribed. But I have a doctor in every city I go to and I always have a prescription. I tell you I never used the hard stuff." He wanted desperately to have me believe him and trust him. He tried many times to convince me that he did not take drugs illegally.

With an impish smile he opened one of the two gray attaché cases he brought each day to court. I was amazed to see a portable tape recorder neatly set in the case. Unknown to anyone in the courtroom, Lenny had been taping the entire trial. He played Ruhe's testimony and then placed the spool in a chaotic pile of partially unwound tapes.

"I have to testify. Please, please, they're killing my act. I wanted you to hear Ruhe's testimony. These judges don't know what my act is."

Lenny was by this time so depressed and fragmented that any performance he could give in the alien atmosphere of the courtroom would only seem to confirm the state's claim that he was incoherent. "Lenny," I said, "you've been convicted once —in Chicago—because you gave your performance in the courtroom. We're also claiming they can't judge you on the basis of the transcripts. That argument's out if you testify."

He whispered, "They're killing me. Why are they doing this to me?" As I left Lenny, he sat on the bed listening, probably for the hundredth time, to the Ruhe tape.

Over the years, author and critic Nat Hentoff had seen Bruce at least forty times and had written many magazine reviews of Bruce's performances. He testified under my direct examination most of July 2, then came back to face cross-examination the following day. He testified repeatedly concerning the artistic value of Bruce's work.

Kuh's dislike for the bearded Hentoff intensified as the examination wore on. Hentoff for many years had been espousing politically radical ideologies, nearly all of which irritated Kuh. From his column in *The Village Voice*, Hentoff had attacked many of the activities of the district attorney's office and of the police. Tempers rose in the examination, which became a verbal pitched battle that would have erupted into a physical brawl had it not been for the decorum of the courtroom.

Kuh tried to establish that Hentoff was not to be believed because he had written favorable articles about an "ex-convict." The ex-convict turned out to be A. J. Muste, the dignified pacifist who was jailed for his beliefs.

Alan Morrison, the New York City editor of *Ebony* and editorial bureau chief of the Johnson Publishing Company, which publishes *Ebony*, *Jet*, *Tan*, and *Negro Digest*, had previously heard Bruce many times in New York. A fan of Bruce's, he thought the comments about black-white tensions in the country were intelligent and true. Kuh, in his cross-examination of Morrison, again tried to show that Bruce could be as effective if he used different words. The attempted shuffling of words was absurd. Ephraim, in his redirect questioning of Morrison, pointed that out. "Mr. Morrison, I call attention specifically to the words about which you were questioned by Mr. Kuh. The Negro saying, 'You are full of shit, you liberal,' would it be as effective to say, 'You are full of excrement, you liberal'?"

"Had Bruce used the word 'excrement' for 'shit' in the context, it would not have been effective but, as a matter of fact, totally ineffective for the purpose; it would be totally absurd."

"Again returning to the statement on page 10—'There's gonna be a change, you wouldn't believe it. Then you'll see an all-black jury and black judge and shit.' Now, wouldn't it have been just as effective for Mr. Bruce to use the word 'ordure' instead of 'shit'?"

"It would not have been effective at all in my view."

"Well, or the words 'bodily waste' instead of 'shit.' "

"Rather absurd, I think."

Judge Murtagh interrupted. "Might not it have been omitted altogether and have been just as effective?"

"Right. Well, I have already answered that question; but—"

Judge Murtagh attempted again. "But this time I am asking the question."

"Well, my answer is the same. I think the addition of those words reinforces the point in a colorful and humorous manner."

Daniel Dodson, professor of comparative literature at Columbia University, testified on the afternoon of July 3, 1964. He had the bearing of an academician, was older than most of our other witnesses, and would not be regarded by the trial or appellate judges as part of the avant-garde culture that some of our other witnesses represented. Having spent most of his life in scholarly work, he could relate Bruce's work to that of writers of the past. It would be difficult for the judges to discount his testimony totally, and perhaps one of the judges would feel that Bruce's work was not obscene simply because Dodson felt it wasn't. Dodson's description of the Jacqueline Kennedy sketch would have great weight certainly at the appellate level, if not for the trial court.

The difference in the judges' attitude was noticeable. Dodson testified with dignity, freshness, and intelligence. In response to Ephraim's questions, Dodson said that he had a Master's and a Doctor's Degree in English Literature from Columbia, that he was head of the Comparative Literature Department at Columbia, and that one of his major interests was satire. Dodson, with his eyes fixed on Murtagh, continued to answer on the direct examination.

"Would you state your opinion with respect to these two transcripts as satire?"

"These two transcripts suggest Mr. Bruce is one of our sharpest, most cogent, articulate satirists writing or speaking today. I think he is in the tradition of our great satirists, Swift and Rabelais. I think he expresses his moral outrage effectively. All satirists have a kind of moral outrage. Mr. Bruce has moral outrage. I think he states it effectively when he speaks of the pomposity, the ridiculousness, the hypocrisy of our society, and he satirizes it very effectively."

"Can you give us any specific example as to satire or expression of moral outrage?"

"Yes. I would choose one which is not popular because the subject matter probably would be considered indelicate. I am thinking about *Life* magazine's pictures showing Mrs. Kennedy on the back of the car at the time of the assassination of the late President Kennedy. Mr. Bruce suggests that the caption under the pictures said Mrs. Kennedy appeared to be helping the Secret Service man onto the car. Now, I felt when I saw that, this was a palpably absurd explanation. It seemed she was frightened and trying to get away from the bullets. I believe Mr. Bruce was quite correct in explaining, as he did, that hers was a perfectly normal reaction. Mr. Bruce was saying that this woman, a brave woman, indeed she was a brave woman, was going to get off the car and run for help under these circumstances. He talks about *Life* magazine's need to make her something she is not, and Bruce then says this is how we create false idols."

"You drew a parallel between Bruce's approach and Swift's and Rabelais' approach. Will you tell us what was intended by that?"

"Yes. Satire, as I understand it, is a rather complex subject. The satirist brings upon his material a certain perspective. Swift did this in *Gulliver's Travels*, in which he used the framework of Gulliver's travels to create a satirical situation. He does the same kind of thing in *The Modest Proposal*. Bruce uses the device occasionally, but his main device is the direct approach to the pomposity of our society—the vernacular of the street. He uses it very incisively, with a controlled, articulate mind. I think a good deal of humor or satirical approach is derived from this method."

"By the way, there is an emphasis, is there not, in the writings of both Swift and Rabelais, on bodily function?"

"Particularly in Swift's. He had an excremental obsession. He had a relatively—a pathological—excremental obsession, owing to the fact that Swift was an ill man when he wrote the last section of *Gulliver's Travels*."

Kuh attempted to discredit Professor Dodson by showing

that his sympathy for the substance of Bruce's satire made him less objective. He did not succeed.

The trial was going into its third week. The anti-pornography crusade had run its course as the stifling summer was beginning. Articles appearing in *The New Republic*, the *New York Post*, and *The New York Times* all questioned the district attorney's decision to continue the Bruce case. Why, they asked, was so much time, energy, and money being spent to prosecute Bruce? Was he such a danger as to warrant the full-time commitment of the district attorney's office for weeks on end?

Frank Hogan, a respected district attorney who had prosecuted some of the most notorious criminals in the country with composure, had become over-involved in the prosecution of the deadly Lenny Bruce. He had put his office's prestige on the line. When it became apparent that his office had misused its authority, he became nervous and irritable. The case touched him in a way that no big-rackets prosecution ever had. The state had originally told the court that the trial would not take more than three days, yet we were in our third week. Hogan and the court were amazed at the caliber of our witnesses. Hogan came to court several times to watch the case and was there for Dodson's testimony. He was visibly upset, especially when he looked about the crowded courtroom and saw many young members of his staff among the spectators, laughing at Bruce's material.

The district attorney's office in New York is in the same building as the courthouse, and when big cases are tried, members of the D.A.'s office often sit in to observe. Hogan knew of the practice and approved of it. The young lawyers in the district attorney's office could learn a great deal from watching experienced prosecutors and defense attorneys at work. But this time Hogan knew that some of his staff—the Harvard and

Yale graduates who were his pride—were not in favor of the prosecution. He was furious when he saw them sitting in the courtroom. When the court called the morning recess, he turned around from his third-row seat and signaled the lawyers to meet him in the hallway. He was livid. "What are you doing here? Is there anyone here who doesn't have work to do? If so, tell me and I'll find things to do. I don't want to see you here again." They stayed away for the rest of the trial.

Later that week, a close friend of mine in the appellate branch of the district attorney's office was called in to see Hogan. I had had lunch with this friend several times during the trial and we had exchanged comments as we saw each other coming and going in the building. Word got back to Hogan, and he accused my friend of fraternizing with the enemy. He told him to stop it. "The performance is filthy. Anyone who doesn't agree with the prosecution can hand in his resignation."

We decided to call Jules Feiffer, the tall, thin, quizzical-looking cartoonist and playwright. I felt he could add yet another perspective to the case.

Feiffer testified, "I think what Mr. Bruce does goes beyond social comment. He's not doing cute parodies about our pet peeves or showing how funny or disagreeable people are in this kind of society. He's going to the very core of what the American experience is today, in terms of my generation. I think also that his work must be judged in the context of the rest of that generation—what is being written today, the films, the plays, the artists producing the novels, and that whole attitude. Like any other performer, he'll have good nights and bad nights. When he's on, there's nothing like him. He's brilliant. One night, a message that he might use will seem pointless, and you don't understand why he's doing it. Another night, he works into it so beautifully that it explodes at you. I can't explain why, except that this is the nature of his art. And I consider Lenny Bruce an artist, and what he's performing is the art of verbal and visual improvisation, built up little by little over a series of performances. I understand it. It's really something new in theater and I consider what he's doing a very personal kind of theater."

Feiffer's earnest voice carried throughout the now quiet courtroom. Kuh, as well as the judges, were so interested that for a brief moment the trial seemed to stop. Feiffer continued: "Lenny Bruce creates a spurt of electricity that's so charged by his presence, his physical presence, what he does to and with the audience, that it becomes theater—and the only other night-club comedians I've seen able to do that were the type of Mike Nichols and Elaine May, who have managed to do it between them. But I've never seen anybody do it alone before. I might add also that Bruce, Sahl, Nichols, and May came along at a time in America when they were desperately needed, because their political and social commentaries existed during the days of the reign of President Eisenhower and McCarthyism, when nobody was saying anything. They were making human and political commentaries that could not be published in this country. But in the nightclubs, the small nightclubs, these people could perform and perfect their art, simply because no-body other than the audience was paying attention. And I think much of the literary development of the last few years has grown out of the atmosphere whose beginning was in these little clubs. I think Bruce has something to do with the history of liberalism in this country."

Kuh's cross-examination evoked mocking answers from Feiffer.

"Mr. Feiffer, I think that you mentioned your cartoon strip, and that I know is not an adequate description of it, but the 'Sick, Sick, Sick' cartoons which are now called 'Feiffer' have been running eight years now, have they?"

"It began in October of '56, in *The Village Voice,* and it be-came syndicated, I think, about three years later."

"And would you say, and that's why I hesitate to use the

words 'cartoon strip,' there's biting, effective, strong, sober satire? At least that's your intent, and they've won prizes as such, have they not?"

"Well, I make that attempt. Not every week, because some of them are just funny and throwaways, but generally I try to give a picture of contemporary American society as I see it, and do it in as hard a way as I can and still make some sense to the reader."

"And you puncture holes in just about anything that you think needs holes punctured in it, is that correct?"

"Only things I don't like."

"Right; and that includes quite a whole area of activities, does it not?"

"Quite a few things, yes, sir."

"It includes some of the racial bigotry?"

"Yes, sir."

"That's very important to you, is it not?"

"Yes, sir."

"And it includes religious bigotry and intolerance, and religious formalism that is intolerant of other religions following different formalisms?"

"Yes."

"And it includes sexual prudery?"

"Yes, sir."

"And it includes undue reverence for position, for title, for governmental authority?"

"I'm sorry, I'm not sure I understand that."

"It includes undue reverence and worship of position and title?"

"Yes, sometimes even due reverence."

"Due reverence?"

"Yes."

"And over the eight years of 'Sick, Sick, Sick' and 'Feiffer,' you've directed some of your effective satire at that?"

"Hopefully, yes."

"And yours is more than humor, yours is more than belly laughs, yours is satire in the great tradition of that word, as best you can do it, is that correct?"

"How do I answer that? I try, yes."

"With your usual modesty, Mr. Feiffer. I do mean that and respect that. Now, have you, in all these years, found it necessary in any of your cartoons to use, and my apologies for using these words, 'cocksucker,' 'motherfucker,' 'fuck,' 'shit,' 'piss'?"

"At the moment, Mr. Kuh, I'm working on a novel . . ."

"No, please answer my question first, Mr. Feiffer. In eight years of 'Sick, Sick, Sick,' now called 'Feiffer,' have you found it necessary to use any of those words?"

"I've found it at—I've found at times that I thought, not those words but other strong words might—would have been necessary, had I been able to get them in a newspaper, yes. Unfortunately, I also know what you can and cannot get in newspapers, so I haven't gotten them in."

"Have you seen the word 'fuck' in *The Village Voice*? Because I have."

"Yes, I've seen the work 'fuck' in *The Village Voice*, yes. But I've never seen it in the papers I'm syndicated in."

"*The Village Voice* is the paper you started in, is that correct?"

"Yes."

"And when you started in *The Village Voice*, did you use the work 'fuck' in any of your reviews?"

"No, but I didn't use the word 'goddamn,' because I was a growing boy then."

After Feiffer finished his testimony, Bruce again asked us to allow him to take the stand. "All those people are interpreting my act and my defense. They're saying they know my act better than I do. I'm just a little guy who says all these things without knowing how profound they are."

Bruce was right. It may have been Feiffer's version of his act instead of Ruhe's, but it was never Bruce's.

We were able to persuade him that he ought not to testify; he might possibly hurt his case, and there was still some chance of winning. Winning is often a lawyer's obsession. It's taken me a while to put winning and losing a case into proper perspective. Sometimes you win the case but hurt the client more in the winning than if you had lost. The strain on Bruce of sitting still each day was intolerable, but I'm not sure the result would have been any different if we had let him take the stand. And our primary responsibility was to Bruce even though we were playing to an audience larger than the trial judges and appellate courts.

Following Feiffer on the stand was Herbert Gans, the eminent sociologist and city planner. This small, chunky, gentle man was our most surprising witness. I spent hours with him at his home discussing his testimony. In private conversation he is often barely audible, says "yes" or "no" with great effort, and exhibits absolutely no emotion. His books, based on his observations about various communities, meticulously detail the lives and habits of those he observes, without the author's judgments or personality ever showing through.

Herbert Gans absorbs and understands. Could he articulate in the alien atmosphere of the courtroom? I was unsure about having him testify. Every one of our witnesses had, I felt, been excellent, and perhaps we were trying to gild the lily. Would the pressure of hostile judges result in his totally withdrawing? How quickly would he be able to think when loaded questions were hurled at him? We found out on July 9.

The listing of Gans's qualifications took at least twenty minutes. I had his four-page résumé before me as I asked about his background. Besides writing hundreds of articles, he had taught at universities all over the United States and had served as consultant to various government agencies. He had lived in different communities throughout the country and had carefully observed the use of language in each of these communities. As he testified about his four different university positions and ten consultantships in six years, a picture of an energetic, involved scholar emerged.

Bruce turned to Alan Schwartz, the lawyer for the Solomons. "Gans is no good. Why bring him here to testify? Look, he can't even hold a job or stay in one place. What's wrong with him?" Alan Schwartz burst out laughing. Murtagh interrupted the trial, called Schwartz to the bench, and said, "Any more laughing and I'll hold you in contempt." Schwartz promised that it wouldn't happen again.

Gans testified that, according to his studies, the word "fuck" and all its derivatives were used constantly by most men in the army, sometimes several times in one sentence and often liberally sprinkled throughout long conversations.

Murtagh looked disbelievingly at Gans and interrupted the questioning. "I was in the army for several years and never heard it."

Spectators in the courtroom laughed. Even Murtagh's fellow judges turned to look at him. Later that day, after spectators kept rushing up to Lenny and saying Murtagh's words were lies, Lenny said to me, "Everyone thinks he's lying. But they're wrong. He probably was an officer and never heard the words because he's not the kind of guy you say 'fuck' in front of. He's telling the truth."

I concluded Gans's direct examination by referring to a study he had made involving certain aspects of the life of Bostonians.

"Have you heard the words 'cocksucker,' 'shit,' 'fuck' used in the Boston community?"

"Yes, I have."

"How were they used?"

"They were used as words of anger and accusation and as words to put somebody else down, so to speak."

"Did they connote sexual imagery?"

"They didn't."

"At what point in the lives of the various people in the community did they first learn these words?"

"I assume that they learned them because they were in daily use; the children learned them from other children, learned them from parents, learned them from neighbors."

"Are these words used commonly where groups of men are together?"

"Yes."

"And have you observed them used with groups of women together?"

"Yes."

"And are they used in mixed company?"

"Yes."

Gans's answers on the direct examination were quietly and thoughtfully given. Kuh, thinking he could bully Gans, tore into him with sarcastic, needling questions. Gans at first answered softly; then, reacting to Kuh, he sat up on the chair, seemed to grow a foot, and proceeded to bury the prosecutor by raising his voice the smallest bit while continuing to give thoughtful answers.

"Are these words, when used, repugnant to the community? In other words, are they just among men or just among women or in mixed company—people who know each other extremely well?" Kuh asked.

"No. I think they're used as words of accusation, of anger. More among men as a group or women as a group, but also in mixed company when the anger is very strong."

"When you spoke to mixed groups, establishing friendship and interrelationship with them, did you use the word 'cocksucker'?"

"I've used it among my own friends."

"I didn't ask you about your own friends. Have you written papers about your own friends?"

"No."

"Well, I'm talking about your field of expertise, Professor."

"Well, the researcher does not use words of anger with people he is studying, because this interferes with his studies. He has to be a very neutral person."

"And he being a neutral person, these words are anything but neutral, is that correct?"

"He would control his anger of all kinds."

"And these words are words that, in your experience in American life, are used under terms of anger, irritation, is that correct?"

"I didn't get the middle of the question. Would you repeat it?"

"In your experience in American life, these are words basically of anger and emotion and irritation?"

"Of accusation, anger, for putting someone else down . . ."

"Have you used the word 'cunt' in your conversations with these people, Professor?"

"As a researcher, no."

"Have you, on occasion, gotten angry in the course of your work as a researcher?"

"Of course I have; yes."

"And when you've gotten angry, have you used the words 'cocksucker,' 'cunt,' 'motherfucker'?"

"I kept the anger to myself. I haven't gotten openly angry; no."

"Have you used them among these people with whom you've lived all of nine months in Boston and Minnesota? Have you used the words in your conversations with these people?"

"Not as a researcher; no."

"You say that they used them commonly, is that right?"

"Yes, yes . . ."

"And these words are only used when the people are wrought up, emotionally disturbed, losing control?"

"I said they used them in anger; they're not necessarily emotionally overwrought. They're everyday words of anger."

Kuh's frustration and anger were manifest when the cross-examination ended.

Several times that day the judge warned us about Bruce's practice of commenting on the witnesses' testimony. Murtagh did not find the comments funny. He made it clear that he thought it was the lawyer's responsibility to quiet the client. Judge Murtagh today is saying the same thing to the lawyers involved in the Panther 21 trial, reminding them that they are, as Lenny said to me when we met, officers of the court first and advocates second.

I think he is wrong about the lawyer-client relationship. The lawyer has a greater obligation to his client than to the court. This does not mean that if his client wants to disrupt the courtroom, the lawyer is obligated to emulate his client's conduct. If the client carries on a course of conduct that can lead either to the loss of the case or to punitive contempt proceedings, then it is the lawyer's responsibility to make sure that the client knows of those consequences.

After Gans testified, Lenny and I had lunch together for the first time since the trial began. His paranoia was mounting. As we were sitting talking in the Italian restaurant behind the courthouse, which is frequented by district attorneys and plainclothesmen, the waiter who brought us our food let the tray slide and dropped the bread. "It's a signal to the cops. They're gonna bust me here," Lenny said. His eyes darted around and he saw that many of the diners in the restaurant were looking at him. He sat helplessly waiting for the arrest that never came.

Dozens of incidents during the day confirmed his fear—from the way he was looked at on the bus by passengers, to the way salespeople reacted as he bought electronic equipment. He never got angry—just sadder—as he withdrew more deeply into himself. He could express his anger on stage during a performance as he mocked cops, churches, and society in general, but he could never personalize his deep emotion so he could lash back at his tormentors.

We went back to court. Murtagh, his hair immaculately parted, his manner that of a man involved in the burdensome task of sentencing another man to die, remained impassive throughout the testimony we offered. Judge J. Randall Creel, trying to catch concepts he was unfamiliar with, smiled quizzically as Bruce's imagery flew by. Judge Kenneth Phipps, as the trial wore on, came to laugh at the new material he heard each day. (Maybe if he enjoyed the performance he would dissent from the conviction?) Whenever he felt like laughing, he would swivel in his chair so his back was to Murtagh and he would cover his mouth with his hand. Though it hardly seemed possible, Murtagh became even more impassive.

While we were on trial, from mid-June to mid-July, the obscenity law changed dramatically in our favor, leaving no doubt that a conviction of Bruce would be overturned on appeal. The most drastic change came with the Supreme Court's 1964 rulings in the *Tropic of Cancer* and Jacobellis cases.

On June 22, 1964, the United States Supreme Court, in an appeal from a Florida conviction based on the sale of *Tropic of Cancer*, found the book not to be obscene. The *Tropic of Cancer* cases showed that "dirty" language could not sustain a conviction. The state, in its prosecution of Bruce, had directed its attack primarily at Bruce's use of taboo words, since the state could not seriously claim that his act was erotic or appealing to the prurient interest.

The Supreme Court on the same day decided each of the issues we had presented on Jacobellis's behalf in his and ultimately Bruce's favor. Five different opinions were written by the justices, as they disagreed about nearly all the issues presented to them. Mr. Justice Brennan, joined by Mr. Justice Goldberg, gave the first opinion.

Mr. Justice Brennan first rejected the argument that the Supreme Court should not review a jury's determination of obscenity, because, he said, we are dealing with the right to free speech and the factual issues are too great not to be reviewed.

Second, Mr. Justice Brennan rejected the argument that "contemporary community standards" referred to local standards. Knowing that a local standard would result in books being banned in one state and not in another, Justice Brennan said the standard must be a national standard, as "it is, after all, a national constitution we are expounding." Any other decision would have been calamitous, for the suppression of a particular book or film in one locality would deter its distribution in other localities where it might not be held to be obscene. Sellers and exhibitors would be reluctant to test the variations in different places.

The last and perhaps most significant legal issue was Mr. Justice Brennan's rejection of the balancing test—of "weighing" social importance against prurient appeal. "A work cannot be proscribed unless it is 'utterly' without social value," he said.

The Jacobellis decision indicated to Bruce's judges that the Supreme Court would examine every obscenity verdict to see whether the material violated a national standard. The *Tropic of Cancer* case illustrated the application of the Jacobellis rules to a controversial work that had previously been found obscene primarily because of its use of "dirty" words. The decisions forewarned that if Bruce's work had any social value, a conviction was improper.

Fifteen days later, on July 7, 1964, we were told by Bruce's Chicago lawyers that the Supreme Court of Illinois had ordered his Cook County case reargued because of the U. S. Supreme Court's ruling in the Jacobellis case. It was unusual for a court to recall a decision on its own motion; it suggested that the Illinois court was going to reverse the conviction.

The following week the New York Court of Appeals, as a result of the Jacobellis and *Tropic of Cancer* cases, held that the book *Fanny Hill* could not be suppressed as obscene. Chief Judge Desmond, in his dissenting opinion, described the book as containing, "to the last intimate physical detail, numerous instances not only of prostitution, but of voyeurism, transvestism, homosexuality, lesbianism, flogging, seduction of a boy, etc, etc. Indeed, the book is 'pornography' in the strictest philological and etymological sense of the word, since it is, quite literally, the narration by a prostitute of the particulars of her trade."

Bruce's severest critics could not claim that his work approached that level. Bruce said, "How can they continue this? Why won't they at least let me work while this is going on, so I can live? I'll let them see my act in advance. I'll do it here and maybe they'll tell me this act, the one I do, is okay. And that's the only one I'll do."

Hogan, representing the People of the State of New York, could and should have dropped the charges against Bruce then because of the changes in the law. But he did not. The trial continued.


We started the next day with Forrest Johnson, the tall, athletic-looking minister of the Edgehill Community Church in Riverdale, New York. He was the first witness we called to the stand who had been in the audience on April 1, 1964, the night of the arrest. Mr. Johnson, a minister for thirteen years, held a B.S. degree from the Presbyterian Theological Seminary in Chicago and a Ph.D. degree from Edinburgh University.

I questioned him: "What time did you arrive?"

"We arrived at the Café Au Go Go I should say sometime between eleven and eleven-thirty."

"Did you see Lenny Bruce's entire performance?"

"I did."

"Where were you seated in relation to the platform on which he was speaking?"

"As you enter the Café Au Go Go, assuming that you enter in the direction I'm facing, I was seated on the aisle, about two-thirds of the way down to the stage."

"Now, during the entire performance that you saw, did Lenny Bruce ever make a gesture pointing toward his crotch?"

"No."

"During the entire performance that you watched, did Bruce make any gesture that was somehow suggestive of masturbation?"

"None whatsoever."

"Either with a microphone or without a microphone?"

"No."

"You're certain of that?"

"I'm certain of that. I think I would be reasonably sensitive to an act of that sort. I don't think I would have missed it."

As the judges saw it, Bruce's act had attacked God and religion. Mr. Johnson said: "Mr. Bruce is making a distinction between the God of the Hebrews and the God of the Christians. He says, 'You can find the Christian God in the five-and-ten and in cereal boxes.' This is an important point. Within our Judaeo-Christian tradition, one of the things we are concerned about is the cheapening of our God, the raising up of false gods. One of the great Biblical stories, you'll remember, is that Aaron built a golden calf, and the people went from worshipping the true God to worshipping the golden calf. I think this is analogous to what he's talking about—a cheapening and idolatrizing of religion. . . . If I may go far enough afield, it strikes me that the movie *The Ten Commandments* was criticized by many of us as obscene, as an attempt to use religion, and hypocritically through it to bring in obscene material. Bruce says, 'The Christian God has appeared in three pictures.' Yes, God appeared in *The Ten Commandments*, and that to me was a cheapening and a misuse of religion; and to this extent I think Mr. Bruce was showing himself to be a very aware social critic.

"I think his routine concerning the mezuzah, which is a religious article of the Hebrews, is a sensitive statement. Among the Hebrews in early times, as distinct from the Christians, the name of God was so sacred it was not even mentioned. The word 'Yahweh' is just an attempt to make the initials for God, which was unspeakable among the Hebrews. I think in referring to this, he's referring to the sin relative to the problem that the Hebrew has with respect to giving a name to God.

"Bruce, in the performance, talked about those who lie for truth. It seems to me that in his book *The Brothers Karamazov* Dostoevsky talks about something very close to this: the Grand Inquisitor meets Christ fictionally in a town square in Seville and he says, 'You brought the people freedom, but we've given them miracles, mystery, and authority, and they want our anthill, so to speak. In other words, you've given them this burden of freedom.' Along with that mentality in history has gone the idea that everything is subsumed under the larger purpose, the larger totality; one can lie for what he considers the bigger truth. He is saying, 'I don't care whether you're talking about lying for Communism or lying for Christianity or lying for anything else—it is still lying.' I simply want to say that I think this man is profoundly sensitive and has shown himself to be profoundly compassionate. He says, 'I'm weak, you're weak, humanity is weak, and therefore we're bound up in a kind of bundle of life that requires that we show each other understanding.' "

Kuh in his cross-examination pressed the point that the larger segment of the New York community would not give the same interpretation as our witnesses had—that what Johnson considered a striking comment on religion would be found offensive by other churchgoers as religious as Johnson. Johnson pointed out that he himself made comments similar to Bruce's from his pulpit, using different language, and Kuh again took up the matter of the taboo words.

"Are those words that you would hesitate to use in ordinary social conversation with your congregants?"

"I—they aren't in my general vocabulary, but I know that individuals whom I consider to be individuals of propriety use them occasionally to make a point."

"Are they words that you would hesitate to use in mixed company—men and women who were members of your congregation?"

"If I wanted to make a point and I felt they were the right words, I would not hesitate."

"Have you ever used any of the words in mixed company, with your congregants?"

"I have."

"Which one?"

"I have used the word 'shit.' "

"Have you ever used the word 'fuck'?"

"I have used that. As a matter of fact, the other day I was discussing this case and my eight-year-old asked, 'Did they use the word "fuck"?' She asked it in a most objective fashion and, I thought, in a way that didn't cause any kind of disfavor to her. I—I'm glad my daughter felt that she could ask that word in company that included my congregants."

What followed next was as unseemly as it was unnecessary.

"And when you go home, tonight at dinner with your daughter, you intend, in order to relieve her of guilt feelings, to use the words 'fuck,' 'motherfucker,' 'cocksucker'?"

The court sustained my objection. Kuh tried again.

"Do you intend to use the rest of the Bruce vocabulary at dinner tonight in conversation with your daughter?"

I objected and said, "Mr. Kuh is just trying to offend this witness." The court again sustained the objection.

We rested the case for the defense on July 9, 1964, after twelve witnesses who had seen Bruce at various performances testified that at no time had they seen Bruce make any lewd gestures; they denied he ever touched his crotch on the stage and denied he ever moved his hands in a masturbatory gesture.

The state called five witnesses in rebuttal: Robert Sylvester, the Broadway columnist for the *New York Daily News;* Dan Potter, executive director of the Protestant Council; John Fischer, vice president of Harper and Row; Ernest Van Den Haag, a professor of social philosophy at New York University; and Marya Mannes, the well-known social critic.

All had disparaging things to say about Bruce's performance, but on the whole their testimony helped our case more than it hurt it. Sylvester said that though Bruce used "some pretty strong language," a number of performers, he acknowledged, including Jackie Cannon, Joe E. Lewis, Jackie Gleason, and Dean Martin, used the same language. Dan Potter, after observing that the only place Bruce's language would be accepted would be "in the back wards of the Rochester State Mental Hospital," said he considered *Tropic of Cancer, Lady Chatterley's Lover, Ulysses,* and *Fanny Hill* to be in the same category. Potter also felt that the words "fornicate" and "sexual intercourse" were obscene.

Marya Mannes, the author of four books, with a well-earned reputation based on her independence of mind and her outspokenness, was the most formidable of the state's witnesses. A contributor to *The New York Times, Herald Tribune, Esquire, Harper's Magazine,* and *The Saturday Evening Post,* she appeared regularly on radio and television. A social critic, she was the state's counterpoint to Dorothy Kilgallen. She testified, in response to a question of Kuh's, that she "did not use the same language as Bruce" because "I don't think it would help." Kuh then asked Miss Mannes if, judging by our contemporary community standards, these materials would in her opinion be deemed offensive.

I objected on the grounds that the witness had not been qualified as an expert on contemporary community standards. I
knew the court would overrule the objection. I also knew Miss
Mannes, hearing my objection, would refuse to declare herself
an expert and would phrase her answer in personal terms.

She answered: "Well, I don't know what qualification one
has to have for knowing or assuming what community standards are, and I admit this is an extremely hard term to define. I
wouldn't attempt to define it at this point. I found, as a
member of the community, that four-letter words are everywhere these days . . . although I might say the performances
were, if I may use the word, cleaned up in San Francisco—the
profusion of four-letter words in the transcripts I found offensive."

I then cross-examined her.

"Would you in the course of your own writing, Miss
Mannes, use certain words if you felt it to be effective?"

"Effective is not the word to be used. I would say whatever
is necessary that I felt needed saying."

"As I understand your testimony, you stated that you would
use those words if it were necessary to get your point across, is
that right?"

"I would if I felt so, but only with the aim of—only if I
could find no other way to express or to prove a point, but not
for the saying of the word by itself."


On July 28, 1964, at 4:30 in the afternoon in the middle of a
blistering New York summer, we completed the taking of testimony. Lenny, Ephraim, and I left the courtroom exhausted.
The court gave us thirty days to file a legal memorandum summing up all the trial evidence.

In September we filed our final brief asking for acquittal, and
the state responded by pressing for conviction. Kuh's brief said
the recent Supreme Court decision did not mean that Bruce's

work was protected. Although he had, during the trial, used the Chicago conviction to justify the New York prosecution, he was silent about the Illinois court's decision to reconsider the case.

Lenny, desperately short of funds to cover his own living expenses, tried all during the trial to find work in New York. No one would hire him. Theater and nightclub owners were afraid of arrests. Finally, when the trial ended, the owner of the Cork and Bib, a nightclub in Westbury, in Nassau County, agreed to have Lenny perform. Lenny was exhilarated and in the week before he was to perform seemed to regain some of his spark. But after the first performance, as he was walking out to the parking lot, he was stopped by Assistant District Attorney Norman Levy of Nassau County and a detective. Levy told Lenny and Marshall Blumenfeld, a close friend of Bruce's who was with him, that the show was not "his cup of tea." Levy said the Las Vegas parody, the "tits and asses bit," was "questionable."

"What is it you don't like?" Blumenfeld asked. "The language or the mockery of Las Vegas?"

Levy, turning to Bruce, said, "He's the expert on obscenity. I'll let him judge that. If you do another show like the one you did tonight, I'll arrest you." Then turning to Hirst, the owner of the Cork and Bib, Levy said, "If you let him go on, I'll pull your license." Lenny walked away, crushed, never to work in New York again.

In October, while we waited for the court's decision, our relationship with Lenny reached a breaking point. He felt we were only interested in making an appellate record and were not trying to communicate with the trial judges. Becoming more tense as the month passed without a decision, he finally fired us in late October.

November 6, 1964, was decision day in the case. I went to court to help Lenny if he needed it. I arrived shortly before 10:00 A.M. The press, assistant district attorneys, and lawyers filled the courtroom. The clerk came out and asked if we were all present. We were—all but Lenny.

We waited, and as the minutes passed, I became apprehensive. I had spoken to Bruce a few days before and didn't know if he was going to show up. He feared the decision—he knew he was going to lose and was terrified of jail and the stigma of being branded a "dirty" comic. He also felt that a conviction would ruin him financially. He was becoming more and more confused.

Shortly after eleven, Lenny came in, clean-shaven and, for the first time since the legal process had begun on April 6, seven months ago, attired in a suit and tie. He looked like the typical defendant!

I told the clerk we could begin, and the three judges left the robing room and mounted their seats behind the bench—Judge Murtagh in the middle and Judges Phipps and Creel on either side. "Is everybody ready?" Murtagh asked. Bruce rose and asked permission to put in additional evidence since the case had not yet been decided. Murtagh said, "The case is closed." Bruce replied, "I'd like to reopen it. How can you decide if my act is obscene if you never saw or heard my act? All you heard was a dirty show presented by the district attorney." He concluded, "I so much want to have the respect of the court."

I sat beside Bruce as he spoke. I wanted to restrain him, to tell him he wasn't getting anywhere. But throughout the trial he had kept still—at great cost to himself. He had listened to us all through the proceedings, and in his eyes we had failed. I could not say for certain that his more human approach was not perhaps better than our way. I've tried enough cases to know that many times the client is right about a particular approach.

Months of welled-up tension and feeling went into Lenny's plea. I found it heartbreaking. It was only then, after my tension and my involvement were over and the wall I had built to keep Lenny at a distance collapsed, that I realized how much I cared for him. The more he spoke, the more love I felt for him. He made a deeply moving plea, and it came to nothing.

Murtagh, with scarcely concealed disgust, ordered Bruce to be seated. He gave his decision. "Ella Solomon is acquitted. Judge Phipps and I vote to convict Howard Solomon and Lenny Bruce; Judge Creel dissents."

All along I had had mixed feelings. I knew the conviction was almost a certainty, yet I continued to hope. When I heard the decision, I leaned over to Ephraim and said, "They didn't hear a word of the testimony. It's as if we had not presented any witnesses. The whole thing was a goddamn waste, and we didn't make it easier for Bruce."

The dissenting vote was, however, a partial victory and of critical importance for the appeal. The appellate court would scrutinize the trial record more closely now than they would have if the judges had been unanimous. It was at that point that our evidence would bear fruit. The record in the Bruce case would run to several thousand pages—probably none of the judges who would preside over Bruce's numerous appeals would have heard of him before.

Theoretically, the judges of the appellate courts read each record with equal care. In the first New York appellate level, the calendars are so crowded that it is difficult to believe the court ever reads the records, or even a fair percentage of the briefs. The dissent, however, pulled Bruce's case out from among the hundreds of unanimous obscenity convictions. At least one of the three judges was convinced of the value of our constitutional argument and of the facts we had introduced concerning the performance.

I was certain an appeals court would reverse Bruce's conviction. Judge Murtagh's decision was a travesty. There are many ways for a judge to write a decision without revealing his prejudices. Murtagh highlighted his by saying that Bruce had made a masturbatory gesture and by resurrecting an archaic concept of obscenity.

Judge Murtagh knew, as Kuh knew, that there was small probability that the conviction would be affirmed by a higher court solely on the basis of Lenny's words. Something more was needed to justify a conviction—some overt act. The state gave the "something more" to Murtagh and Murtagh used it. Ruhe had testified in an offhand manner that Bruce's hands were on the microphone as he performed and that his hands slid up and down the microphone. This, of course, is not unique; but Ruhe, who had heard hundreds of "dirty words" where there were none, for whom it was all "philosophical claptrap," exaggerated Bruce's hand motion and described it as a "masturbatory gesture." Patrolman Lane, attending the performance at the request of Hogan's office, said he saw Bruce touch his crotch. Apparently none of the other license-department employees or policemen who had witnessed Lenny's performances saw any such thing, for they were never called to confirm Ruhe's testimony.

During the trial I had interviewed some thirty-five people who had seen the April 1 performance. Every one of them denied that Bruce made any masturbatory gesture. I had put on the stand the twelve best factual witnesses—best because of their diversity, articulateness, and ability to withstand cross-examination. But, although Ruhe's testimony was contradicted by twelve witnesses, Murtagh found that Bruce had made the criminal gesture. This, he said, "together with language that was not erotic but vulgar," sustained the conviction. Murtagh ignored not only the Jacobellis and *Tropic of Cancer* decisions that had come down during the course of the trial, but all recent legal authority. He cited old decisions that had long since been repudiated by the Supreme Court.

The final irony was the action taken by the legal reporting services and the *New York Law Journal*, which reproduce for distribution to all lawyers the decisions of all trial and appellate courts. They resolved not to distribute Murtagh's opinion because, by its use of language, it was itself obscene. The *New*

*York Law Journal* explained that the words (found in books being sold daily in drugstores and on newsstands, and in plays performed on and off Broadway) were too rough for the sensitive ears of the legal profession. "The majority opinion of necessity cited in detail the language used by Bruce in his nightclub act, and also described gestures and routines which the majority found to be obscene and indecent." The *Law Journal* decided against publication, even in edited form, on the grounds that deletions would destroy the opinion and without the deletions publication was impossible "within the *Law Journal* standards." Bruce's reaction: "Why don't they arrest Murtagh?"

Judge J. Randall Creel wrote a fifteen-page dissenting opinion concluding that Bruce should be acquitted. He found the court's attempt to determine community standards an impossible task.

After Creel read his dissent, Murtagh suggested sentencing for December 16. Everyone agreed but Bruce. He asked to be sentenced immediately, explaining that he could not afford to remain in the city without working and could not afford to travel back and forth to appear in December. I had explained to Lenny before we came to court that defendants can waive the right to a time lapse between decision and sentence.

Murtagh, emotionless as always, rejected Bruce's application. "December 16 for sentencing." He ordered Bruce to report to probation for fingerprinting and a psychiatric examination, and then adjourned court. Lenny was left at the bench inside the court bar, rolling his eyes toward the ceiling and muttering, "If I could just show them my act." He felt that there was malice behind the decision but still believed he could reach the judges. He knew that the morning's developments presaged a punitive sentence. Ignoring Judge Murtagh's direction to report for a psychiatric examination and fingerprinting, he walked out of the courtroom and out of the building.

On November 24, 1964, the Illinois Supreme Court reversed

its previous decision convicting Lenny. The court in acquitting Lenny relied on precedents that had come down during the summer of Lenny's New York trial.

One month later, on December 16, Bruce walked into Judge Murtagh's court for sentencing, wearing a dirty blue trench coat over torn, faded blue dungarees and a blue-striped T-shirt. His shoulders were hunched, his hands in his pockets. He looked at the room as if he were trying to memorize it. The night before, Bruce said, "I know he's a good man. I can talk to him. He's just insulated. He'll hear me. It's my last chance to get through to him." Lenny was frenetic, hysterical. It was not only that he was going to be sentenced but that he was finally going to have a chance to confront his judge. He was scared stiff.

Murtagh asked the formal question the law required, "Is there any reason why sentence should now not be imposed?" There is rarely any answer other than "no."

Bruce exploded with feeling. He began to answer Murtagh at 3:35 P.M. Before he concluded, he had run two minutes over his usual one-hour performance time. He began his attempt to communicate with the judges by advising them that he had filed a suit against them in the Federal Court in Manhattan for half a million dollars each. The suit claimed that the judges' conviction of him violated his civil rights.

"It's twenty-five to four and I speak for the record. Your Honor, the first motion I make, I would like the bench to appoint a referee. The reason being I have sued Your Honor personally for $500,000 under 1983, as Your Honor is aware. You were served personally. I sued Magistrate Phipps and Magistrate Creel, and the civil suit 356474 is still on. The temporary restraining order was denied, but there is still a suit and I feel that perhaps Your Honor might be a bit biased. And I would like Your Honor to appoint a Master for the tape recording that reflects the perjury that Mr. Kuh encouraged. The Master would also listen to the tape recording and see the distortions and conflicts in the record—the transcript which I purchased from the court reporter. I wait to hear Your Honor's word if you would appoint a Master or not."

Judge Murtagh responded, "Your motion is denied. Anything else?"

"Judge, just hear my act once. You convicted me on what someone else said my act is. I know you are all good men and want to do right." Lenny was like a small child pleading to his father. "Just let me show you my act. I know you'll help because this is justice and you don't want to do wrong. Please, please just let me show you my act. It's not dirty." Murtagh sat stony-faced. His eyes never wavered.

A newspaper, reporting on Bruce's monologue the following day, said, "Deeper and deeper Bruce went, declaiming decisions, citing citations, lecturing on the law until it became impossible to tell when Bruce was quoting and commenting on Justice Holmes, or when Bruce himself was quoting and commenting on Justice Roberts quoting and commenting on Justice Holmes."

Bruce went on. He had uncovered new evidence which required reversal of the verdict and he wanted the court to read it. His new evidence was thirty years old—the legislative bill jacket of the thirty-year-old statute he was being tried under, and letters written to Governor Franklin D. Roosevelt in 1931 when the legislature sought to amend the obscenity law to exempt actors from the provisions of the obscene-performance statute. Bruce said this meant he was immune from prosecution. Bruce never realized that the proposed amendment had not been passed.

The most important words that can be said to the court at the sentencing are the words of the prosecutor. The state was brutal. Kuh spoke: "First as to the defendant Bruce: I'm here at the direction of the district attorney, Frank S. Hogan, and ask on behalf of the people of this county that the defendant Lenny Bruce's sentence be one of imprisonment. May I state in support of that request, if it please the court, that apart from the defendant Bruce's conduct prior to the trial, the defendant Bruce throughout the trial, and since the trial, has shown by his conduct complete lack of any remorse whatsoever."

Lenny cried out, "Remorse! For what? I came to court not for mercy but for justice."

Murtagh sentenced Bruce to four months in the workhouse. Howard Solomon, the owner of the Café Au Go Go, was fined $1,000. Judge Creel, who had dissented from the conviction, also dissented from the sentence, saying that he did not believe Bruce should be jailed.

There was a discussion on the question of delaying Bruce's sentence until the appeal was decided. Bruce pleaded for time. He had neither lawyer nor funds. If he was in jail, he said, he could not get the appellate process started before he served his sentence. And then his appeal would be "moot."

Bruce was a first offender convicted of a misdemeanor by a split court. Any prison sentence at all was outrageous. And he was faced with four months in prison. It was incredible that the question of stay pending appeal should even have been an issue.

Kuh wanted Bruce jailed immediately, but the court indicated its willingness to give Bruce time to make the application for a stay. Kuh and the judges argued. Bruce stood by without a lawyer while all this was going on. The trial court, reacting against Kuh's overzealousness, granted Bruce's request.

After the conviction and sentencing, Bruce brought suit after suit in the federal courts. He wanted to perform in Long Island and Manhattan, but nightclub owners, threatened with arrest, would not hire him. He tried to get a permanent injunction barring threatened prosecutions by William Cahn, the Nassau district attorney, and by Hogan's office. After the injunction was denied in the lower federal court, he appealed to the Circuit Court of Appeals.

The Court of Appeals is on the seventeenth floor of the federal courthouse in Lower Manhattan. It is an elegant, large, high-ceilinged courtroom. Because it is in New York, it hears a great number of commercial cases, antitrust cases, violations of the Securities Exchange Act, and the like. By and large, it is the more successful Wall Street lawyers who try these cases. The dozens of such lawyers getting together on a morning in the Court of Appeals to argue their cases make the room resemble a bankers' meeting. It was an incongruous scene when Bruce, in his white Nehru jacket, arrived to argue his appeal of the denial of an injunction. His fellow advocates were stunned.

He walked in carrying a suitcase filled with papers and legal books. When his case was called, he went to the podium and stacked his law books, place marks protruding from many of the pages, all over the counsel's table. The bench he faced consisted of Judge Henry Friendly, a scholarly, conservative judge; Judge Paul Hays, formerly head of the National Labor Relations Board; and Judge Thurgood Marshall, who was later to become the first black judge appointed to the Supreme Court.

Bruce rose and explained to the court, "I want them to stop prosecuting me in the future. I want you to enjoin them from any arrests for my act, and to stop them from putting me in jail. I'll show you some of it so you'll see there's nothing wrong with it. Under the law, before a judge can stop a performance and arrest the performer, he has to be shown the performance is obscene. What I'm doing is the other way around. But I'll have to show you some of what I'm doing."

The judges listened with interest. Lenny first talked about America's misuse of Christ symbols. He then went into a sketch commenting on the kinds of justice all white men can expect from black juries, pointing out that black men would treat whites as badly as they themselves had been treated. He concluded with his imitation of the outraged liberal saying, "They gave me twenty years for raising my voice—those niggers." Marshall's head jerked up and he nearly dropped a pen from his hand. Bruce saw Marshall's face, stumbled, tried bravely to explain the joke, but could not. Then he knew he had lost the case and sat down.

Bruce died a pathetic, incoherent, broken man on August 3, 1966. He died from an overdose of drugs. Before that, he had sustained serious injuries when he fell from a window. But to me his death was in large part due to the inner turmoil, frustration, and overwhelming feeling of helplessness he had experienced as he fought the law during his last five years.

After Bruce died Howard Solomon, who had been convicted along with Lenny, continued the appeal with the help of William Hellerstein, a Legal Aid Society lawyer. On February 18, 1968, nearly four years after Bruce's arrest, the appellate term reversed Murtagh's decision by another 2 to 1 decision. Although it was the finding of Bruce's act as obscene that was reversed, the case entitled *People v. Solomon* does not appear to be part of the Bruce drama. Bruce is not mentioned in the decision and the case does not bear his name.

The appellate court said obscenity had not been proved:

> The court below found that the monologues were "not erotic" and "not lust inciting." Moreover, integral parts of the performance included comments on problems of contemporary society. Religious hypocrisy, racial and religious prejudices, the obscenity laws and human tension were all subjects of comment. Therefore, it was error to hold that the performances were without social importance.

Judge Samuel H. Hofstadter dissented. While agreeing that there are different standards for different media, he said, "This appeal involves a public performance. In this aspect it is to be distinguished from the sale of a magazine, a book or the sale of film." His characterization of Bruce's work as a "public performance" rather than as a nightclub performance for a limited, voluntary audience indicated that he would impose a higher standard on Bruce's act than on a book, magazine, or film. And he did. "The right of the people to regulate public conduct under the police power of the State is of greater scope." Voting to affirm the conviction, he concluded that the monologues were merely a device to enable Bruce to exploit "the use of obscene language."

The state could have let matters end there. But Hogan wanted vindication and he appealed to New York's highest court. Two years later, on January 22, 1970, the New York Court of Appeals, in the case called *People v. Solomon,* affirmed the appellate term's decision by a 6 to 1 vote.

Judge Adrian Burke of the Court of Appeals said Judge Creel's lower-court dissent expressed his opinions on the case. Judge John F. Scileppi, the dissenting Judge who wanted the conviction upheld, drew an analogy between *Fanny Hill* and *Tropic of Cancer* and Bruce, saying they were all dirt. His feelings about the Bruce case can be gleaned in his dissent from a decision that approved the sale of *Fanny Hill.* "The majority opinion here, in my view, sounds the death knell of the long-honored standards of American decency which have remained an integral part of our national heritage." Bruce never knew he had that much power.

I saw Jerry Harris, the district attorney originally assigned to the Bruce case, in 1970, after the case ended, and he told me: "I'm glad I had nothing to do with it. I saw and heard about Lenny during and after the trial. The case helped to kill and destroy him. It was terrible. Looking back on it, all those obscenity prosecutions were a waste of time. We should be doing other things. I'm glad I don't have Bruce on my conscience."

Bruce, if he were alive today, would probably be arrested as often as he was in the sixties. First Amendment law is basically the same as it was at the time of Bruce's trial. All it takes is one ambitious politician or prosecutor. What Lenny would say about Agnew and Mylai, Nixon and Johnson, could lead to his destruction. In the past five years the spirit of the Warren court affected the decision-making powers of lower-court judges and prosecuting attorneys, resulting in fewer "speech" arrests and convictions. Partially as a result of this, society is more open than before. But the pendulum is swinging back. New members of the Supreme Court have indicated that they will not be strictly bound by the Warren court's decisions. More legislation seeking to control speech and conduct is pending today in the legislative halls than at any time since the McCarthy era. The new impetus for repression is part of the law-and-order feeling in the country. The men and forces who prosecuted Bruce still hold the power of the law.

# Three

*Mrs. Sylvester Smith against*
*Ruben King and George Wallace*

ON THE FINAL DAY of the 1968 term of the Supreme Court, Chief Justice Earl Warren delivered what he believed would be his last Supreme Court opinion. A week later the Chief Justice made known his desire to leave the court.

Reporters, constitutional lawyers, academicians, and Supreme Court buffs heard him render his decision in a momentous test case—one that had examined the power of the states to deprive mothers and children of aid to which they are entitled under a federal welfare program. The case had started two years before, in October 1966, when Mrs. Sylvester Smith, a penniless black woman, and her four children were cut off from welfare aid. I took her suit to the Alabama federal court and later the United States Supreme Court. Hers was the first welfare case to be argued in the high court—thirty-three years after the Social Security Act was passed. The decision profoundly changed the welfare system and helped the country move toward a guaranteed minimum income.

The effects of *Smith v. King*, as the case was first called, went far beyond Mrs. Sylvester Smith, plaintiff, and the defendants Ruben King and George Wallace, representing the state of Alabama. Nineteen states had welfare regulations similar to Alabama's, and each year those regulations were invoked in cases involving more than 750,000 children. The decision directly affected every one of those children. Ultimately, it affected laws on the books in every state, laws allowing government employees to degrade the eight million American welfare recipients by delving into their private lives and forcing answers to humiliating questions upon the threat of cutting off aid.

Mrs. Sylvester Smith first applied for aid a few months after her husband was killed "in a fight over a woman." She was twenty-three years old and was left with three children: Ida Elizabeth, three; Ernestine, two; and Willie Lewis, fourteen months. Aid was granted. In January 1957 she had her fourth child, Willie James, the son of Louis Fuller. Willie James was added to the AFDC (Aid to Families with Dependent Children) lists in June 1963, after Fuller left town, presumably for New York. The Smith family received about $45 a month until March 1966.

That summer of 1966 Mrs. Smith moved with her daughters from the country town of Tyler up to Selma, where she found a job as a cook and waitress in a Negro café—3:30 A.M. to noon for $16 a week, later raised to $20. Her two sons stayed in the country with their grandparents, joining the family in Selma on weekends.

One result of the move to Selma in 1966 was that the Smiths were assigned to a new caseworker, a young bulldogged woman named Miss Jacqueline Stancil, whose record bears out the impression she gives of going about her duties in a most tenacious way. Miss Stancil intended to apply all the rules to the letter. After reviewing the Smith file and noting mention of William E. Williams, Miss Stancil questioned a third party and was told that Mrs. Smith was being visited on weekends by Williams, who lived in Tyler, fifteen miles south of Selma. "When I asked who told," recalls Mrs. Smith, "she said, 'It was a little birdie.' I'd like to meet that little birdie."

Mrs. Buster, Mrs. Smith's caseworker during her years in the country, had been content to overlook the visits of Willie Williams; Miss Stancil was not, and in September 1966 she notified Mrs. Smith that her aid would be stopped if Williams kept coming around.

On October 11, 1966, Mrs. Smith was notified that her aid was being stopped. It was a loss of $29 a month, more than one quarter of her income. Not one to suffer rebuffs in silence (a few weeks earlier Mrs. Smith had addressed a letter to President Johnson, complaining about her daughter's being dropped from the aid rolls because the girl had had a baby), Mrs. Smith went to the welfare department and insisted on seeing Miss Stancil. "It's none of your business what I do. I'm not having any more children. Who says I'm sleeping with some man?" Williams was married, she said. His wife worked, they had nine children to take care of, and he had never helped her with more than $4 to $5 a month. "Ain't much he can do," she told Miss Stancil. "You can't make a man take care of his own kids, much less take care of other people's kids."

Miss Stancil said the rule was the rule, and since "you admit he gave you things," the rule applied. Mrs. Smith insisted on speaking to Miss Stancil's superior, a Mrs. Johnson, and to Mrs. Buster. For two hours Mrs. Buster, Mrs. Johnson, and Miss Stancil attempted to persuade Mrs. Smith that her children would be punished for what she did. Mrs. Smith refused to admit that she or her children had done anything wrong.

Though she is able to laugh at the violent argument now— "It was a big mess"—and is quick to concede that caseworkers have, as a rule, been "nice" to her, Mrs. Smith is still angry at Miss Stancil: "She didn't have no right to cut my kids off. Sitting down there in that air-conditioned place and saying my kids can't get aid. She never came around to my house and found anybody there. I told her: 'As long as I'm not having no more kids for you to support, why should you bother me? You shouldn't be so hard on me.'"

When Miss Stancil said Mrs. Smith ought to end the "relationship," Mrs. Smith flatly refused. She was still young, and "If I ain't with him, I'm gonna make a relationship with somebody." She told the three white Alabama ladies: "If God had intended for me to be a nun, I'd be a nun."

In the fall of 1966, Mrs. Smith told her story to Donald Jellinek, a Northern lawyer working for the Lawyers Constitutional Defense Committee who had won a reputation around Selma for standing up to welfare-department officials. The Lawyers Constitutional Defense Committee, a civil-rights group put together in 1964 by the ACLU, NAACP, and other veteran civil-rights organizations, had been the legal arm of the Southern civil-rights movement.

Offices staffed with militant attorneys were opened in Louisiana, Alabama, and Mississippi. The lawyers, unfortunately, were compelled to spend a good deal of time fighting criminal proceedings brought against them by the Southern states, charging them with unlawful practice of the law. The states would not admit them to the local bar—they therefore couldn't go into the state courts—and tried to stop them from practicing in the federal courts. Jellinek's activism had resulted in his arrest, and at the time he saw Mrs. Smith he was facing a criminal proceeding initiated by the state of Alabama. Jellinek could not represent her, and there was no lawyer in Alabama who could.

From Selma, Jellinek relayed information about the case to New York, to the Center of Social Welfare Policy and Law at Columbia University. I had become the newly formed center's co-director a few months before, at the invitation of Ed Sparer, with whom I had worked two years earlier while defending people subpoenaed by New York State's Un-American Activities Committee. Ed told me that Columbia University had invited him to set up a legal program designed to examine the deficiencies in the welfare system. His original approach was study, research, and publication. I became excited by a more activist approach, a chance to test a system of previously unchallenged laws in courtrooms throughout the country.

Ed knew the complexities of federal and state welfare laws; I knew trial and constitutional law. "Let's do it together," he said. "It will be the only program of its kind. It's a year-to-year project. Our funding is only for one year. I don't know what will happen after that."

We saw it as a chance to develop test cases by a unified approach in an area that had recently gone untouched. And if we were successful in having the welfare laws interpreted as we believed they should be and in increasing the number of people receiving aid, we would overload the system and make it so expensive that it could not help but break. This might lead, we thought in 1966, to some kind of minimum family allowance or a guaranteed minimum income.

A difficulty in civil-rights law is that, as soon as a particular problem is attacked, other lawyers bring similar suits around the country, often without thinking out all the ramifications. You can't control litigation that is not your own; often you can't even control your own. But since welfare law was still so new and its complexities are not known to many lawyers, and because Ed was one of the country's leading welfare experts, we might play a guiding role in the development of cases and issues by becoming involved in the seminal lawsuits being tried throughout the country. We might even have some say in deciding which cases went to the Supreme Court.

I left the prestigious mid-town law firm I was then with and the people I had worked with for years. I also left, for a while, criminal and civil jury work. Three weeks after I met Ed, I began working at one third of my previous year's income in the precariously funded Columbia project.

The Smith case was only one of the many substitute-father cases we at the center were looking into at the time. There were cases from Georgia and Michigan, and we reviewed them all, trying to decide which case would be best to attack the regulation with. Racial discrimination played a part in the creation and application of welfare policies in both Northern and Southern states, as well as in the federal government itself. It would be harder to prove in the North, however. Though Michigan's welfare policy was racially discriminatory, this could probably not be proved to the satisfaction of a Northern court.

The Alabama policy had been devised by George Wallace. Soon after taking office as Commissioner of Alabama's Department of Pensions and Security, in January 1963, Ruben King was ordered by Governor Wallace "to work on the AFDC problem." Welfare costs were rising throughout the country and the AFDC program was becoming something its creators never conceived it to be—a black program. "I wanted to get down to the real meat of the coconut," said Commissioner King—he had the shape of a snowman, with a round red head sitting on a round body. He had been appointed to his post by Wallace; it was perhaps no coincidence that he had attended law school with the governor's brother.

King, on Wallace's orders, began to tackle what most whites in Alabama regarded as the welfare commissioner's main task—saving money by denying aid to Negro welfare recipients. A study prepared by the Alabama Department of Pensions and Security indicated the most effective way to do this. A racial breakdown of the entire welfare program showed that in most of Alabama's programs (old age, disability, child care) nearly all the beneficiaries were white—only the AFDC program had a substantial group of black beneficiaries. It wasn't that there were no aged, disabled blacks, but the practice in Southern welfare had always been to deny blacks benefits in these programs by virtue of discriminatory regulations.* King and Wal-

* Alabama, like all other states, would determine the amount of money an indigent needed and, depending on who the indigent was and which

lace concentrated on devising a rule to weed out the black AFDC families, a rule that, on the face of it, would not seem to have any racial overtones.

King appeared before the Alabama State Board of Pensions and Security on June 29, 1964, to inform them of the new substitute-father regulation. "The federal government doesn't like it, but I don't think they can tell us what kind of relationships we have to subsidize. The policy is not aimed at the children; it's to place the burden of support where it belongs." He said the welfare program as it now stood promoted illegitimacy. "If we took a woman off aid when she had an illegitimate child, then they would stop having illegitimate children." George Wallace expressed his concern for the children as he supported King's statement. "I do not want any policy that would deprive a child of care when it was needed. However, I feel these policies will work." The State Board, all appointed by Wallace, approved the policy and it was adopted by the legislature. King had "cracked" the coconut. George Wallace called the regulation a "significant step forward," and in his supporting letters to the legislature he praised King for having formulated it.

From Alabama's point of view, Mrs. Smith's case was the worst possible one to litigate. Alabama seemed to have no proof of any wrongdoing by Mrs. Smith or of support being given by any substitute father. This presented a problem for us, too. Alabama could end the test case as soon as we started it, simply by restoring Mrs. Smith's aid. It was also possible that, with just one plaintiff, the state could come up with some other justification for having terminated aid. Or Mrs. Smith might be

---

welfare category he fell under, would appropriate funds to pay a percentage of the "need" figure. Of course, the largest percentage of "need" was paid in the "white" programs—programs for the blind, disabled, and aged. The percentage of "need" in the AFDC program was scandalously low. Black children were getting less than forty percent of what Alabama said they needed to maintain minimum living conditions.

persuaded through community pressures not to be "a vehicle" for the test case. (The stores later did refuse her credit, and there were many days when her children had nothing to eat.) We tried to find other plaintiffs to join Mrs. Smith's suit but could not. We were not able to get the Alabama welfare rolls with the names of those whose benefits had been terminated because of the substitute-father regulation, and our attempts to make our interest known met with no success. These problems were important enough to make us question the wisdom of bringing suit.

Yet we were attracted to the case by the fact that the Department of Health, Education and Welfare had neither approved nor disapproved the Alabama regulation, although it had approved similar regulations in other states. The Department of Health, Education and Welfare had told Alabama to change the regulation, but it continued to give Alabama funds to carry out the AFDC program despite the defects in the state law. To have cut the program off would have been a greater tragedy, HEW reasoned, for then no federal aid would go to any Alabama children. HEW's past criticism of the Alabama program meant it would not feel forced to oppose us in a legal challenge. In fact, we hoped HEW might even support our argument.

I called friends at HEW and the Solicitor General's office to see if they knew what position the government might take. They had no idea what the government would do, for there were many political considerations over which the government lawyers had no control. I continued to hope they would support us, but eventually I was disappointed. The government sat on a fence during the two years the case was fought. In retrospect we were lucky, for later experience showed that the government generally defended even the most heinous welfare practices.

The federal government's position on this and similar government benefits programs is scandalous. HEW, afraid that any determined resistance to repressive state regulations will lead to across-the-board reductions, always tries to avoid trouble. Though their timidity is appalling, their fear is not groundless. Southern Congressmen routinely terrorize HEW representatives when they testify before Senate committees.

In Washington, for example, under the iron rule of Senator Robert Byrd, at that time chairman of the Senate Subcommittee on Appropriations for the District of Columbia, the Department of Welfare had been forced to acquire nearly as many "fraud investigators," bent upon cutting people off relief, as "social investigators," who are responsible for passing on initial eligibility. In speeches on the floor of the Senate, Byrd proudly reported that, under his aegis, District of Columbia AFDC case loads fell from a peak of 5,628 in November 1961 to 3,823 by October 1963. His request for appropriations with which to hire additional investigators was struck out on a technicality in a House-Senate conference. As a result, he said, "the AFDC case load had gradually crept back up and by August 1966 had recorded a total of 4,767 cases." Bad though he believed that was, Byrd observed that, without the investigators who were on hand, the case loads would have reached 9,600—double the actual rolls. Other welfare suits filed in his district elicited these remarks: "I'm not going to sit by and watch our agency attacked. What business do these lawyers have to question the Department's regulations?"

There was a second reason why we were attracted to the Smith case. Our decision to litigate was dictated in part by the "erosion theory of litigation": take the worst example of a practice or rule, the gross or excessive form in the most highly suspect social setting, and challenge it. The Alabama substitute-father rule didn't just seize on the fact that there was a man with income in the house to disqualify an AFDC family; it disqualified all families in which the mother was *thought* to have any relationship with a man, with or without income and in or out of the house. Mr. Williams, the so-called substitute father in the Smith family, was not, in fact, the father of any of the children; he was not living in their home or performing any of a father's duties. He was under no obligation to contribute to their support and, in fact, he was not contributing.

The erosion strategy, if successful, would not necessarily bring a narrow court ruling—one that would apply only to the particular circumstances of this case. The reach of the Alabama substitute-parent practice was not the only evil we would attack. The suit would be framed to encourage the court to hold that all state rules and practices which disqualified families by virtue of an assumption of income or support from a person without a legal obligation of support are contrary to the Federal Social Security Act.* The court, in examining the history and purpose of the Social Security Act for the first time, was faced with the most sympathetic of "plaintiffs"—750,000 destitute children penalized through no fault of their own. It might use generous, broad language in interpreting the Act, thus providing a framework for hundreds of future cases. If one case had to be the first, if one case were to be the touchstone for all future poverty litigation, then I believed it should be Mrs. Smith's. Few lawyers realized what the stakes were in the challenge to Alabama's substitute-father rule; the attorneys representing the state of Alabama certainly did not.

This patient, analytical approach to change through the test method can be frustrating. You often have to let many cases go by while waiting for the "right" one. And you have to sit back and watch other lawyers file suits that you have decided not to file and that should not be filed by anyone at that point. Sometimes more harm than good is done in the rush to have a law declared unconstitutional. The Office of Economic Opportu-

* While we hoped for a broad ruling, we nevertheless realized that this kind of litigation should have safety valves built in. If the court did not agree with the larger principle involved, there should be enough attractive alternatives to assure a lesser victory. Thus, the future of poverty litigation would be advanced in any case.

nity's legal-services division, then staffed mostly by young, inexperienced lawyers, was often guilty of overzealousness. The experienced civil-rights organizations and private attorneys in this field were by and large more sensitive to the dangers of filing a bad lawsuit that would have long-range detrimental results.

Immediately before we filed the Smith suit, a group of Washington lawyers filed a similar suit attacking the Washington substitute-father practice. (The plaintiff's name in that case, coincidentally, was also Smith.) They brought the case before an unsympathetic judge on an insufficient record, with badly drawn papers, and before they had thought out most of the legal problems. I knew of the suit and of Judge Alexander Holtzoff's reputation, and tried to persuade them not to litigate. They wouldn't listen, and the course of poverty litigation throughout the country suffered for the next three years as a result. Judge Holtzoff, eighty, one of the oldest judges on the federal court (even among those retired), was known as a "pro-prosecution" judge in criminal trials. The small, peppy, caustic man was noted for the heavy sentences he imposed on persons convicted of what he considered to be violent crimes, and for his marked distaste for what he termed dilatory practices by civil-liberties lawyers carefully building a constitutional record. (Upon his death, *The New York Times* said that the United States Court of Appeals had reversed him more times than they had any colleague who served during his tenure.)

Judge Holtzoff wrote a vitriolic decision that lawyers had to grapple with each time they filed a poverty suit anywhere in the country. In this decision, the first to analyze the right of a welfare recipient to attack the welfare program, the judge said welfare was "charity" and recipients had no right to complain about welfare practices since welfare was a privilege the state could dispense as it pleased. If welfare was "charity," the state could impose any conditions it wanted on the recipient, from bedroom checks to making the recipient account, item by item, for the monies received. Judge Holtzoff also said the federal courts should not be called to review the welfare system; it was up to the state courts to do this. If the state courts were to decide, however, there would be little or no chance of winning in the near future, since state judges would defer to state welfare administrators. If these issues were to be resolved successfully, they would have to be tried in the federal courts. As in the civil-rights litigation begun in the early sixties, only the more or less politically free federal courts, with their higher-caliber judges and more modern procedures, were in a position to render better, more knowledgeable decisions here.

Judges throughout the country based their findings on Judge Holtzoff's decision. It was not until two and a half years after the Washington Smith case that the Supreme Court, in our case, *Smith v. King*, for the first time unequivocally rejected the concepts set down by Judge Holtzoff.


The Mrs. Sylvester Smith complaint, filed on December 2, 1966, in the United States Federal Court for the Middle District of Alabama, Northern Division, in Montgomery, against George Wallace, Ruben King, and other state welfare officials, asked the court to invalidate the Alabama regulation on a number of grounds, constitutional and statutory. Its constitutional arguments were patterned on a complaint we had filed a few months before on behalf of Mrs. Virginia Anderson, a Negro welfare recipient denied aid because of Georgia's "employable mother" regulation, a practice as horrendous as the substitute-father policy.

Mrs. Anderson had six children. Her husband had died in an accident, and she was receiving $120 a month from welfare. One of the Columbia Center's lawyers who visited her in Georgia saw starving children covered by flies in a house alive with rats. The practice in Georgia was to cut all Negro AFDC women off welfare about May, suspiciously close to the beginning of the okra harvest, thereby creating a large employment pool. The Southern rationale was that jobs might be available, so the women should be penalized for not working. The white farm owners could then pick and choose the women they wanted to work in the fields at the wages the farm owners wanted to pay.

There were nine mothers for every job, but the welfare agency, in order to exert pressure uniformly during the okra season, did not restore relief to those who couldn't find jobs. The women who did work forty hours a week made less money than they would have received from welfare (they earned about $10 a week) and did not get any federal aid to bring them to the minimal welfare levels. A marvelous practice. The Anderson lawsuit partially stopped it.

The complaint in the Smith case charged that the substitute-father regulation "was conceived to deny aid to blacks, and that it had had that effect." At the time we filed the complaint, we did not have many facts to support the racial claim—just a knowledge of Alabama. We would lose nothing by our allegation, however. If we could not prove it, it could easily be dropped. In motion papers that we filed with the complaint, we asked the court immediately to stop the state of Alabama from cutting off relief to families because of this regulation and to restore aid to those who had lost it. The case was assigned to Judge Frank J. Johnson, Jr., an Eisenhower appointee, whose running battle with his former law-school classmate, George Wallace, estranged him from Alabama society. Judge Johnson's United States District Court had earned the hostility of Alabamians, as it applied federal power in the Montgomery bus boycott, Freedom Rider cases, and other bitter social fights in a state not particularly sympathetic to the exercise of such power.

Years before the Smith case, Wallace had accused Johnson of being an "integrating, scalawagging, carpetbagging bold-faced liar," after Johnson overruled a Wallace directive and ordered a local grand jury to give to the federal government the voter-registration records of Bulleck County. Wallace refused to turn the records over to the "feds" (he called them "snoopers"), said he would jail the agents of the United States government if they set foot in Alabama, and then decided the records were safe if filed with the grand jury. Johnson ordered Wallace and the grand jury to give the records to the federal government. Wallace marched up and down the state, holding press conference after press conference announcing his refusal to do this and his determination to stop the grand jury from complying with Johnson's orders. Wallace was finally cited for contempt.

By the time the case came to trial, the records were in the hands of the federal government. Johnson would not give Wallace the satisfaction of finding him guilty—he decided that Wallace, regardless of his public statements, had quietly surrendered the records. Wallace, outraged, denied it, proclaimed his guilt in court and in the newspapers (it was serious for a candidate, which Wallace then was, to cooperate with the "feds"), but he was not granted his martyrdom, as Johnson intoned, "Not guilty."

I had little doubt that Johnson would stand up to any pressure Wallace could bring to bear. Thus, a major potential stumbling block was out of the way. Win, lose, or draw, we were going to get a fair, intelligent decision by a court that would not permit its orders to be flaunted by the governor of Alabama.

In the last week of December 1966, Judge Frank Johnson granted our motion for a three-judge court but denied us a preliminary injunction. He felt the issue was too new, too controversial, to decide without a full trial. But granting our motion for a three-judge court meant that, if we lost the case at the trial level, we could get a direct appeal to the Supreme Court and thereby avoid an appellate step. The fact that at that moment children were being denied aid compelled us to try and move the case up to the Supreme Court as quickly as we could.

Immediately after receiving the complaint, Alabama sought to have it dismissed. The state pointed out that HEW had allowed these regulations for the last fifteen years. "Who is Mrs. Smith," they asked, "to claim twenty states and the Department of Health, Education and Welfare were wrong and had misconstrued the 1935 Social Security Act?" Judge Johnson denied the state's motion on January 4, 1967, and the trial was set for four months later.

Mary Lee Stapp, an attorney in Alabama's Department of Pensions and Security, was assigned to the case. An honors graduate from the University of Alabama Law School, she was a dignified, attractive, fortyish woman with a soft voice that could put you off guard, lulling you into appreciating the music and missing the meaning. "Why are y'all doing this? These people are just different than we are. If you win, you in the North will be flooded with black babies."

We made the necessary motions to force King, Wallace, and the other members of the Alabama Welfare Department to answer questions, to prove both the racist motivations behind the policy and its arbitrary application.

In February 1967, in the state building in Montgomery, I began to examine the Alabama officials under oath. They at first denied the regulation had anything to do with the sexual conduct of the women. "You don't understand, Mr. Garbus," Commissioner King said in response to my questioning. "We're not interested in the mother's fooling around. We are not in the business to judge people morally. The regulation has nothing to do with sex. We're interested in getting the men to support the children." He patiently explained all that Alabama was trying to do for its poor folks. He also said any mother whose aid was stopped could always choose "to give up her pleasure or to act like a woman ought to act and continue to receive aid. The question is," King concluded, "does the man have the privileges of a husband?" Although I persisted in my questioning, he refused to admit that by "pleasure" and "privileges of a husband" he meant sexual relations.

King denied that the regulation was aimed at Negroes. Two thirds of the 22,574 families on AFDC in 1964 were black, and King said he believed that the cut-off rate because of the substitute-father regulation would probably run two blacks for every white. I thought his estimate was wrong, and if I could prove it, the racial claim would be sustained.

A county-by-county analysis of Alabama was what was needed, but the center did not have the money or staff for it. We decided instead to study seven of the sixty-one counties. Each of the sixty-one Alabama counties was evaluated for median income, percentage of population on welfare, rate of Northern migration, racial composition, and population, as we tried to get a test sample.

We selected Baldwin, Chambers, Clarke, Dallas, Greene, Montgomery, and Russell Counties as representative of the entire state. But the welfare records of these counties were not available. (The material is privileged and no one outside the welfare department, other than the recipient, can see the files.) There was not enough money to conduct a field survey, so I decided to try to obtain the information by examining the people who actually operated Alabama's program. In my questioning I sought to find out how the policy worked from the time it was enacted until January 1, 1967.

In the beginning, neither King nor Wallace took the case seriously. Had not Wallace and the legislature approved the regulation? Had not HEW approved similar rules? "HEW," King said at his examination before trial on April 17, 1967, "stood by since 1964, when we've been cutting off families. If it was as bad as you say, they wouldn't have allowed it. The feds are no friends of ours."

As the lawsuit came closer to trial, King got angrier and angrier. He became evasive, refused to answer questions, and criticized his lawyers, who, because of court orders, were required to give us certain information. The litigation was being run from New York; it was impossible to go before the Alabama court to compel Alabama to furnish facts each time we needed more information. King refused to produce statistics for the twenty months the regulation was in effect, and we agreed to accept information only for June 1966, a month we chose arbitrarily.

One day Mrs. Stapp got all the women county welfare directors of Alabama together in a big room at the Department of Pensions and Security and, one after another, they testified before me. As they sat waiting to be called into the small examining room, they giggled like schoolgirls.

Mrs. Katie B. Shaw, the county director of Greene County, said every one of ninety-one recipients cut off in June 1966 was Negro. "Mr. Garbus, you don't know how it is. They know this regulation is good for them. They want it. We're social workers and we care for our people. Why, Clara Lloyd did her college work at your school, Columbia University. We've all got social-work degrees. Years ago you could be in welfare without any training. That's no longer the case." Her voice rose as she strained to be understood. "The ladies want our help in getting rid of the men who live off their welfare checks and this does it. They really do. Many times I tell them, 'You shouldn't go with Mr. Jones or Mr. Washington because he's no good,' and they appreciate it."

Nan C. Murphy, in whose county (Chambers) seventy-five women, all Negro, were cut off, said, "We just try to do the right thing. You're from the North and can't really understand our problem. These men who see our recipients just won't work. The feds tell us the unemployment rate in my county is seventy-five percent. Now, you know, if a man wants to work, there's a job for him." By the time the examinations were finished, it was apparent that every one of the more than six hundred recipients cut off in the seven counties during June 1966 was Negro.

We confronted King and the court with the results of our study. King said that we had deliberately chosen June 1966 because it was not representative. (He never offered any explanation of why June 1966 was any different from May 1967 or January 1966.) King said, "Let's look at the performance in those counties for an eighteen-month period." We agreed, and he produced his records and computed the figures. The number of cut-offs for the seven counties for an eighteen-month period were put in the trial record. The percentage dropped from one hundred to ninety-seven. King had proved the validity of our sample.

King then said those counties were not "representative" (again he didn't indicate why), and he submitted figures for four counties of his choice. In the four counties he selected (Barbour, Jefferson, Selma, Montgomery), 88 percent of the families deprived of aid were Negro. I told the court at trial, "Your Honor can safely assume that these four counties (out of a total of sixty-one) were handpicked by Alabama because they had the lowest percentage of Negro cut-offs; state-wide figures for all sixty-one counties would certainly be well above ninety-five percent." Alabama's failure to understand that their analysis helped Mrs. Smith's case more than it helped their own case demonstrated their rock-bottom faith in the virtue of their position. Wallace and King would have been better off not submitting any figures at all.

I did my own analysis of the four counties Alabama chose and found additional data that was of help to us. "In Barbour County, where there were ten times as many Negroes receiving aid as whites," I told the court, "the cut-off ratio was forty to one. In Jefferson County, where there were four times as many Negroes receiving aid as whites, the cut-off ratio was twelve to one. The figures for the remaining counties were similar. There is no question but that the practice was created to be discriminatory and has that effect."

Jacqueline Stancil denied under oath that there were any racial overtones to the policy. She testified that, during the period of her employment with the state of Alabama in Dallas County, she had closed nineteen cases because of the substitute-parent regulation. She was surprised when the records revealed that all of them involved Negro families. Through the testimony of Alabama's witnesses, we showed that, of the 184 cases closed in Dallas County between July 1964 and the end of January 1967, 182 of the cases involved Negroes. The ratio was ninety-one to one.

This was 1967, before a summer of riots in the Northern cities. Pressure to cut back on relief rolls was mounting as the legislative committees and politicians charged fraud and corruption. Harried commissioners demanded more money to keep the welfare system from collapsing. The Kerner Commission found the Northern welfare system to be largely responsible for "the tensions and social disorders that have led to civil disorders." The Alabama lawyers held that this confirmed George Wallace's view that Alabama handled its Negro problem better than the North and that we Northern troublemakers had better tend to our own backyard.

Mrs. Stapp, in what she regarded as an answer to our assertion that welfare recipients have constitutional rights, told the three-judge federal court in the brief she submitted:

> . . . Alabama suggests that establishing such "rights" would give the Welfare Law and Policy Center of the Columbia School of Social Work more opportunity to pretend Harlem is not in New York and spend more time assisting Southern Negro recipients in being liberated from circumstances which still permit them (nearly three years after adoption of the substitute-parent regulation) to comprise only 97 percent of the case load in Dallas County.

Alabama's brief contended that the regulation stopped black women from having illegitimate children. Although the illegitimacy rate had risen since the regulation went into effect, the Alabama attorney general held that, were it not for the regulation, the state "would be overrun." Illegitimates, Alabama claimed, were the "unworthy poor" and they should be treated differently from the "worthy poor," the white legitimates, who were entitled to benefits. There are no worthy poor or unworthy poor in this country, we asserted. Illegitimate starving children are as needy as legitimate starving children. No one should starve merely because Alabama law calls him a bastard.

"It is not our fault that children are born bastards," was Alabama's reply, "and that they lose money for food because of it. Alabama did not make them illegitimate in the first place." *My Fair Lady* was cited as authority for their position.

> . . . Eliza's father, in *My Fair Lady*, poignantly illustrates this in the later Victorian Age as he describes himself as one of the "undeserving poor," and later, when confronted with the fact that he has never given Eliza (his illegitimate child) anything, he counters, "I gave her the sunsets over Hyde Park." The court in *Zepeda* in the course of its opinion points out that: ". . . laws cannot temper the cruelty of those who have the epithet 'bastard,' nor ease the bitterness in him who hears it knowing it to be true."

According to Mrs. Stapp, Mrs. Smith's case was not typical. And it did not warrant the reconsideration (and perhaps the invalidation) of the entire regulation. A dedicated lawyer, Mrs. Stapp presented inconsistent arguments earnestly, convinced as she was of the righteousness of her position. It was probably deliberate that Alabama chose this motherly-looking woman to argue the case: the court might find it hard to believe that a woman like her could defend a rule as bad as we said this was.

In most of the families covered by the substitute-father rule, Mrs. Stapp contended, the man involved was, in fact, the father of the recipient children and he was keeping up a connection with the family. In any case, Mrs. Smith had not "exhausted her remedies," the Alabama lawyer said. "If an incorrect determination of her status has been made, it would be up to the Alabama Welfare Department to correct it on appeal. Mrs. Smith's course was to inform the state that she had broken with the father and to have this news corroborated by, as the regulation said, at least two 'acceptable references in a position to know.' Singled out by the regulation as persons in a position to know were 'law enforcement officials, ministers, neighbors, grocers.' "

"With Mrs. Smith's permission," Mrs. Stapp continued, "an investigator would have gone to her favorite policeman or grocer to inquire whether she was still enjoying sexual relations with Williams and, if so, where and how often."

Although much of the regulation was unclear, there was agreement among King, Wallace, and myself on some of the particulars. Even if a woman with a five-month-old child swore under oath that she had not seen the father since the hour of conception (fourteen months before), she and child could be cut off, the Alabama officials all testified, on the grounds that she still had a continuing relationship. To have the aid restored, the mother would have to get affidavits from her friends and neighbors showing that the relationship had terminated. The affidavits would say, "Miss Jones lived and slept with Mr. Thomas for six months, but it is now over." Since most of these women "don't exactly know what cohabitation means," one caseworker explained, she would ask them: "Do you have sexual intercourse?" or, "Do you have sex relations with this man or that?" This, despite King's statement that "the regulation doesn't deal with sex."

One of the mothers we spoke to in the course of the suit said,

"Our kids were asked whether we were sleeping around, and they tried to get them to sign affidavits against us. They lied to the children about the use of the affidavit."

The language of the regulation became a bone of contention. It said the single welfare mother could not "regularly and frequently cohabit" with a man. Although King and Wallace denied it, for those who had drawn up the regulation, "cohabit" meant "fornicate"; what "regularly" and "frequently" meant was anybody's guess. King and Wallace felt it was all right for a woman to go out once or twice a month—"People are human." However, one of their female county directors thought that a sexual encounter every six months would be a bar to aid, assuming that it was with the same man. All caseworkers in Dallas County are white, virginal-looking ladies of a certain age. Describing those who are attracted to the job, one Alabama official observed: "They wouldn't be likely to know what constitutes frequency in sexual matters."

However one cares to interpret the rule, in Alabama a man could be judged a substitute father without ever having seen his substitute children. In speeches around the state, and during the trial, former Governor Wallace and Commissioner King set forth a time-honored legal principle not exactly out of Coke or Blackstone: "If a man wants to play, then let him pay."

My position was: "Before Mrs. Smith, Mrs. Jones, or any other welfare client can lose aid, she must be given notice of the reasons for her threatened termination, and a hearing. Faced with the need to live, she will scarcely be able to devote the time and energy necessary to prepare for trial, interview witnesses, and do all that is necessary to win a case. This is why recipients rarely request a hearing after termination of payments. If states were required to grant reasonable notice and opportunity for a hearing before termination of benefits, a sense of care and caution in the administration of the regulation might arise, which would make it possible for the recipient to have a meaningful hearing."

The particular issue, the right of welfare recipients to a hearing, had not yet been raised successfully in any court, and the Alabama court would probably decide this case without ever grappling with that issue. My arguments were not critical to Mrs. Smith's case but were presented to set a background for later arguments which the Alabama three-judge court, and perhaps the Supreme Court, would hear in future welfare cases. It is good to acquaint courts and lawyers with arguments and theories they will later hear more of. The newness and radicalism gradually disappear, and they become conditioned to the arguments and will listen more respectfully on hearing them again in subsequent cases.

King, in response to my questions, said, "I never knew of Mrs. Smith's case. She could have appealed to me. I wouldn't have cut off her benefits if she were right. My ladies sometimes make mistakes; I correct them. People, black and white, know they can come to me." We went into the details of the Alabama appeals system, which, according to King, now under oath, "made sure that all poor people got what was coming to them." It turned out that not one of the 18,000 women cut off because of the substitute-father regulation ever appealed—probably because no one ever told them they had the right to appeal.

The only people who knew about the appellate procedures were King's employees. However, the existence of an appeal procedure was rendered meaningless by the generality of the language in the notification of reason for termination ("substitute-father policy") and the failure to advise recipients of the right of appeal. There had been five appeals in the entire Alabama welfare system (covering perhaps 75,000 terminations) since King took office three and a half years before.

The trial before the three-judge court in Alabama was set for May 8, 1967. I reviewed the evidence we had uncovered in our preparation for trial and decided to submit all the evidence (including the testimony of King and his ladies), rather than go through a full trial. There was nothing to gain by a full trial; and Mrs. Stapp agreed. It is an unusual procedure—I had never done it before, nor have I since. We submitted all the evidence to the court in Montgomery on May 15, 1967.

Immediately after argument, I left my job at the Columbia Center. John Pemberton, Jr., the director of the American Civil Liberties Union, had called me in early that year and asked me to be associate director of the ACLU and the first director-counsel of its newly formed tax-exempt foundation, named after Roger Baldwin, the man who established the ACLU. According to Jack, the Baldwin Foundation was to begin litigation in what he described as "the frontier areas of civil liberties," in some twenty states throughout the country. The foundation was going to be a large legal operation, with nearly two dozen lawyers and a first-year budget of nearly three quarters of a million dollars. Jack assured me that the ACLU was behind the new organization and wanted it to go into areas, such as welfare, that the ACLU had scarcely touched.

I knew of the ACLU's tensions as it set off in new endeavors; to a lot of people not familiar with the organization, the ACLU is radical, but it actually has its base in the conservative principle of strict adherence to the Bill of Rights. As in many other primarily volunteer organizations with a paid staff, there is often a continuing power struggle over who actually runs the organization. Because of these and other limitations, the American Civil Liberties Union had been left behind in the sixties as a legal explosion took place in many areas of law. Here, I was told, was an opportunity to bring this organization "up to date." I accepted the position and continued to represent Mrs. Smith from my new office.

I felt that a quick decision in the Smith case would be favorable and a delayed decision unfavorable. I reasoned that if the court was moved by the injustice of the regulation which was being invoked to let children starve, it would decide quickly. I was unhappy, therefore, when the decision had not come down by June, and I braced myself for defeat.

The spring, summer, and fall of 1967 were sad seasons for those who were trying to help the nation's poor. Vietnam was draining the poverty programs. A greater percentage of the poverty dollar was going into high-visibility projects, as the Johnson Administration felt forced to come up with dramatic results. In 1966 Sargent Shriver, the head of OEO, had confidently told the public that American poverty could be eliminated in a decade. The following year he said, "The war on poverty is not fought on any single, simple battlefield, and it will not be won in a generation." People were beginning to realize that $10 million additional in 1967 for OEO legal services, though it represented a 100 percent increase from the previous year, was not going to make much difference.

The summer passed. *Smith v. King* was the country's first major welfare court case—many of the concepts that would evolve in this new area of the law were being tested here, and lawyers all over the country were waiting for the verdict. Many had other welfare cases pending which they didn't want to bring to court until after the Smith decision. But they could not, in good conscience, delay the suits indefinitely. By fall I had virtually no hope.

Then, on November 8, 1967, on a clear, cool day nearly a year after the complaint was filed, United States Circuit Judge John C. Godbold and District Judges Virgil Pittman and Frank Johnson delivered their unanimous decision in favor of Mrs. Smith. The Alabama federal court declared the Alabama regulation unconstitutional, calling the substitute-father rule "arbitrary and discriminatory" and stating that it violated the equal-protection clause of the Fourteenth Amendment by permitting Alabama to "pick and choose the mothers and children it will aid through the use of some classifications which are not rationally related to the purpose of the applicable statutes."

The court commented on the racial argument and the proof we had offered. Though they were persuaded that discrimination played a major part in the creation and application of the regulation, they nevertheless did not want the case to turn on the racial issue. They wanted neither black nor white children to be punished.

> . . . While the plaintiffs placed considerable emphasis upon facts strongly indicating that the "substitute father" regulation was designed to discriminate and has the effect of discriminating against Negroes, by reason of the facts presented, this case does not rest upon racial considerations and, therefore, the decision should not rest upon such considerations. On the contrary, this decision should be, and will be, designed to enure to the benefit of all needy children, regardless of their race or color.

Both from a political and from a legal view, the court neatly answered each of Alabama's arguments. It reaffirmed the right of Alabama to regulate the morality of its citizens and approved of its concern with stable family situations based on legal marriage. It tried to blunt, as well as it could, the wild cries that were sure to follow; the court would surely be accused of sanctioning black sin.

> . . . The expressed interest of the State of Alabama in not desiring to underwrite financially or approve situations which are generally considered immoral is a laudable one; the State's argument that this regulation is a "genuine attempt to place the responsibility for taking care of children on persons who bring them into being" is, however, wholly without any realistic or rational basis insofar as this "substitute father" regulation is concerned. The punishment under the regu-

lation is against needy children, not against the partici-
pants in the conduct condemned by the regulation.
The State is not without means of attempting to solve
the problem which it recognizes, short of depriving
children of aid because of immoral conduct of the
mother.

The court concluded:

> . . . The Alabama "substitute father" regulation de-
> prives those children of the equal protection of the
> laws in violation of the Fourteenth Amendment to the
> Constitution of the United States.

The "equal protection clause" has traditionally been invoked
to protect the rights of blacks as a "class." The court here defined a new class—needy, dependent children, white or black—
stating that the equal-protection clause is not restricted in its
application to the rights of Negroes. However, the decision was
only the first step, though a big one. It is the court's order that
directs the litigant to comply with the court's finding. *Brown
v. Board of Education*—the sweeping 1954 school desegrega-
tion case—had clearly shown that, unless a court order is specific and provides a concrete way for the decision to be imple-
mented, the decision's effect will be undermined.

The order, as framed by the three Southern judges in the
Smith case, was firm and did not allow for the kinds of delays
that have plagued civil-rights reform. Alabama was ordered to
"immediately reinstate upon the Alabama Aid to Dependent
Children rolls, regardless of their race or color, each of the
children who has been declared ineligible for Aid to Dependent Children Financial Assistance through the use of the regulation entitled 'Child Ineligible if There is a Father or Mother
Substitute' provided the said children are now otherwise eligible and entitled to receive said assistance."

The court went even further, agreeing to cooperate with me

in supervising Alabama's compliance. Alabama was given ninety days to restore aid to the 21,000 children; the state was ordered to "file with the Clerk of this Court within not more than ninety days from the date of this order a list setting forth the names and addresses of the individuals who have been restored to the Alabama Aid to Dependent Children rolls pursuant to the opinion and decree of this Court." I was to check the lists of names to make sure Alabama had complied, and this gave me one of the happiest moments of my life, as I sat in King's office in Montgomery checking off the names of the children and mothers who were to receive welfare money once again.

Alabama had thirty days to decide whether to appeal. I hoped they would take the case to the Supreme Court. By winning the Supreme Court decision, we could do so much more than we could in winning a case even for 20,000 people of Alabama. A Supreme Court decision might wipe out all forms of the substitute-father regulation in all twenty states which had them.

But Alabama had other options. King and Wallace might simply drop the law that had been rejected and adopt a new one with some other definition or combination of definitions of "substitute father,"—one that did not terminate aid on the basis of the mother's sexual conduct. Our "victory" could be canceled with the swipe of the pen used to write a new rule. Southern legislators had developed this practice to perfection in school, voting, and jury cases. Fewer than 5 percent of welfare suits ever reach a decision, because the welfare departments, rather than litigate, will capitulate on a given case. We would then have to start a new suit with a new plaintiff to attack the new regulation and the regulations of the nineteen other states. The cost in money and manpower would be beyond us and other private agencies.

The newness of welfare litigation and of the concepts we were setting forth, and the blind faith of Alabama's officials (and most other welfare officials) in their welfare practices, led to quite different results. Would the Supreme Court, King and Wallace asked, not uphold a welfare regulation in effect in Northern as well as Southern states? Senator Eastland expressed the same thought when he said, "They won't be for integration and giving money to them in the South if they also have to do it in the North. Let's put it to them. Then they'll understand the problems of the South." And so Alabama filed a notice of appeal to the United States Supreme Court. Their gamble, and their faith that racism would obscure the justness of Mrs. Smith's claim, would eventually benefit thousands of children.

Wallace and King did not fully realize that an adverse decision by the Supreme Court could be disastrous to their cause. The three-judge court had struck down the regulation because it cut off aid to children on the basis of the mother's sexual conduct. The Supreme Court might carry the decision to its logical conclusion and hold that the state could terminate aid to a child only where there was a father present and legally obligated to support the child.

HEW had so far ignored the case. The department refused to enter the lawsuit, even though Judge Johnson directed it to do so early in the litigation. Judge Johnson, furious at the government, directed John Doar, then attorney in charge of the Civil Rights Division of the Department of Justice, to file a brief. Doar filed an insipid two-page letter, saying nothing meaningful and thereby increasing Judge Johnson's anger. Not only did the federal government refuse to put a halt to a discriminatory practice; they refused to help anyone who was trying to do it. We began to be afraid that the U. S. Solicitor General might enter the case on Alabama's side because of the pressure in Washington. As it turned out, Doar's letter was the federal government's last word on the merits of our claim.

One of the claims we made in our lawsuit was that HEW acted improperly in failing to stop Alabama from applying the regulation. Would HEW now come in and defend the regulation? Commissioner King's description, when testifying on the federal government's position, was correct. "Well, to be honest and frank about it, the federal government has never liked the policy, but they have never had enough guts—and I say this for the record—the federal government has never had enough guts themselves to define what a substitute-parent policy would be. They were about ready to until Senator Byrd's investigation of the ADC problems in Washington D.C., and after that they have been afraid to."

On November 15, 1967, Alabama asked the three-judge court to stop enforcement of the order (in legal terms, to "stay" the order), pending the appeal to the Supreme Court. "If Alabama is forced to pay benefits pending the appeal (the monthly cost is in excess of one million dollars) and then wins in the Supreme Court, we would have lost monies wrongfully paid," Mrs. Stapp said, "and, of course, the Mrs. Smiths of Alabama would get a windfall." Mrs. Stapp said that Alabama would win in the Supreme Court, that substitute-father regulations more stringent than Alabama's had been approved by HEW, and that the three-judge court was wrong. I filed opposing papers in the Alabama federal court and, taking advantage of the federal government's indifference, I pointed out that "although the federal government, not the state, would pay most (83 percent) of the benefits in Alabama and more than half of the benefits around the country, HEW was not joining in the application for the stay." Judge Johnson denied Alabama's application.

Alabama's next step was to seek a stay from the Supreme Court. Each of the nine Supreme Court justices has jurisdiction over a different area of the country. Hugo L. Black was the justice from whom Alabama had to seek the stay, and three days after Judge Johnson denied their motion, they filed an application in Washington. This application was of great significance. If Justice Black denied a stay, judges at the federal

district-court level in other states would grant motions enjoin-
ing the other substitute-father regulations. Although the denial
of a stay application is not technically precedent, it would be
obvious to the lower federal judges that a justice of the Supreme Court had such grave doubts about the regulation's constitutionality that he would not allow it to be enforced pending
an appeal.

Alabama and I both offered the same arguments in Washington as we had presented to Judge Johnson in Alabama. In addition, I asked that if the stay was granted, the court should ex-
pedite the appeal. I cited the plight of the children who were
being deprived of support daily. Alabama stated that giving
money to Mrs. Smith and the others like her would deprive
"moral" welfare recipients of benefits; Alabama would have to
apportion the available money among more people.

On November 27, 1967, Justice Black granted Alabama's
stay application on condition that Alabama file all the papers
necessary for consideration of the appeal on an expedited
schedule. Argument was set for April. This meant that 21,000
children would have to wait at least another six months for aid.
By speeding up the appeal, however, Justice Black made sure
that it wasn't a year. Also, his action made Mrs. Smith's case
the first welfare case that would be heard in the United States
Supreme Court.


We began to prepare for the Supreme Court. I decided to present a "Brandeis" type of brief, analyzing not only the Alabama
regulation but also the regulations of the other states and the
political, economic, and social realities behind the regulations.
Law students from the Arthur Garfield Hays Civil Liberties
Program at New York University and attorneys from the Columbia Center on Social Welfare Policy and Law researched all
the decisional and statutory laws from the nineteen other states
that had substitute-father regulations. We went back to the

1935 legislative history of the Aid to Dependent Children program and the ensuing debates during President Roosevelt's first term of office.

After many meetings with law professors and poverty lawyers throughout the country, I decided to plead the case on different grounds from those advanced by the lower-court decision. The three-judge federal court had decided Mrs. Smith's case on constitutional grounds—holding that the equal-protection clause was violated by the regulation discriminating against a particular class, and they described that class as "needy dependent children who are ineligible or whose mothers engage in illicit personal relationships, or who have an illegitimate child born in their family." This made it too easy for state legislatures to pass other regulations as stringent and discriminatory as the substitute-father rule but which would not violate the court's findings in Mrs. Smith's case.

Alabama could enact a law that held that if a man took a child to school, or to church, he was to be considered the father. Other states had such laws. The District of Columbia regulation attacked in the case before Judge Holtzoff, for example, was not based solely on the sexual relationship between the mother and the substitute father. A man would be regarded as a substitute father if he did any of the following:

> . . . Visits the home to see the children . . . Donates gifts to the children . . . Was the father figure in the home . . . Acts "at home" with the children by dressing, feeding, carrying or fondling them . . . Takes the children on walks, excursions and the like . . . Shows concern about the health of the children and uses health facilities in the community to restore the health of the children . . . Shows interest in the educational progress of the children . . .

The federal statute said a needy child is entitled to benefits when the "parent"—more particularly, the father—is dead, absent, or incapacitated. The critical term was "parent." Alabama claimed that although Mr. Williams had not fathered and did not support any of Mrs. Smith's children, he was in fact their parent, and since he was neither dead nor absent nor incapacitated, the children were not entitled to aid. I was prepared to argue that "parent" meant the natural or adoptive parent, one who is under a legal obligation to support the children. Any state regulation that defined as a "parent" a person who was not legally responsible and on that basis denied aid was, I asserted, in violation of the Social Security Act.

This argument, requiring an interpretation of a key provision of the Social Security Act, as well as its history, not only would, if successful, win the case for Mrs. Smith but in its construction of the Social Security Act would affect all future welfare cases. It was not without risk, however. There was a body of case law and statutory history giving states great latitude in interpreting welfare regulations. In fact, the easiest way to argue an appeal in the Supreme Court is to ask the court to affirm the lower-court decision. If an appellee presents a new basis for the decision he is asking for, the court must explore the whole question anew, and the appellee no longer has the precedent of the lower court.

Congress was working on the Social Security Act of 1967 as it prepared for its December recess. Christmas was near, and the plight of the children of Alabama was very much on my mind. One particularly distressing section of the proposed new Social Security Act seemed relevant to Justice Black's stay order and might, I felt, be used to persuade Justice Black to reverse the stay he had granted. This was the provision known as the "welfare freeze." Under pressure of increasing ADC rolls and increasing welfare costs, Congress had decided to put a ceiling on the amount of federal money that could be used for ADC programs. The states, if they could no longer count on federal contributions, would have to limit the number of ADC recipients. The freeze was to become effective January 1,

1968, and would make it nearly impossible for even one name to be added to the welfare rolls after that.

Senator Robert Kennedy, during the Congressional debates, called the freeze a "disgrace," and Daniel P. Moynihan termed it a "retreat to brutality." If passed and signed, the legislation could affect Mrs. Smith, her four children, and the other 750,-000 children throughout the country who were being denied aid under substitute-father regulations. Even if we won in the Supreme Court, Alabama (and the nineteen other states) could refuse to restore aid because of the freeze. Alabama could say that they would restore aid to Mrs. Smith when there was room for her family on the welfare rolls, which would have a specified ceiling. The Social Security Act would freeze the ADC rolls at the January 1, 1968, level, so we had to have the stay vacated before that.

I knew of no analogous situation in court history. I decided to go back to Justice Black and ask him to remove the stay. I was aware of the obstacles that faced us. It was mid-December; the Social Security Act of 1967 had not yet been voted out of committee and there was always the possibility that it would not be. Moreover, the fact that the federal government was not going to pay for the additional children did not necessarily mean that Alabama would not. Of course, we knew Alabama would not: with its record in the welfare and civil-rights areas, Alabama would certainly not be spendthrift in this instance. There was also a remote possibility that President Johnson would veto the new Social Security Act because of the freeze provision.

The Senate and House committees approved the joint bill on December 21, 1967, the day before the Christmas recess. President Johnson had ten days in which to sign the bill and was expected to do so at his Texas ranch on January 2, 1968. On December 22 I filed papers in the Supreme Court asking Justice Black to reverse the stay he had granted. The court was in recess, and Justice Black was in Florida. Edmund Cullinan, the gravel-voiced Chief Deputy of the Supreme Court, was reluctant to present the application to Justice Black on the holiday weekend and tried to find reasons not to. "The matter is moot if President Johnson does not sign the bill," he said. "HEW hasn't filed any papers and it doesn't look like they agree with your interpretation of the manner in which the Supreme Court decision would be rendered null and void. There are too many speculative factors. I'll hold the papers until Justice Black returns after the New Year." All my efforts to move him were unsuccessful.

President Johnson signed the bill on January 2, 1968. My motion to vacate the stay was presented to Justice Black the following day, and he immediately asked Alabama to state its position. Alabama, naturally, opposed our application. "Mrs. Smith's lawyers are using the freeze provision as an excuse to seek reargument of the original stay application. The law does not operate the way Mr. Garbus interprets it and the conflict he describes will never come into being." Mrs. Stapp said she did not know what Alabama's position would be if the freeze provision were part of the new Act and the Supreme Court invalidated the substitute-father regulation.

I had anticipated Alabama's response before filing the December 1967 application to vacate the stay. Every effort was now made to have the Department of Justice join the application, since they could have cleared up many ambiguities about the freeze provision. I went to Washington and was given an administrative runaround. Going from HEW's offices to the Department of Justice and then back to HEW, I tried to persuade the federal government lawyers at least to file papers clarifying the legislation, if they would not directly support my application.

I told Mr. Cullinan of my efforts to have the government in on the application. "I don't see how Mr. Justice Black could rule in my favor if he does not have a clear understanding of the freeze provision," I added. The following day Mr. Justice

Black asked the government to submit an analysis of the new law. Finally, on January 10, 1968, HEW submitted an affidavit which interpreted the freeze provision much as I had done. After many pages of convoluted thought, the government lawyers ultimately concluded that a favorable decision in *Smith v. King* in the Supreme Court would be meaningless if the stay were not now vacated. But they did not have the courage to take a position in support of our motion and did not ask that the stay be vacated.

The next days were anxious ones. Hugo La Fayette Black, now eighty-one years old, with eyes as bright as his hair was white, had come from the red-clay hills one hundred miles from Selma. He knew the South and Alabama most intimately and would not be misled by false arguments. His decision would be based on the facts.

On January 29, 1968, nineteen days after the HEW affidavit had been submitted, Mr. Cullinan called to tell me that Justice Black had vacated the stay. The Alabama children were to be given aid immediately. Decisions are generally read in open court, but since court was not in session and the matter was urgent, Justice Black issued the decision from his chambers. I flew to Washington that day, read the decision, contacted the three-judge Alabama court, and started the mechanism to restore aid.

Justice Black's decision read:

> . . . I have concluded that in light of this factor, not present when I considered this case in November, the stay entered at that time should be vacated. The new amendment places a ceiling on the number of dependent children for whom federal sharing in state assistance programs is available. Although this ceiling will not go into effect until July 1, 1968, a crucial figure in determining the level of the ceiling is the average number of children for whom monthly payments are made during the first three months of this year.

The impact of the stay on welfare recipients in Alabama is thus considerably more serious now than it was prior to enactment of the new statute. If the judgment below is affirmed, appellees and the class they represent, a group estimated by the State to total 15,000 to 20,000 persons, will be restored to the welfare rolls for the future, but federal contributions will remain fixed in relation to the past level. The State of Alabama will then be forced either to reduce the level of payments to *all* children or to approve a great increase in the state and local funds available, so that the previous welfare allowances, ordinarily supported up to 80% or more by federal funds, could be granted to the new recipients without any federal support. . . . Under these circumstances, the possibility of injury to the State from the judgment below would appear to be more than offset by the possibility under the stay of decreased federal welfare assistance to all dependent children within the State for an indefinite period. Thus, the stay is vacated.

The effect of the decision was startling. Alabama was forced to put Mrs. Smith and her children, and 21,000 others, back on the relief rolls immediately. At the same time, the courts of Georgia and Louisiana issued orders prohibiting the application of their substitute-father regulations. Aid was restored to 24,000 children in Georgia and 36,000 in Louisiana, and within the next ten days, lawsuits were filed in four other states. The Supreme Court argument was still to come.

The "explosion" of the welfare rolls (and the increasing number of dependent blacks) was featured all over the daily press. Fred Graham, the *New York Times* Supreme Court reporter, wrote several articles, before the Smith argument, pointing out the vast amount of welfare money that would be needed for the 750,000 children if we won. The articles spoke in terms of dollars only. Graham quoted the heads of welfare departments in the North and in the South on the impossibility of finding funds for the additional names on the rolls, but he never once mentioned the plight of the needy who were hurt by the regulation. The articles reflected the temper of the country in those months.

I was notified in March that the case would be heard in the Supreme Court on April 22. Dr. King's Poor People's March on Washington was set for Sunday, April 21, 1968, and I thought it fitting that the dates coincided.

The briefs submitted to the Supreme Court at the end of March were different from the briefs we had submitted to the three-judge court—the arguments were both sharper and fuller. I wanted to delve into the motivations behind the rule in the other states, because we were now seeking a court decision that would affect all twenty states. I spent weeks in the library reading Southern papers and culling quotes from former Southern governors and legislators. In January 1951 Georgia Governor Herman Talmadge had been quoted in the *Atlanta Constitution* as being "willing to tolerate an unwed mother who makes one 'mistake' but not when the 'mistake' is repeated two, three, four or five times." He proposed restrictive policies which the state welfare director claimed would "save the state $440,000 a year, mainly by limiting aid to children of unwed Negro mothers." The Georgia director further noted that "70 percent of all mothers of more than one illegitimate child are Negroes . . . Some of them finding themselves tied down with one child are not adverse to adding others as a business proposition." Other states sang the same tune. The *Arkansas Gazette* in September 1959 reported:

> . . . in addressing a convention at Hot Springs, Governor Faubus mounted the well-worn hobby horse of criticizing welfare payments to mothers of illegitimate children: "By taxing the good people to pay for these programs, we are putting a premium on illegiti-

macy never before known in the world." To any one
who has ever heard this line before, which includes
all of us in Arkansas, there was little doubt that Mr.
Faubus was referring primarily to Negro unwed mothers and not to any "good, honest, hard-working"
white folks who have been remiss in getting down to
the licensing bureau. . . . It is a fairly safe theme. No-
body, of course, wants to be put in the light of defending both bastardy and Negroes in the same breath,
and the few who might point to lack of educational
opportunity and generally depressed economic and
social conditions as a factor in illegitimacy are soon
shushed into silence.

Even though I thought the distinctions between legitimacy
and illegitimacy were not meaningful, I wanted to address myself particularly to the claim that illegitimacy could be stopped
by threatening welfare recipients with loss of aid. Although
there has never been any evidence to support this argument, its
proponents stand on its "logic." I concentrated on how best to
present arguments to counter this stand, though there is very
little concrete evidence bearing on it. Winifred Bell, a former
professor of social work at Columbia, in her book *Aid to Dependent Children* reported on studies which showed that when
aid was cut off, families became poorer and less stable, and this
ultimately gave rise to a higher incidence of illegitimacy. This
was the best we had.

Alabama's substitute-father regulation and the regulations of
the nineteen other states, I asserted in the brief submitted to
the Supreme Court, violated the constitutional right to privacy. "A welfare recipient should not lose her right to privacy
merely because she is getting funds from the state. There is no
'waiver' of her right because she is dependent on the state for
aid."

The Supreme Court in 1965 had established a right to privacy when it declared unconstitutional a Connecticut law pro-

hibiting advice on the use of contraceptives. Two years later
California's highest court found that a state welfare department
could not require, as a condition of continuing welfare, that
mothers receiving benefits allow welfare workers into their
homes to search "for purposes of detecting the presence of
'unauthorized males,' " California's equivalent of substitute fathers. The court stated, "By their timing and scope those
searchers pose constitutional questions relating both to the
Fourth Amendment's strictures against unreasonable searches
and seizures and to the penumbral right of privacy and repose
vindicated by the United States Supreme Court in 1965."

"Snooping" by welfare investigators, common in both the
North and South, is a part of the degradation in the welfare
system, and a broad decision in our case could put a stop to it.
In Cleveland, the Police Department's Bureau of Special Services (BOSS), whose main function was to hunt out men in the
house, cooperated with the welfare department. A favorite
BOSS tactic was to interrogate the children of welfare mothers
about undeclared income of their mothers' male companions.
Commissioner King described the Alabama practice: "If the
mothers or children can't prove to us the man is not giving
money—off they go."

Few regulations specify what evidence a local welfare official
must have before determining that a man appears to be having
or intends to have sexual intercourse with a particular mother
receiving ADC. Therefore, a woman's relationship with almost
any man whom she sees frequently—even a childhood friend—
could be and was used as a basis for terminating aid. We had
examined Alabama's reasons for cutting off the relief rolls
thousands of women and children, and the reasons were rarely
even as substantial as what Miss Stancil had heard from her
"little birdie."

To keep the aid that enables her to get food for her children,
the mother, under the regulation, must persuade welfare officials that each man she sees is not interested in her sexually. If

the official is not convinced, the mother must make her relationships known to neighbors, law-enforcement officials, even "grocers"—all of whom are free to spread the story through the community.

Furthermore, the caseworker might not be satisfied with the affidavits of these witnesses. After reviewing the affidavits, the caseworker can go out and cross-examine (with or without the woman's consent) the supporting witnesses to find out, as one caseworker put it, "how they know the relationship is broken." A woman's efforts to convince state or local welfare officials of the propriety of the relationship may well drive her man away.

Many children were asked whom their mother was "seeing" or "sleeping with." "Does a man come around here to visit your mother? How often does he come? Does he stay overnight?" Malcolm X, speaking of his childhood in his autobiography, told of such painful experiences. "When the state welfare people began coming to our house, we would come home from school sometimes and find them talking to our mother, asking a thousand questions. They acted and looked at her, and at us, and around our house in a way that had about it the feeling—at least for me—that we were not people. In their eyesight we were just things, that was all."

In many states the giving of information about a welfare mother's sexual conduct can lead to a determination of unsuitability (with the mother losing her children), and even, at times, to prosecutions for criminal adultery, fornication, and welfare abuse. Faced with having to divulge their private lives, terminate all relationships with men, and expose themselves to criminal prosecutions or legal proceedings in which they could lose their children, many mothers chose not to get involved with the welfare system. I submitted the results of a Florida study which concluded that many mothers so feared to lose their children that they did without money rather than "take a chance" in the welfare system.

Early in 1968, while the Smith case was being prepared for the Supreme Court, many state prosecutors instituted punitive actions against welfare recipients. In several New Jersey towns, fornication prosecutions were commenced against a thousand welfare mothers who had one or more illegitimate children. Paterson Municipal Court Judge Kushner reasoned that this type of criminial prosecution of the mothers would "make the fathers of illegitimate children pay support." He desisted after he realized that the women could not force unemployed men to support their children. Some states also began to prosecute unemployed men under criminal nonsupport laws, which carried severe jail sentences. In Maryland, two hundred fraud prosecutions were instituted against welfare mothers who claimed that they had no financial support; the district attorney presumed that male friends were supporting the women and their children.

The district attorney of Prince Georges County, Maryland, began proceedings (over the objection of the welfare department) to take children away from their mothers on the grounds that they were neglected, when the mother indicated in her application for welfare aid that one of her children was illegitimate. Six mothers, with a total of thirty-one children, were convicted of criminal neglect in 1968, following their completion of routine welfare applications. Maryland Judge Bowen did not take the children away from their mothers, but he warned the mothers that he would if they became pregnant again. He said, "The minimum acceptable standard in this community for men and women who wish to live together, to have sexual relations, and to bring children into the world is that they be married." Black leaders saw Judge Bowen's attempts at birth control as being aimed primarily at their race.

In preparing to argue a case in the Supreme Court, a lawyer will usually study what each of the nine judges has said in similar cases, to determine how many judges are likely to agree with his arguments. The legal approach that is most likely to persuade a majority of the judges might not bring the desired ruling, however, so the attorney must decide how closely the court can be asked to follow the path he wants it to follow.

Since *King v. Smith* was the first welfare case before the Supreme Court, none of the nine justices had written an opinion that would shed specific light on the question at hand. However, one rarely has a completely clean slate in law. Many of the issues in *King v. Smith* had been litigated in other contexts. Mr. Justice White's opinions on the applicability of the supremacy clause might be relevant to some of the points raised in *King v. Smith*. Before being appointed to the Supreme Court, many of the justices had expressed views that gave an idea of how they might react to the Smith case. In a lecture entitled "Equal Rights for Whom?" given on March 29, 1966, at New York University, Justice Fortas seemed to be anticipating cases like ours. After describing the substitute-father rules, and a 1961 Louisiana attempt to reduce the welfare rolls by cutting off aid to black children, as practices that could not be tolerated, he said:

> . . . Whether or not these practices affront explicit constitutional rights and if so, whether there is a remedy for the invasion or denial of the guarantees available to the indigent will undoubtedly be the subject of litigation for some time to come.

One week before the appeal hearing in the Supreme Court, I met with several groups of lawyers who "moot-courted" me—fired questions at me which they felt the court would ask. Lunch with a former professor of law at New York University turned into an exciting two-hour moot-court, presided over by J. Lee Rankin, former Solicitor General of the United States. Rankin's parting remark was, "It's a difficult case and Mr. Justice Harlan is going to be concerned about the federal-state relationships." In fact, Justice Harlan questioned me on that very subject. Finally, I met with lawyers formerly with the

Columbia Center and now with Mobilization for Youth, and they posed questions and discussed the issues with me for five hours.

When I arrived in Washington on April 21, the day before the scheduled hearing of our case, the city was funereally quiet: Martin Luther King had been assassinated two weeks before, and the people of Washington, after tumultuous days, walked the streets uneasily.

That evening I read Alabama's final brief (it had been served on me just as I was leaving for Washington) and was pleased to see that they were still advancing the same old arguments. Alabama's brief quoted Tillich, St. Thomas Aquinas, Malcolm Boyd, Gunnar Myrdal, Plato, Abraham Lincoln, and Kinsey, as well as *Redbook* magazine, among others. Alabama claimed that there are always inequities in the law, and that that, by itself, does not mean that a law is bad. Alabama quoted Paul Tillich as authority for the substitute-father rule, claiming that individuality and inequality go hand in hand.

In a section called "An Incentive to Say No," the brief said:

> . . . Although, as pointed out by the appellees' briefs, the Alabama regulation does not require complete chastity as a condition precedent to public aid in Alabama, it does seem to require that the mother agree to some degree of continence. Is there anything really *bad* about continence? Is there anything bad about requiring the mother to say no? Does the literature of the New Morality or the Kinsey Reports actually prove that continence is not a better way of life? Unbridled sex in this country recently has been more stylish.

I had visions of the Alabama brief being passed out to all of King's ladies in the welfare department, who would say, "The

Supreme Court will finally understand that we're trying to help the black folk." And I could see George Wallace editing and adding to the brief to give it his distinctive touch. Alabama's brief continued with a ringing defense of chastity:

> . . . Appellants submit that there is a lot to be said for continence whether it is being expressed by a low income person from New England who has his roots in puritanism, whether it is expressed by a low income member of the Negro race who has risen from the sexual abuses practiced during slavery and recognizes that "to be free at last" also means giving up the practices which may now be described as a form of self-imposed slavery, or whether it is expressed by the poor Bible-belt white Southerner who knows he has not solved all of his problems either, or the low income Westerner who recognizes somehow that the Hollywood image of sex life is not really what everybody wants.
>
> Without being moralistic, hypocritical or puritanical, there is much to be said for continence. It would be a most refreshing breeze to blow over this country. Imagine turning on television and listening to programs which not only extolled continence and chastity but which also pointed out the attractive aspects of purity. Appellants submit that the important reason that married low income families and the public want the ADC mother to be able to say "no" is really because there is a great longing in everyone for all mothers, poor and affluent, to say "no." There is no government grant or service which would give more to an ADC child—or any other child—than a social order which, again, makes it wholesome and stylish for a mother to say "no" to adultery and fornication.
>
> Nature places a great privilege and a great responsibility on women. Neither Appellees nor *amici* have shown exactly why saying a judicial "yes" to co-

habitors out of wedlock is going to help a deserted mother, widow, or unwed poor mother or affluent mother, get a husband—particularly one who is apt to be helpful with the children. It may be an extremely old fashioned notion, but Appellants advance that the opposite is more nearly true (not that merely getting a husband would necessarily solve all of her problems).

In the long run continence and chastity make better homes. Continence and chastity make better mothers and fathers . . .

There appears to be a belief held among many that sexual relations are necessary to health. This belief could have been the motive for Appellee Smith's statement that she intended to maintain a relationship with some man. Appellants deny the validity of this belief and assert that chastity does accord with good health.

On April 21, 1968, the Sunday night of the weekend on which Dr. King had planned to lead the Poor People's March into Washington, the Hay Adams Hotel was the scene of an unusual meeting. My wife, a friend of ours, and I had dinner with Mrs. Stapp and her assistant, Mrs. Carol Lee Miller. I had called Mrs. Stapp a few days earlier and suggested that we meet to discuss our arguments. We would have a half hour each (she was to argue first), and because the case was a difficult one for such a short presentation, I felt it would be better for Mrs. Stapp to set the statutory, factual, and constitutional framework for the case in her argument, as well as to outline the lower court's decision. I was afraid that, unless she did this, the court would not be ready for my argument presenting different reasons from those heard by the lower court. If the court was not clear about the setting of the case, I would have to spend valuable time clarifying the facts. The arrangement would be to Mrs. Stapp's advantage too, since she would be spared many questions.

The mood at dinner was cordial. Mrs. Stapp wore a navy-blue dress with a white trim, and her hair was pulled back. Her conversation was full of literary allusions; her voice soft and girlish, with a pleasant drawl. She was excited about the Supreme Court argument—it was her first—and she hadn't slept soundly in weeks. She agreed that her presentation should give the background of the case. And she talked on about how poor Alabama was, how hard it was for the state administration to be fair in distributing the little money it had, and how upset the "good people" of Alabama were to learn that the vice-ridden black people of the state expected welfare aid. It was the voice of the Bible-reading, magnolia-scented, good Southerner, with all his biases and defenses. "What would the good taxpaying people say if we had to take money from some needy people to support illegitimacy? Now, Mr. Garbus, you know the Seventh Commandment. How do you reconcile your position with the Seventh Commandment?"

The problem was crystallized, at least as Mrs. Stapp and the welfare department of Alabama saw it, in the assertion that their regulations were "anti-fornication," not anti-black. "Good Alabama citizens don't think there should be sex outside of its 'proper' domicile—the wedded couple. You know that they aren't like us."

"Mrs. Stapp, they can't afford to see a lawyer to get a divorce. There are no black lawyers in Alabama they can turn to to get legal advice or help—and white lawyers don't want any part of them. It's been that way for years. Their common-law marriages are entitled to respect. And if they have an 'illegitimate' child, it is the state that calls it that."

Mrs. Stapp countered with the rallying cry of all white people living in the better parts of town: "It's just wrong. They can do like other folks. What about the Seventh Commandment?" And she went on: "They're not like you and me. They manage somehow. Their mothers' friends don't let them starve. I've been living in Alabama for forty years, and I never saw a starving child or heard of any starvation. Only the

Northerners, who've never been there, say it is so. Why don't they get married? We don't have the money to support all those children."

The dining room of the Hay Adams Hotel is pleasant and luxurious. Woods, velvet, large spaces between tables are conducive to quiet, civilized dining. The following day Mrs. Stapp would argue the impoverishment of her state treasury, and I would argue the impoverishment of her people. Regardless of the decision, the people of Alabama would not believe that Mrs. Smith's children were worthy of state money.

Our case was the fourth on the calendar for Monday, which was "decision day" at the Supreme Court. That Monday the decisions took several hours to read, and it became apparent that the Smith case wouldn't come up until Tuesday, so the clerk gave me permission to leave and I went back to the hotel. Calls had come in from lawyers throughout the country who were coming to Washington to hear the argument and wanted to know when it would be heard. The other welfare cases were to be argued the week after, and all the lawyers in these cases had come to hear *King v. Smith*, for it would show the court's first reaction to the welfare issues. I met with some of these lawyers Monday evening, gave them copies of my brief, and discussed various aspects of my case that were relevant to their clients' cases.

I wasn't nervous before I went to Washington. Having lived with the case and its legal problems for eighteen months, I thought I was thoroughly prepared for the argument, even to the point of thinking that I knew what each of the judges would ask. However, I have always been afraid that one day I would get up to argue and forget all my preparation. I had tried many cases and argued many appeals, yet I still had that nagging fear.

Of course, each trial lawyer responds differently to pressure. While going to law school at night, I had apprenticed with one of the country's best trial lawyers, who had tried thousands of cases and argued hundreds of appeals. One morning I took the train with him to Albany, where later that day he was going to argue a minor case in the New York Court of Appeals. His nervousness astonished me: his hands shook, he could not eat or sit still and paced back and forth continuously. He was inarticulate and inaudible as he and I spoke early that morning. In court later that day, I saw that as he walked toward the bench to present his argument he was even more nervous than before. Although I was at the counsel table, I could barely hear his first tremulous words. And then, magically as if a string were pulled, he became self-assured and eloquent. His argument was brilliant.

In Washington, during the days before the Smith case, I withdrew into myself. I did not show much tension and seemed to be entirely composed, but I was in many ways completely isolated from the people around me. My wife Ruth and my one-year-old daughter Cassie had come with me to Washington. The morning of the argument, Ruth tearfully told me that the baby-sitter had been drinking and she was afraid of leaving Cassie with her. I paid little attention.

The night before the argument, nervousness and excitement took over. I couldn't sleep and paced and read briefs until four in the morning. I thought of the dozens of suits I had tried that had never made it to the high court. None of them had the scope or complexity of Mrs. Sylvester Smith's case. I knew that there was nothing I'd rather be doing than arguing Mrs. Smith's case before the Supreme Court.

The first case on Tuesday, a cold, bone-crackling Washington day, began promptly at 10:00 A.M. The courtroom was filled and lines stretched out into the hallway, as poverty lawyers from all over the country, HEW's Washington lawyers, and representatives of the poor came to hear the argument. They all rose as the crier signaled the approach of the justices with his familiar, "Oyez, oyez, oyez. All persons having business before the Honorable Supreme Court of the United States are admonished to draw near and give their attention, for the Court is now sitting. God save the United States and this Honorable Court." The nine justices, who knew they had an explosive political issue scheduled for that morning, filed in and took their places on the bench.

The first case that day involved Midas Muffler's claim that a franchiser was selling products not manufactured by Midas and selling them as Midas products. Midas said they invested in these franchises, helped support them until they could make a profit, and then this particular franchiser had started selling competitive products and stopped selling Midas goods. The argument ended shortly before eleven.

The Chief Justice called *King v. Smith*. Commissioner King was with Mrs. Stapp, and he came up to the counsel bench and sat down as Mrs. Stapp began. When we approached the bench to argue, the mood of the courtroom changed from one of expectancy to one of tension. Mrs. Stapp went to the lectern, outlined the statutory scheme, and presented her arguments with a minimum of questions from the bench. Her hands shook and her voice indicated her nervousness, but after a minute or two she took hold. "We're doing the best we can for these children. We've got a problem, and I know you judges know about it." During her argument she never looked at Justice Marshall. She spoke as one white person to eight other whites, and when she said the judges knew of the problem, she implied that they were sympathetic to it. Justice Fortas looked sharply at her. He knew it was a "black" problem she was referring to, and he was annoyed that she had so misjudged the court. She pointed out King and told of the part he had played in formulating the regulation in question. She spoke for half of her alloted thirty minutes and reserved the remaining fifteen minutes until after my argument, to answer any questions I raised.

I approached the lectern, and Justice Fortas began question-

ing me about the political realities that prevented HEW from
ruling out unacceptable state programs. I was never to get into
the formal legal argument I had spent weeks preparing. He
asked: "Why hasn't HEW done something if the regulation
does what you say it does? What can HEW do once it decides,
as it seems to have done here, that a regulation is unacceptable?"

"All it can do," I said, "is to withhold funds from the entire
program."

"In effect, then, they can't do anything."

He then asked how the regulation worked. "Do you mean
that even a legitimate child can lose aid if the mother is thought
to have a male 'friend'?"

"Yes."

"Do you mean that they claim the regulation is aimed at support and they don't even ask before they cut off the aid if the
man supports the child?"

"Yes."

Justice Fortas already knew the answers to the questions he
was asking. He was drawing out information favorable to Mrs.
Smith's case for the benefit of the other judges, who were not
as familiar with the regulation. The answers to his questions
showed the regulation at its worst.

Justice Harlan peered at me through thick lenses. He put
down the brief he was holding six inches from his eyes and
questioned the right of the federal government to set standards
for a state program. This was the area Rankin had said would
bother Harlan. Over the course of his judicial career, Harlan
has shown a concern for the rights of states to be free of federal interference. Politically, the issue of states' rights in the
welfare area was one of great significance. I did not want the
same kind of deference paid to state welfare-agency procedures that had previously been accorded state criminal procedures. He asked about the percentage of federal funds in the
program and seemed surprised to learn that 83 percent of Ala-

bama's ADC funds were contributed by the federal government. As we discussed what a Southern state had done to thousands of its poorest families, the courtroom became charged with emotion.

I then told the court I wanted a new basis for the decision, not just an affirmation of the Alabama federal court's decision. "The Social Security Act was passed in 1935; the first of the substitute-father regulations was passed in 1947. It's taken us all this time to get a case, the first welfare case, before the court, and if the decision goes off as the lower court's did, then very little will have been accomplished. Even if we win in Alabama, HEW will not stop similar practices in other states." This argument, correctly emphasizing the political and social realities, was not, as stated, a persuasive legal argument for the decision we wanted. However, the statutory argument—the redefining of the word "parent"—would allow the court to decide the case in such a way as to affect all twenty states.

All courts prefer to decide cases on the narrowest grounds possible. Some judges consider this imperative. The problem in *King v. Smith* was to suggest a way in which the narrowest of rulings would have the broadest of implications. I started to introduce the statutory argument, the one that would give us all we wanted—but I was interrupted by the friendly questioning of Mr. Justice Brennan.

I emphasized, in reply to his questions, that the class being discriminated against consisted of "helpless children" who were being deprived of essentials necessary to their lives. The night before, I had thought a long time about whether to argue that the Constitution obligated the government to furnish the necessities of life. But this novel approach, fascinating in its implications, had not yet been adopted by any court; it was too risky to try to develop it here. I simply stated the point and, referring to Justice Fortas's previous law-school speech, went on. "The degrading search for the 'phantom father,' for a man, any man, whose presence in the household can justify the termination of payments to mother and child, suggests Alabama and the other nineteen states are motivated by factors other than a concern to save the state funds. It is suggestive of the days when the stocks and the pillory and public disgrace were considered suitable for the women caught in illicit love.

"Our acceptance of a measure of state responsibility for the poor dates back to the Poor Laws of Tudor England. But from the earliest times to the present, the poor have been indiscriminately classed as vagrants, vagabonds, and rogues. They have been regarded as offensive by their mere existence. They have been considered a moral pestilence. The Articles of Confederation denied paupers, vagabonds, and fugitives from justice the privileges and immunities of citizenship, and the right to move from state to state. Until the very recent past, it was assumed with little protest that the indigent were, for many purposes, outside of the scope of the Bill of Rights. Under the common law and the laws of the states, they could be seized and jailed because of their status as poverty-stricken.

"This case affords the court an opportunity to interpret the Social Security Act so that we will stop treating the poor as nonpersons, upon whom every indignity can be visited. More than Mrs. Smith, the 21,000 children, or even the substitute-father regulations in nineteen states, is at issue here. The court now has an opportunity to interpret the Social Security Act in such a way as to affect the lives of every one of the eight million welfare recipients in this country."

Justice Brennan asked, as time was running out, how I would like the decision written. The question did not mean that he would vote in Mrs. Smith's favor. He simply wanted to know how the decision would be most effective if ultimately he agreed with us. I was exhilarated, and a joyful murmur swept through the spectators. This was the question I had hoped for but had never believed would be asked. "Give us a decision interpreting the Social Security Act as having rejected the concept of a worthy and an unworthy poor," I said. "Your reading of the statutory history of the Social Security Act should lead you to hold that states may treat as 'parents,' for the purpose of ADC eligibility, only persons with a legal obligation to support." I sat down.

Mrs. Stapp rose to present her rebuttal. She pointed out what she held were the political realities. "If we are required to put those children back on the rolls, it is possible that the entire ADC program will be dropped by Alabama and other states, Northern as well as Southern, and those children now getting aid will lose it." It is up to the individual states to decide whether or not to participate in the federal ADC program. If they participate, they receive federal funds. The ratio of federal to state funds has always been too seductive to turn down, but Mrs. Stapp indicated that Alabama might forgo federal funds rather than give aid to black children.

"Are you threatening us?" Mr. Justice Brennan barked.

"No, of course not. I just want you to know our problem."

"I thought you were. Don't threaten the court." He placed another question, as much to show Mrs. Stapp that his anger had subsided as to obtain an answer. Brennan, a small, soft-spoken man, seldom exhibited such strong feelings.

"What can we do to help you?"

"Reverse the lower court," Mrs. Stapp said.

Brennan was furious. I thought he had asked the question thinking Mrs. Stapp would want to propose a decision that would invalidate the regulation without creating political problems. For a moment he may have felt that Mrs. Stapp was defending a regulation she was out of sympathy with and, realizing the mood of the Supreme Court justices, she would try to help work out a compromise. Her answer, "Reverse the lower court," showed him, and any other justice who shared his feeling, that they had been mistaken. The court's attitude toward Mrs. Stapp changed; the questions became incisive, hard, and flat.

As the hearing continued, Justice Brennan looked through the briefs. In my brief I had pointed to the recent reports of malnutrition, hunger, and starvation in the country; I had asserted that a delay in this decision would result in untold deaths. Mrs. Stapp countered, "If the issue in this case is whether or not the children in question shall live or starve, it does not look as though the ADC grant will play a particularly large part in alleviating malnutrition, hunger, or starvation, for the ADC grant has never insured any child of a balanced diet."

In cutting off aid to mothers involved in illicit relationships, she went on, her state was providing more money for qualifying families. However, the court interpreted this as an attempt to justify giving money to white families at the expense of black families. Justice Marshall, sitting impassively, observed, "Before, you said you needed this regulation to save money. I don't see how you save the state money. You give more milk to some children by giving none to others."

"Those that qualify," Mrs. Stapp answered the black judge.

Justice Douglas, ruddy-complexioned and looking like the outdoorsman he is, spoke for the first time: "You argue that this regulation is not aimed at morality."

Mrs. Stapp quickly said she did.

Justice Douglas then asked, "You're concerned about the child's environment?"

"Yes."

"Do you cut off aid under this regulation if the woman is a criminal, or beats her child, or is an alcoholic?"

"No."

"It seems to me you're making a moral judgment. Isn't it worse for the child if the mother is an alcoholic, a criminal, doesn't care for the child, is never around the house?"

"It may be worse, but the regulation does at least try and stop one source of conduct dangerous to the child. We can't solve all the problems at once," Mrs. Stapp answered, and Justice Douglas stared. He often leaves the courtroom during the middle of an argument. But he was not to do so in Mrs. Smith's case.

There is a pattern in the high court's procedure. The justices hear arguments from a semicircular bench, with the Chief Justice in the middle, the senior justices next on either side, and the most recent appointees at the ends. Often, the newer justices question the attorneys first, with the senior justices and the Chief Justice saving questions for the middle or the end of the argument. Chief Justice Warren had not asked Mrs. Stapp any questions. His eyes never left the lawyer at the lectern, however; he was totally absorbed in the argument. Before she sat down, he said he wanted to ask three short questions. He began them in an even tone, cutting through her legalistic argument, reducing it to human terms.

"Do you mean, Mrs. Stapp, that a woman and her children can be cut off for having a substitute father even though the children have never seen the 'father'?"

"That can't be answered that way. It depends . . ."

"It is a simple question and can be answered 'yes' or 'no.' As I understand it, the answer is 'yes.' "

"It depends on which part of the regulation you look at. I can't answer just that way."

"It seems like a simple answer to me. Let me ask you another question. Is the regulation applicable where the man sees the children and is friendly with the mother, definitely does not sleep with the mother, and does not give the children any money?"

"It depends on the  . . ."

"Mrs. Stapp, I think that can be answered 'yes' or 'no' and I think I'm entitled to that answer."

"It can't be answered that simply. We're not just concerned with the morality. This is a problem that bothers us."

The Chief Justice's face flushed, and his mounting irritation was obvious to all.

"Mrs. Stapp, I think your answer is 'yes.' I have one last question. Can the man be called a substitute father even though he is not the father of any of the children?"

"That just doesn't happen. That's the misunderstanding."

"I just want to know if the regulation can be applied in that manner."

"It depends . . ."

The Chief Justice, in a rare display of anger, lifted a book off the bench in front of him and slammed it down. "Never mind, never mind, never mind," he shouted. Mrs. Stapp sat down.

The argument ended at 11:40. The court runs on a precise timetable and normally would take the next argument. But the level of emotion reached in the courtroom was so high and the members of the court had become so involved that they could not go on. The Chief Justice adjourned court until afternoon.

Now came the wait for a decision. I continued to work on setting up other welfare cases for the Supreme Court, and I came across Northern judges who shared some of George Wallace's views on black welfare recipients.

In May 1968 I presented an application for a preliminary injunction to Judge Thomas Murphy, the former police commissioner of the City of New York, who had made a national reputation as the prosecutor of Alger Hiss. He was then sitting as a federal judge at Foley Square in New York. Several New York mothers claimed that their welfare benefits had been cut off for reasons no more substantial than those given to Mrs. Smith—some because they allegedly lived in tenements where addicts lived; others because they allegedly lived with men who were not married to them. Their school-age children, deprived of adequate food for two weeks, were being kept home. Some had no shoes.

Before we went into the judge's chambers, we presented to him and to the three lawyers representing the city agencies affidavits from several workers, psychiatrists, and school leaders describing the condition of the children. We asked only that a child not be cut off from aid before someone checks on the accusations made—that the benefits continue to be given until a fair hearing had been held to determine if the welfare department's claims were true.

The judge, a bulky, balding man with a handlebar moustache, looking very much like the bass in an 1890 barbershop quartet, spoke to me as soon as I entered his chambers, even before all the lawyers had come in and before any had sat down. "What's this all about, Mr. Garbus?"

"We're seeking a temporary restraining order stopping the welfare department from cutting off payments until they hold a hearing." (Had he read the papers I'd presented?)

"Why do you want a temporary order? It's an extraordinary remedy."

"This is exactly the kind of case for the remedy," I replied. "The families are without the necessities of life. The affidavits prove . . ."

"In a welfare case? This is not the kind of situation where an injunction should be issued."

"It's precisely the kind of case."

"No."

"This is exactly the case where an injunction is necessary— children not getting food, people being put out on the street. What kind of case requires it? Where one record company claims another record company released a record copying its song and it is going to lose some money?"

He looked down at the complaint (apparently for the first time), saw that Mary Kelly was the first plaintiff on the list, and asked, "How long ago was she cut off?"

"Two weeks ago. Her children have been . . ."

"She's managed all right for the past two weeks. She can wait until the case is reached in its normal order."

"If the case is reached in its normal order, there won't be a decision for another six weeks. She has no money. Her children . . ."

The judge stopped me before I could go on.

"She'll manage. They always do. She can borrow money from her boyfriend. How has she been living the past two weeks? I won't sign the order."

"From her boyfriend? What boyfriend?"

"Your application's denied. That's all. Good day."

"Your Honor, this is . . ."

"Good day."

As May passed, the end of the Supreme Court term approached, and I thought about the possibility of reargument at the next term of court. On June 17 I received a telegram from Chief Deputy of the Supreme Court Edmund Cullinan telling me that we had won. The question still open now was the manner of the court's decision. Was it unanimous? How far-reaching would it be? Would it affect the other nineteen states? Would it tell legislators and welfare administrators that a new day was dawning in the welfare system? Would it prohibit the degrading inquiries that Malcolm X, Mrs. Sylvester Smith, and thousands of others were subjected to? And if it did all this, would it make the welfare system so expensive that the more humane guaranteed minimum income, which would not cost that much more, would become a reasonable alternative?

The next day we received the opinion in the mail from the Supreme Court. It was a 9–0 victory, with Chief Justice Warren writing the decision, and it went far beyond my wildest hopes. The Chief Justice decides who shall write the opinion in each case before the court. Chief Justice Warren, believing that this was his last day as Chief Justice, had reserved the Smith case for himself and had handed down a decision that invalidated the substitute-parent regulations in all twenty states.

The Supreme Court ruled that the term "parent" in the Social
Security Act included only those with a legal duty of support.
It said:

> . . . Alabama's argument based on its interests in dis-
> couraging immorality and illegitimacy would have
> been quite relevant at one time in the history of the
> AFDC program. However, subsequent developments
> clearly establish that these state interests are not pres-
> ently legitimate justifications for AFDC disqualifica-
> tion. Insofar as this or any similar regulation is based
> on the State's asserted interests in discouraging illicit
> sexual behavior and illegitimacy, it plainly conflicts
> with federal law and policy. . . .
>
> A significant characteristic of public welfare pro-
> grams during the last half of the 19th century in this
> country was their preference for the "worthy" poor.
> Some poor persons were thought unworthy because
> of their supposed incapacity for "moral regenera-
> tion." This worthy person concept characterized the
> mothers' pension welfare programs, which were cus-
> tomarily restricted to widows who were considered
> morally fit. We reject this concept. . . .
>
> Congress has determined that immorality and ille-
> gitimacy should be dealt with through rehabilitative
> measures rather than measures that punish dependent
> children. . . . All responsible governmental agencies
> in the nation today recognize the enormity and the
> pervasiveness of social ills caused by poverty. The
> causes of and cures for poverty are currently the sub-
> ject of much debate. We hold today only that Con-
> gress has made at least this one determination: that
> destitute children who are legally fatherless cannot be
> flatly denied federally funded assistance on the trans-
> parent fiction that they have a substitute father.

"This signals the beginning of the end of welfare and will
help lead to a guaranteed minimum income," a leading consti-

tutional lawyer said. "It has exposed some of the worst vices of
the welfare system. It will result in the system's becoming so
expensive that it will break down, forcing an alternative way
of dealing with the problems of poverty." *The New York
Times* in a June 22 editorial, when the impact of the decision
became clear, called it the most important constitutional law
decision since the 1954 segregation case and said it would "set
in motion profound changes in American society."

Senator Robert Byrd (Democrat from West Virginia)
pointed out that his colleagues in Congress bore part of the
responsibility for the Smith decision. He declared, "I don't
think we can say much unless we are willing to stand up and be
counted when it comes to confirmation of judges."

The conservative press reacted as expected. Three days after
the Smith decision, David Lawrence headlined his column "Supreme Court by Its Decision Makes Sin Pay." He wrote, "The
Supreme Court of the United States has just rendered a decision
that appears to make adultery profitable and seems to disregard
laws designed to discourage immorality. The Supreme Court
did not base its decision on Constitutional grounds. It merely
held that the Alabama regulation was inconsistent with the language of the federal law—a ruling not unusual in these days of
dedication to technicalities rather than to moral principles."
Weeping crocodile tears, he went on, "States and cities have
welfare departments. It is illogical that the granting of federal
funds should have become involved in the enrichment of 'substitute fathers,' while the poor children suffer the tragedy of
being reared under circumstances that can hardly contribute to
their future well-being. The whole thing has gotten tangled up,
however, in the technicalities of the Supreme Court, which
seems more interested nowadays in the equivocal phrases of
law than in adherence to accepted principles of human behavior."

Most federal and state legislators and governors simply accepted the decision and agreed to enforce it. Many, sympa-

thetic to our cause, were glad to see the court make a decision that politically they could not make. But there were, of course, some state legislators who claimed that the United States Supreme Court had "told us that we must subsidize not only illegitimacy but also adultery."

Representative Sharpe, a Democrat in the Michigan House, asked for strong state legislation dealing with Aid to Dependent Children payments. "The Court's puzzling opinion that an ADC mother can live with a man who is not her husband, or with a series of such men, and that the resulting atmosphere constitutes a suitable home for children who are, in effect, financial wards of the state is beyond doubt as incomprehensible to you as it is to me. What the Supreme Court has told us, in substance, is that we can no longer regard the family as a legal unit." Sharpe suggested that the full force and wrath of the law be focused on the men who prey upon these lonely, deprived women and who trade the questionable value of their companionship for publicly provided money, food, and lodging intended for the children.

Other states indicated that they would try to get around the Smith decision. The Washington *Post*'s lead story for its July 12, 1968, edition, headlined "Virginia to Use Pressure in Welfare Cases," advised: "The State Department of Welfare has decided to let its controversial 'man in the house' policy pass into oblivion but still continue to bring pressure to bear against those to whom it normally would apply. Otis L. Brown, the director of the state agency, said the agency should 'bring charges, such as contributing to the delinquency of a minor, against a mother when it is determined that her actions are detrimental to the well-being of her children.' "

I went to Selma three weeks after the decision. The day after the decision the Birmingham papers, in an effort to make it appear that Mrs. Smith, like all other black welfare recipients, was thriving, reported that she owned a "neat, spotless white frame house" at the edge of town. The truth was otherwise. She rented one half of a dilapidated white-and-green shack. I drove from the center of Selma, past stately Southern mansions and brick homes, and came eventually to wooden frame houses. Then the paved sidewalks and streets ended, and a wide, muddy road with brick houses on either side announced the beginning of the black section. I drove another half mile. The brick houses ended, and the configuration of the street became jumbled. Wooden houses and then wooden shacks began to appear. The road narrowed to a path, and at the end of it was Mrs. Smith's house, in the middle of a red-dirt field.

I stepped over the puddles to get to the house to talk to Mrs. Smith. She had three rooms—a four-by-five kitchen and a slightly larger living room and bedroom. Six people lived there: Mrs. Smith, her four children, and her granddaughter. The beds in the bedroom and the cots in the living room took up all available floor space. The kitchen, which smelled of antiseptic, was clean and bare—there was not a morsel of food in the refrigerator or on the shelves.

A religious meeting appeared to be in progress, and the children were all in the living room. Two of the children had no clothes; none had shoes. Outside, it was over 110 degrees; inside, it was worse. I could barely breathe in the room, so we went outside to talk.

"They haven't put me back yet. It takes a month to get back. They tell me it'll take to the end of the month."

"Do you have any money?"

"No, but I'll manage. Someone is bringing bones tonight."

"Have you spoken to Miss Stancil? There's a way you can get emergency aid."

"Miss Stancil's not my worker any more. I guess they transferred her, or me, because of the trouble. There's a new lady.

She knows I don't have any money and we haven't ate right in a long time. They tell me I've got to behave if I want to get aid."

Mrs. Smith's life had changed very little. The winner of one of the most momentous legal cases of the decade, one that supposedly would change the lives of nearly half a million people, she was still being denied her rights.

I went back to Selma to speak again to Ruben King's ladies. I met some of my old friends and I met Mrs. Marshal, Mrs. Smith's new caseworker.

"They had it better before the welfare system," she said. "They used to live on the owner's land. He gave them food and they lived rent-free. We looked after them. I know you don't believe that. They didn't need welfare."

"Do you know she has no money at all? The kids haven't really eaten in weeks?"

"She didn't tell me that."

"Did you ask her?"

"I told her about the food-stamp program. All she needs is $15 and she can get two-weeks' food."

"But she doesn't have $15. Even if she did, she couldn't get into Selma to carry those cartons away."

"Mr. Garbus, they always manage."

"What about your emergency-aid program? She's entitled to it."

"She never applied for it."

"She told me you said she has to behave to get her benefits. What does that mean?"

"Well, we're going to pass a new law. The Supreme Court didn't understand our regulation. They were confused. Mr. Garbus, I heard you had confused them. It really doesn't work that way. We treat these people well and they need us to stay out of trouble. If we don't do something, there'll be colored babies all over Alabama—and the North too."

I threatened to bring a new suit, and within a week Mrs. Smith was receiving welfare aid again.

Before, during, and after the Supreme Court argument, we were very much aware that some hostile states, when faced with larger ADC rolls, might simply disburse the same sum of money among the greater number of people, thus hurting old recipients to help new ones (as Mrs. Stapp suggested in her argument before the Supreme Court). This was the gamble the Supreme Court had taken. But few states did this. And no state dropped the ADC program as Alabama had predicted they might. Several, including Texas and Louisiana, did reduce benefits to all recipients. But legal moves forced them to conform to the philosophy of the Smith case.

Joel Cohen, a lawyer in HEW's Chief Counsel's office, estimated some six months after the decision that approximately 750,000 children were receiving benefits as a result of the Smith case. But no court has forced any state welfare officials to find those who had been wrongfully denied aid.

Immediately after the Smith decision, hundreds of cases were filed, on the basis of the Smith decision, attacking other onerous aspects of the welfare system. The court's rejection of the concept of "unworthy poor," the court's opinion that it could look into and reject portions of state programs, and its assertion that the Social Security Act required "all eligible persons to receive aid" heralded the beginning of a "Bill of Rights for the Disinherited." It opened the door wide for federal judicial examination of inequities in the welfare system.

"Like Linda Brown, the school girl from Topeka who won the 1954 school integration decision, and Clarence Gideon, the Florida convict whose right to an attorney was upheld in 1963, Mrs. Sylvester Smith has set in motion a dramatic change in American society," wrote Walter Goodman in *The New York Times* on August 25, 1968.

Mrs. Smith put it differently: "A lot of the ladies who got

aid because of my case thank me. They do. They call me or sometimes come over. I was even on television. They had no right to do that to me. I'm glad we did the case. I'll bet Miss Stancil ain't so hard on ladies any more."

# Four

*The People against Manfredo Correa*
*and Frederick Charles Wood*

I FIRST SAW MANFREDO CORREA, Puerto Rican, aged twenty-six, in the Sing Sing death house in April 1961. An addict whose desperation level rose as his need for drugs became greater, he had been convicted after killing a grocer, Anthony Graniella, during a holdup. The gray stone death house, an entirely separate split-level structure, was in the southwest corner of the prison compound. Armed guards watched me as I left my car and walked the hundred feet to the death house.

I proved to the guards at the door that I was a lawyer—I had made arrangements earlier—so I did not have to go through the normal inspection. The pockets and handbags of visitors are examined for poison pellets, knives, razor blades, and so on.

On the first floor I passed the three special visiting cubicles. Each has two parallel screens of heavy gray wire that separate inmates and their families by about four feet.

On the second floor of the death house there is a room with tables and chairs where inmates can sit with their lawyers without intervening screens. I was led in and told that Correa would be brought down.

I've been to Sing Sing many times during the past ten years to see my clients as they waited for death. I've always been impressed by the fact that the guards in the death house are the quietest and most courteous prison guards anywhere. They show extraordinary concern for their prisoners and have a closer relationship with them than the guards outside the condemned cells. They seem to know, as I know, that the men sentenced to die are less "criminal" than most of the other men in our prisons. Over 70 percent of convicted murderers have no previous record. They usually have led exemplary lives as working men, often being overly conscientious. For many of them, their encounter with the law has come within an emotionally charged situation. They impulsively killed someone very close to them—husband, wife, lover, brother, or sister—in an outburst of uncontrollable hostility.

I've often walked down death row. Thirty-nine cells are set aside for condemned murderers; fourteen of the cells were occupied that day. Each measures eight by twelve feet, with three steel walls, a sliding barred door, and a cage-like front. A man is allowed to go out to a walled yard alone for an hour each day; occasionally a guard will play handball with him.

Each cell has a ceiling light fixture, an iron cot with a mattress, a backless stool, a writing surface affixed to one wall, a toilet bowl, and a sink. The sink has a cold-water tap only. In the mornings hot water is provided for shaving, and a razor is passed through the bars. "We make sure the blade is in the razor when we get it back," an officer told me. They are vigilant against suicide attempts. If an inmate wants to smoke, a guard comes along and lights his cigarette. All meals are served in the cells. Knives and forks, once forbidden, are passed in and reclaimed later. Pens and pencils are provided on loan.

On one occasion, I was taken past the "dance hall," so called because the prisoners who won't walk to the chair, or who put up a fight, have to be dragged or pushed in by half a dozen guards. The "last mile" is a short one—twenty steps through three steel doors to the chair.

The prisoner is strapped in the chair. The power comes through moistened electrodes that are fastened to one leg through special trousers and to a shaved spot on the back of the head. The "fair, sweet mercy of electric death" (of which the *New York World* wrote shortly after electrocution replaced hanging in New York State) comes after an executioner, paid a $150 fee "on a piecework basis," pulls the big black switch. Life ends with a 2,000-volt shock.

Today New York is building a new death house in Greenhaven Prison, thirty miles north of Sing Sing. When I recently asked the warden whether they would move the Sing Sing chair to Greenhaven or provide a new electric chair, he said, "Well, I think they'll move it, but it's a hard job. It's a whole lotta apparatus—not just an electric chair. It's not like a toaster that you can just plug in."

In all his years in prison, I was the only visitor Correa ever had. On that first visit, we spent the entire day talking about the crime, the trial the year before, the conviction, the appeal, and the wait for death.

Correa had become puffy and sluggish in jail, adding forty pounds to his five-foot ten-inch frame. As the cold April air came in through the window bars, he shook his head to break out of the death-house stupor. As he spoke, I could see the Hudson through the window.

Correa denied that he had intentionally killed Graniella. He told me the gun that killed Graniella was a homemade weapon that had never been fired before. The weapon was amazingly crude—a simple wooden stock powered by rubber bands. When I later examined it, I could not understand how it could possibly have been fired.

Correa had gone to Graniella's store with the idea of getting money for a fix. He demanded one hundred dollars. Graniella refused and picked up a club. When Correa again demanded money, Graniella came after him. Correa pulled out his gun just as Graniella struck him on the arm. Correa was amazed when the ridiculous weapon fired. Graniella went down with a bullet in his heart.

Correa was arrested three days later and taken to the 92nd Precinct in Brooklyn, where, according to him, he was beaten by four cops. His request for a lawyer was ignored, and when he started to go into drug withdrawal, the police promised him narcotics if he confessed. He made a confession in which he admitted the deliberate, intentional killing of Graniella.

On the basis of the confession, Correa was convicted of first-degree murder and sentenced to death. Because the jury might hear of his criminal record of petty burglaries, he could not take the stand and testify about the murder and the confession. He made an appeal to the highest New York court and lost. Before the date of his execution the Supreme Court changed the procedures to be used in determining whether or not a confession is voluntarily given. This meant that Correa, for the first time, would have an opportunity to give his version of what happened in the station house.

Later, in a procedure in the Supreme Court of New York County, I moved to set aside Correa's conviction. I tried to show through his testimony that the confession he had given was false and coerced, that a confession made by an addict in the throes of withdrawal is, by its very nature, an involuntary confession. The implications extended beyond Correa's case. The outcome could affect the lives of dozens of men in death houses throughout the country.

In response to my questioning, he told what had happened to him in the precinct house: "I was taken from the big squad room to the small commanding officer's room. I was told to sit down. They handcuffed me to the chair. And then they started to question me."

"Did you have any discussion with any of the policemen before they started to question you concerning your right to a lawyer?"

"Yes, sir. He said I didn't need a lawyer."

Correa testified that not only had no one ever advised him that he had a right not to talk to the police; he had been told

just the opposite. He described what happened to him at the police station and the pain he was in at the time the confession
was taken.

"Well, there was—this commanding officer . . . He says,
'You killed a man in Manhattan. We know you killed a man in
Manhattan.' So when I went to answer him, there was a detective with a scar on the side of his face who slapped me com-
mando-style, both ears. The reason I say it is because—they
have a certain way of killing people: when you hit a person
like that, with the hands cupped, if you hit him that way you
can bust his eardrums, with the hands cupped. He had his
hands flat."

"Where was the officer standing when he hit you like that?"

"Right behind my chair."

"How many times did he hit you like that?"

"I can't count."

"What was the officer saying when he was hitting you?"

"He was telling me to give him a confession. And I was asking him for this lawyer—to call my mother. This was refused."

"How many other people were in the room at that time, if
you remember?"

"There was about—about seven or eight detectives, I believe, at the time."

"How long did the officer keep hitting you?"

"He kept hitting me for—I stayed there for about a half an
hour, and I was worked over. Then I started—the withdrawal
—that's when I asked for a fix."

"Before you started to withdraw and asked for your fix, did
anyone else hit you?"

"This officer was the only one that hit me on my face at that
time. The man with a brown suit on, leaning against the
window, with the chair, the detective—the man with the scar
on his face punched me in the stomach. I fell with the chair,
because I was handcuffed to it."

"Then what happened?"

"This detective was leaning there with his foot against the corner of the table, and he just lifted the foot, dropped it on my chest with all his weight, see? Let it drop hard."

"What did Detective Scire tell you?"

"He told me to talk; that this man behind the desk will help me; that he will talk to the district attorney for me if I tell him the truth. And all I was begging for was a fix. I asked him for a fix to relieve the pain."

"What happened after you gave the statement to Scire?"

"I was taken back into the small cage in the big squad room on the same floor, and locked in. I was left there for close to an hour. I was curled up around the floor there, in the small space I had left for myself. I was curled up because I was cold and in withdrawal. I had chills, I had pain; I couldn't stand up."

"Did you at that time feel any pains in your legs?"

"Yes. It hits you behind the knee and your muscles there—your calf—your legs, your toes of your feet hurt. Every joint in your body hurts."

"What happened next?"

"While I was being questioned, this detective with the scar on the side of his face—he was taking boxing lessons with me because everywhere I turned he was slapping. 'Talk,' and, 'Say the right thing. That is not the right answer.' Pow! Slapping me. He slapped me across the face many times; punched my stomach. I got hit so many times, I couldn't tell you how many times.

"Then I was taken back, like I said before—I wasn't put in the cage this time. I was handcuffed to a chair."

"When you asked Detective Scire for a fix, what did he say to you?"

"He said I would get a fix if I gave him a statement."

"Did he tell you where he would get the fix from?"

"He didn't tell me where he was going to get it from. But when they took me out of the room, out to the big squad room, there was a drawer, and it was full of all heroin bags, quarters, eighths, five-dollar bags. And this Puerto Rican or Cuban detective that was there started playing with them. And I was dying for a fix. They put me in a cage."

"While they were playing with the bags, did they indicate to you that you would get one of the bags if you gave a statement?"

"Yes. He said, 'One of these could be yours.' So I was holding out, because the pain was coming in too great—"

"What kind of pain were you getting this time?"

"At first you get—it starts like a dull headache, see? Your eyes start getting watery, and your nose starts running. Then your back—all your back muscles, the small of your back, all of this here [indicating], your leg muscles hurt. And you get the cramps in your stomach, like someone is breaking your guts, or pulling your guts."

Correa had then told of the extent of his heroin habit—four bags of "horse" a day, first at 5:30 in the morning, again at 11:00, then at 4:00, and then for the last time each day shortly before going to sleep. His life centered on taking drugs and getting funds to feed his $40-a-day habit. Correa said he had been in withdrawal several times prior to his arrest and this made him "scared to death of the pain of withdrawal." According to Correa (and witnesses I later called confirmed his testimony), this terrifying fear of withdrawal never leaves the addict.

I continued: "What happened after you were hit in the stomach and fell to the ground?"

"When I was hit in the stomach, I vomited. I vomited on one of the detective's suits. Then from there they took me toward the bathroom."

"What did they do for you in the bathroom?"

"Well, they didn't even let me go into the bathroom. It was like a bed. There's a bathroom attached to two rooms, like. One is a bed. They just took me there, stood me up. There was a sink. And the guy took off his jacket, the guy with the white hair. He said, 'I haven't had a workout in a long time.' I got another workout."

"What did they do?"

"Punched me on the stomach. The worst place you can punch a drug addict is in the stomach when he gets cramps; places where it wouldn't show. They know how to do it."

"Do you know how many times you were punched?"

"I can't count them. All I know is I got worked over."

"How long did this workover take?"

"About fifteen minutes they kept me there. Then they took me back to the big squad room and put me in the cage. There was a small cage there, where you can't even stretch your legs out."

"You were suffering withdrawal at that time?"

"Yes."

"What happened after you were taken to the cage?"

"This Detective Lorenzano came up with this gun, and he says—he says, 'You put your initials on there and I'll give you a fix.' I says, 'I'm not putting my initials on anything until I get a fix. You guys have done enough to me already.' So I was practically kneeling on the floor, not because I was begging but because I couldn't stand up."


During Correa's testimony I tried to show that when the gun killing Graniella went off, Correa's need for drugs was such that he was not capable of "deliberation" or "premeditation." The legal distinction between first- and second-degree murder, the difference between death and perhaps five years' imprisonment, is "deliberation" and "premeditation."

Most states specify that the killing of a human being, unless excusable or justifiable, is murder in the first degree when committed with a deliberate and premeditated design to effect death, or by any act "eminently dangerous to others and evincing a reckless abandon of duty regarding human life, or without a design to effect death but by a person engaged in the commission of certain named felonies: robbery, rape, burglary, arson, or larceny." Murder in the second degree is defined as the killing of a person with a design to effect death but without premeditation or deliberation. Correa could have been charged with second-degree murder but was not.

The state's decision to indict and the jury's decision to convict a defendant for murder in the first degree, rather than murder in the second degree, is an arbitrary one. Deliberation means, as one court long ago put it, "that the act of killing is done in cool blood." The jury, to find deliberation, must determine that the killer was sufficiently rational to know what he was doing. The killer need not have been totally devoid of emotion or passion, however. The jury, then, must perform a mystical psychoanalytical feat that is probably beyond the ability of most, if not all, psychiatrists.

"Premeditation" relates to the time between the decision to kill and the actual killing. It may be an instant, a time lapse of one one-hundredth of a second, or it may be months or years. Was it totally spontaneous—had some modicum of thought passed through the killer's mind? Here, as in every case I was involved in, I tried to show that the murder trial was nothing more than "an island of technicality in a sea of discretion."

Correa, as he was "confessing," knew nothing about these distinctions, although his questioner, the district attorney, aiming for the murder-one conviction, knew exactly where his questioning was leading.

Correa went on answering my questions.

"What happened after you left your detention pen?"

"Well, from there I was taken back into the small squad room, and I was again interrogated. And this time I was so far gone, in need of a fix, that I was ready to sell out the President of the United States to Russia for a fix."

"Tell me your condition at that time."

"Well, they had to drag me in."

"Were you able to walk from the detention pen to the squad room?"

"No, I was not able to walk. I was able to crawl."

"Did somebody pull you along?"

"Yes, Detective Scire, the one that testified here, and another detective which I didn't see before."

"What happened when you were taken to the squad room?"

"Well, there I was—Detective Scire took a statement from me. While I was still sick, he took a statement from me, wrote it down on yellow paper."

"What happened then?"

"Then he took the statement away, and I was kept there. He came back and he told something to the commanding officer there, and the commanding officer says, 'Look, bastard, don't lie to me. I know you're lying.' And I was worked over again."

"What happened after you were questioned by Scire about the homicide?"

"After I was—I gave him that statement, and I received no fix that he promised me. I did not receive it."

Correa did not know that the police weren't yet satisfied. The practice is first for the officer in the station house to get the essentials of the confession. Then the officer calls the district attorney to take a more formal confession in the presence of a police stenographer.

"What happened then?"

"Then I was handcuffed outside to a small chair, like a cowboy's chair, and I was left there right next to the drawer with the—I couldn't reach it—with the heroin, the bags of heroin."

"About how far were you from the drawer with the bags of heroin?"

"About half a foot. But I couldn't reach it, because I was handcuffed to the chair."

"Was the drawer with the heroin open or closed, while you were sitting there?"

"It was open. It was the last drawer on the bottom of the desk, and it was open."

"Did you have an opportunity to see the color of the narcotics?"

"You can't see inside the envelope, or color, but you can see the tape, which was yellow, so from there I determined it was very old—"

"Which indicates that it was good heroin. Is that right?"

"Yes."

Before calling Correa to the stand, I had taken the testimony of Dr. Carl McGahee and offered it to the court. Years before, McGahee, then staff psychiatrist at Sing Sing, had seen Correa in the death house. On the basis of his knowledge of Correa's drug habit, McGahee said Correa would have been at the peak of withdrawal between 8:00 P.M. and 12:00 midnight if he had not had any drugs since the time of his arrest. McGahee testified that an addict sitting in front of a bag of heroin would do and say almost anything to get the drug.

Correa admitted he had signed the confession.

"How long did you sit by the drawer with the bags of heroin?"

"They kept me there for about a half an hour or a little over a half an hour. From there they took me—they untied my handcuffs and took me to the 24th Precinct."

"What time was this?"

"This was right after the district attorney—whatever his name is—Damico—came in, around—he came in around—I seen him around about eleven o'clock, about there, in the precinct. He came in to identify himself when I was in the small squad room."

As Correa answered my questions, the district attorney walked into the courtroom and sat beside the four policemen who Correa claimed had beaten him. Correa saw him, shook slightly, expelled air through rounded lips, and then went on, knowing they would say nearly everything he said was a lie.

I continued: "When you saw District Attorney Damico, did you tell him you were in withdrawal?"

"Yes. I told him that I was a drug addict and I needed a fix."

"What did he say to you?"

"He said, 'Give me what I want and I give you what you want.'"

"What were your symptoms at that time?"

"At that time I was crying; I was in horrible shape: as if they ran me through a grindstone."

After Correa and Dr. McGahee testified, each of the policemen and the district attorney swore that virtually every aspect of Correa's testimony was false. They had seen Correa crying, but it was not from pain—it was from remorse for his crime; he wanted to confess to clear his conscience. And so forth and so on.

A judge, given this conflict in testimony, will almost always believe four or five police officers and a district attorney. In nearly every case involving a confession, it is only when a person not in law enforcement is present at or before the taking of the confession (and this rarely happens) that the confession is truly open to serious challenge.

In Correa's case, as in so many others, the assistant district attorney who took the confession had a commitment to defend the confession. The district attorney often does not know what transpires before he is called to take a confession. He cannot tell if the defendant has been beaten or threatened before he comes into the room. The defendant is primed to talk to the district attorney; all the district attorney knows is that he saw nothing to indicate that the defendant did not confess readily.

An assistant district attorney in Frank Hogan's New York County office explained the procedure in 1964. The office had just admitted the falsity of George Whitmore's "voluntary" sixty-one-page confession of the rape-murder of Janice Wylie and Emily Hoffert. "You have to understand the way the system works," the assistant district attorney said. "As far as I know, it works the same way in every borough in New York City. There's an assistant district attorney on duty twenty-four hours a day in the Homicide Bureau. When a murder suspect is picked up by the police, the assistant is notified. But he isn't asked to come into the station house until the police are 'ready' for him. Translated, this means he doesn't enter the picture until the accused has given a statement to the detectives—or worse, as in Whitmore's case, until the detectives have given a statement to *him*."

Hogan had used the Whitmore case as an example of the need for fewer constitutional restrictions on the taking of confessions. Shortly before his office admitted that Whitmore's confession was false, Hogan told a reporter, "Let me give you the perfect example of the importance of confessions in law enforcement. This, more than anything else, will prove how unrealistic and naïve the court is." His fingers pierced the air. "Whitmore! The Whitmore case. Do you know that we had every top detective in town working on the Wylie-Hoffert murders and they couldn't find a clue? Not a clue! I tell you, if that kid hadn't confessed, we never would have caught the killer!" After it was conceded that the confession was false, Hogan's attacks on Supreme Court decisions became more restrained.

Something of such seeming insignificance as the date a trial begins can mean the difference between life and death. Correa's confession if taken today would be inadmissible, because the police had not advised him of his right to be silent, his right to have a lawyer, and his privilege against self-incrimination. But the Supreme Court's decision changing the law came down five years after Correa's trial and was not applicable retroactively. The officers in Correa's trial all admitted that they had failed to give him the constitutional warnings. The chief of the 92nd Precinct said, under oath, that it was not the practice of the police in his precinct in 1961 to give the constitutional warnings. Under the law today, a case like Correa's would probably have never been brought to trial.

There is no way to eliminate false confessions entirely. The court decision requiring police to advise suspects of their rights will help if the police observe the rules. The intrusion of a "third eye" (tape recordings, sound films, or an impartial observer) in the station house will help even more. It would be better still if the police were required to take suspects immediately before a magistrate when a confession is in the offing. Removing the interrogation from the back room will result in fewer beatings and less friction between the police and the community, and in greater respect for the law. Even if this is not done in every case, certainly it should be done in every case that may involve a heavy sentence.

A month after we presented the last of our proof, the judge gave his opinion—he did not believe Correa's story. He found the confession admissible. After we lost the hearing on the confession, we began preparing a clemency appeal to Governor Rockefeller. Correa's life now depended on the whims and prejudices of one man. It was Correa's last chance.

Graniella's widow had known Correa before the killing. There was a possibility of saving Correa's life, I felt, if she asked Rockefeller to stop the execution. Two weeks before the execution day, I went to 874 Amsterdam Avenue in Manhattan, where Graniella had lived. There I learned that the family had left the neighborhood after the killing and had sold the store.

I spoke to former neighbors of Graniella, but no one knew where Mrs. Graniella and the two children were. Mrs. Graniella had told her neighbors only that she wanted to get away from the place where her husband had been killed. She had said that she was selling the Amsterdam Avenue store and buying another store in the Chelsea area of Manhattan. I walked the streets of Chelsea, stopping in dozens of stores, and finally found hers at 26th Street and Eighth Avenue.

A dark-haired, strong, sorrowful-looking woman stood behind the counter as I walked in. I waited until she was through with her customers and then introduced myself. "I'm Martin Garbus; I'm a lawyer."

She was immediately frightened, as if the only news I could possibly bring her would be bad.

"I'm representing Manfredo Correa. I'd like to talk to you for a moment," I said.

She blanched, and an expression of sadness and fury came over her face. "What do you want from me?"

"He's going to be executed and you may be able to stop it."

"He killed my husband—left two children without a father —ruined my life and the boys' lives."

"Please—"

"Leave me alone!"

"Can I just talk to you sometime? Perhaps in your apartment?"

"No. I want to forget it—it's over—four years ago."

"A boy's life is at stake."

It took a long while to convince her. "I'll be home tomorrow—resting for a few hours. Come over then. But I won't do anything. This is Cruz. He still works for me; he lets me go to lunch and I see my boys then." Cruz Zamet, who was in the grocery store when Graniella was killed and who identified Correa at the trial, shook my hand.

I met Mrs. Graniella the next day shortly after one o'clock. She lived around the corner from the store, on the first floor of a four-story gray building so like all the others in the Chelsea area. Mrs. Graniella had opened the store that morning at seven, carried in the heavy wooden milk cases, set up the outside sales displays for the fresh fruit, waited on the customers, and then had taken a two-hour break to eat and get some rest. She would go back at two and would close the store at one in the morning. This was her routine six days a week.

She started to cry as soon as I walked in. "Please, please leave me alone. I had a wonderful life, and now this," she said, opening her hand and showing me the small, dingy apartment.

She went on crying as she fed her four-year-old child. "Why bother me? Hasn't he done enough?"

"He's twenty-seven years old. He's set to die in the electric chair in a few weeks. You know the boy; he's not a killer. You saw him grow up."

"He's not a killer, but he murdered my husband. Why shouldn't he die? What can I do? Why should I try to save his life? He's got a mother."

"Because a plea from you asking that he not be killed would mean more than a letter from his mother. It could make the difference. Just a letter from you. I'll write it."

"I can't do it. How can I tell my children I saved their father's murderer?" she said.

The longer we spoke, the more torn I felt. She was remembering things she had long since forgotten and thinking of the life she could have had. "You just don't know, Mr. Garbus. My life, since Anthony died, has been terrible. Before that, we had a wonderful life."

I wanted to go, I wanted to leave her alone. I didn't know if Correa's life would be saved by an emotional plea to the governor and by fine-spun legal arguments later in court. When she quieted down, she tried to change the conversation to the store she ran, the store that was ruining her feet and taking her from her children, to whom she should be devoting her time.

It was time for her to go. I told her I wanted to see her again and talk to her a bit more.

"It's no good, leave me alone," she said. But she agreed to see me the following week.

At our next meeting she asked, "What would Tony's

brother say? They still want to kill Manfredo. They went to the police station to get at him."

It became apparent as we spoke that she was less resolute than before. Graniella, many years older than she and very close to his brothers, had married her late in life and had drawn away from his family after his marriage. A strong-willed woman, she had not gotten along with them and now they refused to help her and her children. They felt she was a demanding woman, that the only reason Graniella was in the store late at night when Correa came in was to make more money for her. They blamed her for her husband's death.

She had been thinking about Manfredo. "I know he's not a bad boy. I don't want to see him die. They would kill me if they knew I tried to save the boy's life. He killed Anthony and then I save his life."

"They needn't know about it."

"They'll find out."

"They won't."

"I don't want anyone but you to see the letter. Promise me."

"I can't promise that. I want to give a copy to the governor, and if I do that, I will also have to give a copy to the district attorney."

"No. I won't do it."

I left without the letter, came back the following day, and again left empty-handed.

I hated to go on pressuring her, trying to break down her resistance. In all probability the letter would not change anything; Correa's life probably would not be spared. But there was a chance. I could not say that the wrong man had been convicted or that it had been an accident; the evidence at the trial had been fairly clear. I could not say that Correa had lived a virtuous life; she knew better. But I felt that capital punishment ought to be abolished, and I felt that Correa should not be killed, and so I kept at Mrs. Graniella.

I realized how hard all this was for her: having to relive

the whole thing, and having to raise her children alone and earning a precarious living at best. My own parents had owned a similar store in the Bronx—I worked in it from the time I was in grade school until I graduated from college. Mrs. Graniella might have been my mother, and in a way I might have been Manfredo Correa.

Finally she broke down. She cried and she gave me the letter.

> Dear Governor Rockefeller:
>
> I am the wife of Anthony Graniella, the man killed by Manfredo Correa. I write this to ask you to spare his life.
>
> I have known Manfredo for many years. I saw him grow up. His father left home when he was three. He's not a bad boy and not a killer. He and the other boys in the neighborhood started taking dope when they were nine and ten. They were dead then. Instead of being home, they were out in the street all night.
>
> It's hard for me to say it, but Manfredo's mother did not care for him at all. She ran around with men all the time. Many of these men beat her and the boy knew about it. Sometimes the boy was locked out of the house because the mother had men. He never had a family.
>
> I don't want revenge. It will not bring my husband back.
>
> Mrs. Mary Graniella

Governor Rockefeller's reaction to the letter and the other background information presented on Correa's behalf at the clemency hearing was a curt, cold, angrily snapped sentence: "A lot of Puerto Rican kids have broken homes, have lives like this, and don't become killers." The man who had publicly said all the right things about race and poverty did not grant clemency.

However, as a result of the work done in other capital-punishment cases, work that ultimately led to the virtual abolition of capital punishment in New York, Correa's life was spared.

Correa's conviction, like nearly every murder conviction, is based on the defendant's confession. In New York, twelve of the last fourteen men executed for murder were convicted on the basis of their confessions. Nationwide, 70 percent of the country's executions over the last ten years were based on confessions.

People confess to crimes for many reasons. On April 14, 1968, Charles Horvath reported to the police in Queens, New York, that his wife, Margit, was missing. Two months later Horvath "confessed" that he had beaten his wife to death with a rock and tied a sack of stones around her body before tossing it into the East River. Horvath was immediately charged with murder. On August 8, 1969, a diligent reporter found Mrs. Horvath living in Toronto. Horvath, despondent because his wife had left him, had decided to kill himself but didn't have the courage, so he was going to have the state do it for him.

Ignorance, fear—even honesty—can produce false confessions. In 1953 three men confessed and pleaded guilty to a Philadelphia murder. The men had been in jail sixteen years when a judge ordered them released because in fact no murder had occurred. It seemed that in 1953 no one had asked the medical examiner what the cause of death had been.

At a 1968 hearing the examiner testified that the victim had "died as a result of a coronary heart disease which was not caused, contributed to or aggravated by the assault." All the defendants knew was that they had been in a fight with the victim and that he died immediately after.

This is not an uncommon situation. The police, under pressure to solve crimes, may unwittingly set up a chain of cir-

cumstances that lead to conviction. I saw it when I tried a
murder case in the Supreme Court in the Bronx involving three
boys—one eighteen and two nineteen—who had confessed to
killing Howard Simpson, forty-eight, an alcoholic. Rather than
have the defendants trade a guilty plea for a lesser sentence
(maybe twenty years), we decided to fight the charge.

The facts were as follows. One Saturday evening in 1966,
after leaving a party in the East Bronx, six boys saw Simpson
about a hundred feet away, drunkenly lurching toward them.
The six had had a few drinks themselves and started to taunt
Simpson. They yelled at him, surrounded him, jeered at him.
Then another nine boys joined them. Simpson got frightened
and tried to run out of the circle of boys. He was pushed back.
The pushing got rough, and Simpson fell. The boys went off.

Early Sunday morning, passersby saw Simpson on the street
and assumed he was "sleeping it off." Finally, about nine hours
after Simpson had fallen, a policeman who was trying to clear
the streets discovered he was dead.

The police and the coroner assumed at first that Simpson had
died of natural causes. He had a long history of drinking and
brawling. Although his face and body were bruised, the original police report indicated the bruises were probably suffered
in a series of falls preceding his death. An autopsy showed that
the deceased's internal organs had been destroyed by alcohol
and abuse. The ruling was: death by natural causes; and the case
was closed.

The following week the policemen on the beat heard rumors
of a fight and beating involving Simpson. The policeman investigated, and soon most of the fifteen boys had been found and
questioned at length. On the basis of what the boys were told,
they believed that they had killed Simpson.

A second autopsy was then performed. This time the coroner said death had been caused by the assault. Three boys were
arrested and two weeks later they were indicted for murder in
the first degree. We went to trial. Because of the uncertainty

surrounding the manner of death, the jury "compromised"—the boys were found guilty of manslaughter and sentenced to three years.

Did the defendants kill Simpson? No one knows. Was Correa beaten the way he says he was? Again, no one knows. Any system of criminal law has inadequacies in its truth-determining procedure, but men should not have to face execution because of these defects.

Every murder defendant in this country comes before a stacked jury—one set up to return a verdict of death. Although almost every person sentenced to death is non-white, poor, barely literate, and young, almost all jurors are white, middle-class, and middle-aged. Until recently, jurors who were opposed to capital punishment were removed from juries—even after polls showed that nearly one half of the people of this country were against the death penalty. The constitutional right to trial by one's peers has never been adequately exercised in murder cases.

Statistics cannot indicate the importance of a racially representative jury. Take the case of the three youths tried for the killing of Howard Simpson in the East Bronx. The defendants were Puerto Rican. The case was heard in the summer of 1966, a summer of racial conflict throughout the country, and in a white immigrant area that was fast becoming almost exclusively Puerto Rican. The racial change was so great that what had seemed impossible five years before had become a reality: Herman Badillo, a Puerto Rican, was borough president. The voting lists reflected the fact that Puerto Ricans were predominant, but the jurors lists were frozen at the 1946 figures and our jury did not have one Puerto Rican. Rather, the jury was almost completely middle-class white—representative of the people who were then leaving the Bronx in great numbers as a result of the Puerto Rican influx. These were whites who had invested their savings in small private businesses and homes in the area and who were frustrated and angry—not exactly the kind of people from whom three Puerto Rican boys could expect the fairest of trials.

The states, until 1968, were not satisfied with excluding from jury lists a substantial percentage of the defendants' "peers." In one lawsuit after another, I confronted—and attacked—the inherently discriminatory practice of excluding every potential juror who had "conscientious scruples against the imposition of the death penalty."

People who are opposed to the death penalty are apt to be much more careful about determining guilt and sentencing—they are less quick to discount the defendant's testimony and believe everything a policeman says. By removing them from the jury, by not allowing them even to pass on the question of guilt or innocence, the states have been presenting capital defendants with juries predisposed to finding them guilty.

I saw this in Correa's case. Helen Chinlund, called to sit as a potential juror, was questioned by the prosecutor. A small, neat, gray-haired lady, Mrs. Chinlund had served many years in the Protestant welfare agencies. Her son, she stated, was a minister and her husband a vice president of Macy's. She was the kind of juror who would probably be sympathetic to Correa's version of the killing and of the confession. The prosecutor was tempted to exercise peremptory challenge against her, but a few more questions showed that he needn't. She admitted she had "conscientious scruples" about the imposition of the death penalty, and the judge excused her "for cause."

Mrs. Chinlund's views were not uncommon. At the beginning of the sixties, the Gallup Poll indicated that one third of the population was opposed to the death penalty. On October 19, 1961, a New Jersey prosecutor urged the court to accept something less than a plea of guilty to a charge of first-degree murder, because "two days of interrogation of thirty-seven prospective jurors failed to seat even one." The prosecutor attributed this to "a general reluctance on the part of all talesmen [jurors] to ask for the death penalty."

Still another obstacle to a fair capital-punishment trial is the often prejudicial conduct of the trial judge. With rare exceptions, trial judges throughout the nation have joined district attorneys and the police in leading the anti-abolition forces. Such judges see their role as that of law enforcers rather than dispensers of justice. And in a capital case the judge can make the difference between life and death. By his "judging," a judge can see to it that the most impartial jury will return a verdict entailing death.

One notable judge earned his legal reputation defending hired killers. As a defending lawyer he displayed great and righteous anger when he felt that prosecutors were persecuting his clients. Later, as judge, he showed himself capable of displaying the same passion on behalf of the state and its "needs."

After both sides had presented their evidence, he would, in his charge, squash any chance the defendant might have of acquittal. It is in the charge that the judge sums up for the jury the essential facts and the applicable points of law. The jury believes that the judge, at least, is objective. The charge is the last thing the jury hears before retiring to the juryroom. They often accept as true the picture of the case drawn by the judge. A judge can slant the case, then, by way of the facts he includes in his charge. That kind of bias shows on the case record.

However, this judge operated differently. After years of deliberately trying to make mistrials out of his clients' cases, he knew, as a judge, how to keep errors out of a trial and still let the jury know his bias. He assembled all the facts fairly, and the trial record made it appear that he had done all he could to protect the defendant's rights. However, he made his preference clear to the jury by using all the histrionic devices he had cultivated as a trial lawyer—the raising and lowering of his voice; large, expressive hand movements; exaggerated facial gestures. And none of it showed on the record. "Now the defendant claims he was beaten"—a look of disbelief and contempt for anyone who could claim he was beaten. "And the facts are as follows"—he would race through the facts in a low voice, letting the jury know that the defendant's facts weren't worth considering in their deliberation. But he would dwell on the facts introduced by the state. And another defendant would be convicted.

The factors that result in a man's facing execution are arbitrary and irrational, I have come to believe, and the worst defects of our criminal system are magnified and distorted when the stakes are life and death. A large number of men and women face death, as did Correa, for killing in the course of a felony. A felony murder is regarded as murder in the first degree, even if the judge and jury are convinced that there was no intent to kill. Yet the argument in favor of the death penalty is that capital punishment is a deterrent to those who intend to kill. Why then apply it to a man who did not intend to kill?

In most states a felony may involve an unsuccessful attempted robbery of over $100, or merely breaking in at night, even if nothing is taken. A felony charge may be applied to an accomplice who has no idea that a gun was carried. Under New York law, such an accomplice is accorded the same treatment as the man who kills while attempting to steal $10 million in an organized bank robbery. The state's punishment, based primarily on a deterrence theory that entails execution of a man who never intended to kill, is intolerable.

After I had represented several defendants charged with murder, I became counsel to the Committee to Abolish Capital Punishment. We tried to stop every execution we could. In the next eight years I became accustomed to being notified by the state of the dates on which executions were scheduled, and by 1970 I had received fifty such notifications. Still, the sight of those envelopes chilled me. Sometimes, because of an oversight, a notification would not arrive. I soon learned not to rely on the official notices and began to follow every murder case in New York, so that I would know when a man was to die by the hand of the law. Generally I received the official notice four weeks before the execution. The letters did not give the date or time of execution—only the week; executions always took place on Thursdays at 5:00 P.M.

My first step was to contact the warden or the condemned man, or his former lawyers, to find out if the defendant had a lawyer. Few did. The men stood alone, facing death without friends, family, or funds. The state assigns and pays a lawyer to represent the accused at the trial and on the first appeal, but no further. Often I would find the defendants in a psychiatric hospital. Some would talk to me; others wouldn't. Reduced to a state of torpor by years in the shadow of the electric chair, they would not allow their hopes to be roused again. They had already died "inside" and could not fight any more. Getting the defendants to allow us to represent them was often our greatest problem. The last two men executed in New York State might have been saved, but they refused our help.

Once we represented the defendant, we did everything possible to stop an execution. When clemency was not granted by the date of the execution, we went into the Federal Court for a stay. We would wait until the last day even if we might have gone earlier—a judge will always stop an imminent execution to allow time for a hearing, when faced with an application raising substantial legal and factual questions. The execution could be reset only if the district attorney made a formal motion to the New York Court of Appeals on adequate notice. Then the Court of Appeals would set a new date, at least four weeks later. If we applied for a stay too early, the hearing could be held and decided immediately. An expedited appeal might be heard the following day, and the condemned man would die on schedule.

Our campaign to stop executions while we tried to change the laws that helped to kill employed several strategies. We planned suits in several states directly attacking the constitutionality of capital punishment. We raised issues unrelated to the death penalty itself (the validity of procedures for determining the admissibility of confessions; the composition of grand juries) which, if we were successful, could affect death-house defendants throughout the country. By temporarily stopping executions, we knew we would be congesting the death houses, thereby building up moral pressure for abolition, under threat that there would be mass carnage once the stays came to an end. Moreover, it would be difficult politically for any state administration to have large numbers of executions when for years there had been none.

The committee did not have funds (our annual budget was never more than $500) or a paid staff. We couldn't, at first, enlist the help of socially involved organizations or, with few exceptions, men elected to public office. From 1960 to 1965, before we were joined by other organizations, we fought virtually a lone battle. Yet the work done in those five years saved scores of lives and played a large part in the eventual abolition of capital punishment in New York and other states. And it helped prepare the way with the public and in the courts, not only because the work of the committee convinced many people that a society which sanctions the killing of criminals loses its own dignity thereby, but because the suits we filed helped lay the groundwork for future litigation.

On December 19, 1962, I received a letter from the warden of Sing Sing: "This is to inform you that Frederick Charles Wood is going to be executed January 23, 1963." For the next four months Wood did everything he could to get rid of the volunteer lawyers (myself included) who were trying to save his life.

I had been following his case for years before I got the letter, and I knew that his conviction could be challenged on one important aspect of the execution procedure. The law clearly states that an insane man cannot be executed. (Yet in fact most if not all of the men put to death are something less than sane before their sentence is carried out.) It is somehow not quite decent, the law tells us, to execute a man who is not sane. And once the state finds that a death-house resident is insane, thousands of dollars are spent to give him excellent psychiatric aid and the services of the best mental hospitals, so that he will be sufficiently cured to be killed.

Although all states in 1962 had insanity proceedings, they were nearly all antiquated or ignored. A successful challenge to these procedures in the Wood case would be one more step in the fight for life—gaining us time during which new court decisions might be made that would affect old cases; time during which new evidence might be uncovered in a case or the death penalty be abolished in that state.

Wood's record in murder was bizarre. In 1925, when he was fifteen, he injected arsenic into cream puffs he sent to a sixteen-year-old girl who had rejected him. She died immediately. Six years later, when he was twenty-one, he plunged a knife 140 times into a woman he had picked at random. The reasons: a few days before, a doctor had confirmed that he had contracted syphilis and gonorrhea from a prostitute. Wood had taken his anger out on a woman he had never seen before. In 1942, when he was thirty-two, Wood committed a third murder. This time it was a friend, John Loman, who had made a disparaging remark about one of Wood's girlfriends. Wood bashed his head in, then hid the body and cut it into small pieces to try to get rid of it. Eighteen years later, while on a drunken binge, Wood killed John Recigno and Frederick Sess, sixty-two and seventy-seven, and cut up their bodies with broken glass. It was these last offenses that brought him to trial for the last time.

Originally, Wood had not been found competent enough even to stand trial. The state produced two psychiatrists who stated that Wood was legally sane although mentally ill at the time of the killings. Wood's trial lawyers based his defense on a plea of insanity. Four defense psychiatrists, including a court-appointed, "impartial" psychiatrist, adjudged Wood insane. They all testified that Wood at times thought he was Christ and spoke directly to God. He had been in mental institutions for all but a few weeks between the ages of twenty and fifty.

Wood, sensing that the finding might be not guilty by reason of insanity, insisted on testifying. Against the advice of his attorneys and the judge, he told the jury, with a sneer and a giggle, "At the time I committed the crime, the two murders, I knew the nature and quality of my act. I was sane then, perfectly sane, and I am perfectly sane now." The state did not cross-examine him.

On September 27, 1961, Wood stood before Judge Albert Bosch in the Supreme Court of Queens County after the jury came back with the verdict Wood wanted: guilty of murder in the first degree, with a mandatory death sentence. The court clerk asked for information which by law he was required to place in the file before the judge passed sentence. Wood proudly told the judge that his IQ was 146. The transcript is chilling:

COURT CLERK: What is your trade or occupation?

WOOD: I am a wine sampler.

COURT CLERK: Use intoxicating beverages?

WOOD: If I can get them.

COURT CLERK: When you do, do you drink to excess?

WOOD: Just moderately.

The court clerk then got down to the business at hand.

COURT CLERK: Frederick Charles Wood, do you have any legal cause why the judgment of this court should not be pronounced upon you?

WOOD: Well, I got schizophrenia and I was wondering if the judge could prescribe some shock treatment for me.

JUDGE BOSCH: I don't think that's very funny, Mr. Wood. It's bad enough when a judge has to do what I have to do this morning.

WOOD: I feel sorry for you.

JUDGE BOSCH: I know you do . . . The judgment of this court is that you, Frederick Charles Wood, be turned over to the Commissioner of Correction of the City of New York and by said commissioner delivered to the Warden of Sing Sing State Prison at Ossining, New York, and by him put to death in a manner provided by law, on some day in the week beginning January 29, 1962, at the Sing Sing State Prison. May the Lord have mercy on your soul.

WOOD: That's real sweet of you, Judge. Thank you.

The state assigned lawyers for the purpose of an appeal. The case was appealed, and on December 6, 1962, the Court of Appeals, in a divided opinion, affirmed the conviction and sentence of death. Four judges voted not to upset the jury's determination that Wood was sane. Two judges, including the chief justice of the Court of Appeals, said, "We vote to reverse," because by the "clear weight of the evidence this defendant is insane."


Killers, like Wood, may commit murder so that the state will kill them. Lacking the courage to take their own lives, they bring the state in as a partner. It is as difficult to prove with any degree of certainty that capital punishment encourages killing as it is to prove that it discourages it. But I believe that in many cases murders can be prevented if the potential killer knows the state will not help him kill himself.

I started our defense after receiving the warden's letter in Christmas week. Wood had had a sanity hearing December 8. This final legal step before he was to be killed was set forth in an obscure section of New York's Code of Criminal Procedure entitled, "Proceedings when a person under sentence of death is declared insane"; it had been part of New York law since at least 1876. It had never been challenged and, as we were to learn, had never properly been applied.

The statute began, "If a defendant in confinement under sentence of death *appears* to be insane, the governor *may* appoint a commission of not more than three disinterested persons to examine him and report to the governor as to his sanity at the time of the execution." The law required the district attorney to be present at the examination and stated that "counsel for defendant *may* take part." The statute continued, "When the defendant is insane, the governor *may* send him to a state hospital for the criminally insane, have him treated and if and when cured, returned to Sing Sing for execution."

Wood's case reminded me of Erwin Walker's case. When Clinton Duffy, the former warden of San Quentin, came to New York in 1964 to help support our legislative battle for abolition, he told me about Walker. Sentenced to die for a 1946 police killing, Walker arrived in San Quentin in 1947 and remained on death row as his case was appealed. His sanity was not questioned at the trial, and he behaved as normally as is possible under the circumstances. But he began to go to pieces in death row, and by April 15, 1949, the date of execution, he was dazed and incoherent. He tried to kill himself two days before the execution by winding the cord from his radio headphones around his neck, cinching it with his fingers.

He succeeded only in putting himself into a state of mild shock. Warden Duffy, visiting him two hours before the execution, saw him sitting in a corner staring into space. "As I watched, he suddenly heaved a great sob and fell on his mattress. He rolled back and forth, whimpering and moaning and clawing the wall. Then, like a frightened animal, he tried to hide under his mattress, first putting his head under, then trying to cover his whole body, while he continued his awful sobbing."

Duffy called in seven psychiatrists while at the same time ordering the execution to proceed. The witnesses had begun to file in and the bags of cyanide had already been hung over the wells beneath the chair in the gas chamber when the psychiatrists told Duffy that Walker was "exhibiting definite signs and symptoms of insanity and we recommend a stay of execution and an insanity hearing." After conferring with Governor Earl Warren, Duffy ordered the execution stopped.

Several months later Walker was found to be insane by the Marin County Superior Court and sent to the state mental hospital at Mendocino. For twelve years he was given the best of medical treatment, and finally, on March 1, 1961, the Marin County Superior Court found him once again sane. The psychiatrists' report indicated his cooperative nature and his desire to be well. As a reward, the court set a new date of execution: April 15, 1961, the twelfth anniversary of the first date on which he had been scheduled to die. Walker, faced once more with the gas chamber, again began to exhibit signs of insanity. As the appointed date drew near, his disintegration became worse. Finally, after a clemency hearing on March 27, Governor Brown determined that Walker's mental break was real and commuted the sentence.

Section 495-a, "Proceedings when a person under sentence of death is declared insane," was and—since it is still in effect—is barbaric. Similar provisions in the law allow the governor to make the sole decision as to whether a man "appears" to be insane or not. And the governor can go ahead with the execution even if the man in death row does "appear" to be insane— the governor is not required to appoint an examining commission unless he wants to. (What in fact does "appear to be insane" mean?) The governor can, if he wishes, rely on the least substantial evidence to come to a conclusion—a phone call to the warden, a conversation with the district attorney. And, under the law, no one can review the governor's or the commission's decision or even demand to know what that decision is.

Of course, if a man was executed, we knew he had passed and had been given 2,000 volts as a graduation present. Although the district attorney was *required* to attend the examination, there was no one present who could be expected to question seriously a determination of sanity. This was not entirely surprising since most of the men executed were indigent and did not have funds for a lawyer.

During the first week of January, I met with two of Wood's former lawyers. I asked whether they had been present at the sanity hearing of December 8; they had not. I asked whether they had been invited to attend the sanity hearing; they had not been invited. "Do you know whether such a hearing took place?" I asked. They did not. "Will you tell the court you knew nothing about it?" They would not. "Wood requested that we not do anything on his behalf," the lawyers said.

In my efforts to find legal cause to save Wood's life, I sought out people who knew Wood and who might ask that his life be spared. Emil F. Winkler, the state's chief expert psychiatric witness, wrote to Governor Rockefeller asking for clemency for Wood.

Legal points we had brought up in other cases might be useful here too—but Wood's lawyers, although they were no longer doing anything on his behalf, refused to withdraw formally from the case. They had been assigned by the Court of Appeals to represent Wood, and the assignment entailed a fee of $2,000 as well as the promise of future assignments. Wood's counsel did not believe any of our legal arguments could win. But they would be open to criticism if they left the case after losing the appeal, and they were reluctant to let us represent him now. They did not want to waste time on what they saw as useless, and they had had enough of Wood; they refused to file any proceedings on his behalf.

Wood's death drew nearer. Howard Jones, the governor's counsel, knew that if Wood's lawyers stayed in the case, Wood would die on January 23 as scheduled. He told the lawyers that they had an obligation to hold on until the end. We told them that they had an obligation to leave the case if they weren't going to make any move on his behalf. Jones criticized them for dealing with us and for even thinking of leaving their client. I was aware that Governor Rockefeller's office, embarrassed by the Wood case, did not want the battle for Wood's life to be as extended as had been some some other cases I had been involved in. The governor was hard put to explain how his parole board had released Wood after a third killing, to kill again.

Wood heard of our efforts to save his life, and he wrote the court and the governor:

> My four lawyers assigned to the case prior to trial want to withdraw and I wish no further legal action. I am all set and prepared to go Thursday night at 10:00 and I don't want any do-gooder to interfere.

He began a barrage of letters asking us not to get into the case.

James Donald French, the only man executed in the United States in 1966, had a history similar to Wood's. He was convicted in Oklahoma of strangling his cellmate while serving a life sentence for a previous murder. When the lawyer in the first murder case had French's first death sentence reduced to life imprisonment, French tried to have him disbarred. He told his psychiatrist after he killed for the second time that he had committed the second murder because he wanted to be put to death. He asked the governor and the Supreme Court not to allow anyone (lawyers were at the top of the list) to delay or prevent his execution.

As Wood's date of execution approached, he continued to resist every effort made on his behalf. He wrote his lawyers:

> It grieves me to have to write but I have been instructed to do so if I really want to ride the lightning. Thursday evening sans further delay because of an unwanted stay of execution . . . I do not welcome

intrusion into this stinking case of mine—I have no
desire to live out the rest of my life in confinement.
You must (or should) understand that capital punishment is, in the final analysis, more merciful than a
tortured existence of a lifetime in prison or in an
asylum. I should know, sir, as I've done 31 years of
suffering in these noble institutions. So, in the language
of the artist, please cease and desist.

We chose to ignore Wood's requests. That decision has
troubled me more than any other I've made concerning a
client. I think we were right.

Our approach was to have the legal system find him insane,
although I do not believe that the question of sanity can be
determined in a courtroom. The best we could do for Wood
was to have him spend the rest of his life in a mental institution
for the criminally insane. Wood, having spent over thirty years
in the best institutions the state has to offer, was driven to desperation by the possibility. But by challenging the state's right to
kill him, we might establish a precedent that would save others.

Wood's antagonism toward us raised a legal as well as a
moral question. Did his letters to us and to the court constitute
the "intelligent" and "understanding" waiver which the Supreme Court requires before the constitutional right to counsel
can be relinquished? The chief judge of the New York Court
of Appeals, Charles Desmond, said that, unless Wood requested
a lawyer, he would not get one. But this begged the question—
whether Wood was mentally capable of making the choice.

One of the lawyers working on the case pleaded with
Wood's mother in Elmira to try to convince her son not to
take his life. She refused. "He knows what he wants. He never
listened to me anyway. Perhaps it's best for him. He's too
smart just to sit in prison."

Wood said again and again in his letters that the decision he
had made proved that he was rational. Each time his sanity was
questioned, he reacted with a passionate outburst. He did not

object to being called a brutal killer, but when it was suggested that he was not sane and might be incapable of making the choice for life, he was outraged. When his letters were not heeded, he wrote to the press, the district attorney's office, the judges of the federal and state courts, and the governor. He argued he had the final decision whether he should live or die and that, given the choices (mental institutions and jail for the rest of his life, or death), he would rather die.

While all this was going on, I learned all I could about Wood and his case. The court file in Queens County contained, in addition to the trial records, hundred of pages of psychiatric reports, some of which had never been admitted in evidence. Included in each psychiatric report was a full description of the psychiatrist's method, diagnosis, and conclusions. The court record showed a history of quarrelling between Wood and every lawyer he had had. The conflict, often violent, was understandable. The various people had different goals: the lawyers were committed to keeping Wood alive; Wood was trying to die. But there was nothing in Wood's file about the Sing Sing examination. Who had examined Wood? Had his full psychiatric record been available? Had Wood himself been examined, or just his records? Wood certainly would never help us get the answers to these questions.

I went to one of the Sing Sing psychiatrists who was part of the prison medical team. He had examined Wood and dozens of others before him. I asked the doctor what he did at a man's last hearing before his death.

"I examine the man and give the warden a report," he said.

"What do you do next?" I asked. "The law requires the state to hold a hearing on the sanity issue. Someone representing the defendant should know the contents of that report. I believe there must be an adversary hearing but the courts have not yet said so. The state is obligated to have an impartial, knowledgeable trier of the facts, then make a decision based on a full record."

"I didn't know that provision of the law," he said. "We send the report on to the Lunacy Commission. No one ever told me the law required any kind of hearing. I didn't know it was part of the execution procedure."

"How do you get the facts to make your determination?"

"We have a probation report and take a history from the patient. Many of the fellows aren't too bright and don't give me any information," he said in his New York-tempered Southern drawl. "We give our report to the Lunacy Commission. I don't know who they are. I've never seen them. They never question me on my report. I don't believe they take it too seriously. As far as I know, it's completely ignored. One fellow I examined in 1960 was clearly insane. I submitted my report. The next thing I knew he was executed. I think the Lunacy Commission feels all these guys are malingering or something. Our reports have no weight or authority."

As we talked and I explained what he had been doing and what the State of New York had not been doing, he blanched. "I never knew any of this," he repeated.

"It's incredible," I said. "This practice has been going on for at least fifty years. Hundreds of people have been killed in the electric chair in New York State. Before you find a person mentally incompetent so that his monies can be looked after by a court or by a relative, you must go through a long, technical incompetency proceeding—with lawyers on both sides, and in New York a judge of the highest trial court must sit on the case. But before we put a guy to death—nothing!"

The entire procedure seemed senseless. Dr. Harvey Bluestone, then the Chief of Psychiatric Services at Sing Sing, agreed: "The procedure is crazy. It's based on the idea that only if the man is sane can he appreciate the experience of electrocution. It's not cruel enough to execute a man who doesn't know exactly what's happening to him. We all treated the procedure as one that had no reason behind it. What was the sense of endlessly shuttling the men back and forth to Mattawan? After a short time in the death house they would be the same as before."

I looked into all the legal cases in which sanity procedures had been challenged before a man was put to death. If the law is ready to accept that a man is entitled to have his friends, relatives, and counsel present when he is tried, it should no less recognize his right to have someone speak for him at a sanity hearing. It is in the very roots of our English common-law heritage not to execute an insane man any more than we would convict him without a hearing. Yet statutes similar to New York's have been on the law books for hundreds of years, and thousands of men have been executed. And the United States Supreme Court has never spoken clearly on the issue raised by Wood's case.

We worked long into the night of January 18, five days before the date of execution, preparing papers seeking a stay of execution so that we could present our claim to the high court. On January 20 we filed a petition for habeas corpus on Wood's behalf before Judge Dudley B. Bonsal of the federal court sitting in Manhattan. Our petition stated: "The State is bound by the Constitution to assign counsel to an indigent defendant such as Wood, in the post-appellate period of a capital case." It was not difficult to show that denial of this might operate to Wood's prejudice. We said: "Wood's present lack of counsel, in what may be the last few days of his life, operates to his actual prejudice. It is most likely that assigned counsel would seek to initiate proceedings to determine whether Wood's execution is prohibited by law because of insanity."

The state opposed the application. It claimed that since Wood was sane enough to be found guilty of a crime he was sane enough to be executed. We countered that the issue of sanity at the commission of a crime was unrelated to the issue of sanity before execution, that the standards, as well as the dates, were different. Our petition was argued before a federal judge in Manhattan on January 22, 1963, the day before execution.

The judge denied the application but granted a stay to allow for an appeal from his order. Wood's desire that he not be represented, the judge said, constituted a waiver of his rights.

The day after the decision, the *Los Angeles Times* said, "The case of Frederick Wood as it progresses becomes a case against the entire concept of capital punishment. It may accomplish what Chessman could not—the abolition of the death penalty."

The stay was granted to February 4, 1963, primarily because of the Coleman case, a suit pending in a higher court raising the same point—the right-to-counsel issue. We breathed a sigh of relief at Judge Bonsal's order because we did not expect the Coleman case to be decided until midyear. That could put off Wood's execution for at least a year.

We were wrong. The day after Judge Bonsal granted the stay in Wood's case, the Coleman case was decided against the condemned man. Wood's execution was immediately rescheduled for March 21. Any chance of winning an appeal from the judge's decision in *Wood* was ended by the opinion handed down in the Coleman case. To keep Wood alive, we would have to start a new legal proceeding challenging on wholly new grounds the procedure for determining insanity.

What grounds? We weren't sure until mid-February. Until then we believed that the inadequate procedure required by the law had been followed. But we were wrong again. A telegram sent to Benjamin Jacobsen, the district attorney, from Sol Neil Corbin, the new counsel to the governor, indicated that the district attorney, required by law to be at the hearing, had not been present. Jacobsen never even knew of the hearing. Although the district attorney would be adverse to the defendant, he might still be expected, as a lawyer, to insist on a constitutionally acceptable method of conducting the inquiry. I later learned that district attorneys were rarely if ever present at such examinations.

On March 15, a second petition for habeas corpus was filed

in the United States District Court in Manhattan, arguing that the examination by the three psychiatrists on December 8, 1962, had failed to meet the "requirements of the Fourteenth Amendment to the Constitution." The petition questioned the validity of the proceeding "which permits the sanity of a condemned man to be determined without a voice raised on his behalf."

Wood's next letter went to the federal district judge now sitting on the case, Harold C. Tyler. "I have had three stays of execution thus far effected by well-intentioned lawyers as do-gooders. I want no more." On March 19, 1963, the judge denied the petition but granted leave for an immediate appeal because there were "significant and serious" questions. A California newspaper reported: "Wood won a partial victory in his battle for quick extinction."

The following afternoon a law professor from New York University argued for a stay of execution. He lost, in a 2 to 1 decision. The dissenting judge said, "There are too many important federal questions to justify their foreclosure by execution of the accused." A stay of execution was sought from Supreme Court Justice John M. Harlan, the justice responsible for passing on stay applications from the New York area. When he refused, our last chance was gone.

The spectacle of lawyers trying to save a man's life while he sought to "ride the lightning" made front-page news, and the publicity helped the fight against the death penalty. If a man like Wood could kill three people, face the death penalty, be jailed, be put in mental institutions, then be declared sane and freed to kill twice more, something was very wrong with the way we disposed of people like him.

Throughout January, February, and March, while litigation to stop Wood's execution was being fought through the courts, the New York senate and assembly and the legislators of a dozen other states again began to consider the abolition of the death penalty. I traveled around the country—California, Illinois, Michigan—debating and discussing the issue of capital punishment. Legislators who favored abolition brought up Wood again and again as an example of the kind of man we were executing and the inefficiency of the death penalty as a deterrent. Members of the Committee debated district attorneys, Congressmen, and policemen on radio, television, and in the press. This was more than just the yearly legislative debate on abolition. In 1963 Wood's case was in the public eye almost every day for as long as the several state assemblies and senates debated the issue.

On March 21, 1963, Wood entered the execution room. Finding a dust spot on the chair, he interrupted the procedure, borrowed a handkerchief, and cleaned off the electric chair. He removed the cigarette dangling from his lips, but not the smile on his face, as the black hood was pulled over his head. As they strapped him into the electric chair, he said to his executioners with a rasping voice in the midst of a riotous laugh, "I got a little speech to make, gents. This is an educational project. Gentlemen, you will finally see the effect of electricity on Wood. Enjoy yourselves."

The 2,000 volts went through his body. His head jerked straight up, his fists clenched. Sing Sing claimed Wood as the 613th electrocution victim since 1894. "He killed five people, slicing pricks, tits and arms; a man like that deserves to die," said a state trooper, one of the witnesses to the next-to-last execution in the state of New York.

By the time Wood won his dreary battle to die by the hand of the law, his fixed, angry stare was well known to newspaper readers throughout the country. The *Newark Star* said, "Lust Killer Wins: the most celebrated capital punishment case since Caryl Chessman ended when Wood realized his most pressing ambition—to die in the electric chair." There was a national reaction of revulsion toward Wood's headlong rush into death.

The day after the execution, the *Boston Herald,* in its lead editorial, "State Aided Suicide," said:

> The person bent upon killing himself is ordinarily regarded today as mentally ill and deserving of appropriate treatment yet the State of New York in electrocuting Frederick Wood yesterday for the murder of five persons utterly denied the validity of this approach. For Wood was, indeed, a man desperately bent upon self-destruction. "I want no more stays," he said. "I really want to ride the lightning." And New York, hearing this, pushed him into eternity. It was not an act to make any human being proud.

This revulsion set in motion a change that we had all been seeking. The day after Wood was executed, members of the New York State Assembly spoke of the "spectacle of Wood's killing" as they voted 110 to 12 to remove the mandatory death penalty on first-degree murder cases. On April 1, the bill was passed in the New York Senate by a vote of 55 to 2. And it was shortly signed into law.

Wood's case and the spirit of the 1963 New York law played a significant part in the final success of abolition in New York and four other states in 1964 and 1965.

Gallup, Roper, and Harris polls in 1964 showed increasingly large numbers of people opposed to the death penalty. In more and more murder trials, considerable numbers of potential jurors had to be excused for "death scruples." Legislators began to take note of the change in public opinion.

A number of organizations reconsidered their positions, among them the American Civil Liberties Union. In the early sixties I had gone before the New York board of directors to try to persuade them to commit their resources to the fight against capital punishment. They had refused, saying that this was not a civil-liberties issue. The American Civil Liberties

Union is the sole national organization that devotes itself exclusively to interpreting and securing the enforcement of the Bill of Rights. Many people believe that if the ACLU regards a law or practice as unconstitutional, then it is. When in April 1965 the ACLU issued a statement condemning capital punishment, we knew we had gained a valuable ally.

Among legislators, there was a groundswell for abolition. The Committee to Abolish Capital Punishment, to maintain the momentum, began to hold private and public meetings attended by criminologists, penologists, psychiatrists, legislators, lawyers representing death-house inmates (both committee-sponsored cases and "private cases"), and the public. It was the first time that such groups had been brought together, and legal and legislative strategies were planned for a nationwide assault on capital punishment.

When the final chapter of the struggle to end executions in New York opened, only four men had gone to the Sing Sing chair in four years, by far the lowest number of executions in any four-year period since the first man was electrocuted there on a July morning seventy-four years before. Yet the New York death house had twenty-four occupants. Legislators were not unaware of the prospect of mass executions if a new bill was not passed.

The prestigious New York State Temporary Commission on the Revision of the Penal Law, headed by Assemblyman Richard J. Bartlett of Glens Falls, greatly influenced by the Wood and Whitmore cases, heard from all interested lobbies, from our committee, the police, and political leaders, penologists, and psychiatrists, and concluded that there was no reason to uphold the death penalty.

Then the various forces involved took sides, as they do in every "law and order" legislative battle fought today. Police associations rejected the Bartlett commission recommendations and vowed to establish a fund for legislative lobbying against abolition. Although their arguments were devoid of both fact and logic, this opposition created a serious problem, since legislators were convinced that it would be politically risky to vote against them. The District Attorneys' Association joined forces with the police. This was even more serious. The D.A. had the respect of the legislature, the citizenry, and the judges and probation and correction officers who implement the criminal system.

To our surprise, Frank O'Connor, then district attorney of Queens, came out on our side. "The police are in no greater danger in cities where capital punishment has been abolished (Detroit and Providence) than in New York and Chicago. . . . The death penalty, rather than deterring murder, actually deters the proper administration of criminal justice." O'Connor's statement—coming from one of the most respected district attorneys in the country—was of enormous significance.

In the first week of March 1965, the New York State Legislature announced that a public hearing on capital punishment would be held on March 25. On March 11 the Committee to Abolish Capital Punishment called a meeting to adopt a concerted plan of action. Executive secretary Ruth Kitchen set up press headquarters in Albany and organized some two dozen representatives of civic, religious, and political groups—including the NAACP, Americans for Democratic Action, and the National Council of Churches—to testify on behalf of total abolition.

A bill substantially abolishing the death penalty was passed by the New York State Senate by a 47 to 9 vote on May 13. The size of the affirmative vote startled political observers. "Sentiment has changed a good deal in the last month or so," Senate Majority Leader Joseph Zaretzki noted.

The Assembly began debate at 12:19 on the afternoon of May 19. Five and a half hours later the abolition bill cleared by a vote of 78 to 67, only two votes more than the constitutional minimum of 76 needed to pass a measure.

Nelson Rockefeller spoke up for the first time, opposing the bill. He said the bill was inconsistent because of the two exceptions in it (the killing of a police officer and the killing of a guard or fellow inmate by a life prisoner were still punishable by death). Rockefeller said the bill undercut the two fundamental precepts of those who favored it—the moral argument that the state has no right to take a life and the pragmatic argument that capital punishment is not a deterrent to murder. "If the proponents admit that it's a deterrent in some cases, then why not in others?"

Rockefeller's position was outrageous. Those exceptions were in the bill as a concession to the police, and Rockefeller knew it. His invocation of an inconsistency to justify his veto was a shabby evasion. If he considered the bill defective, why didn't he lead a fight to eliminate the exceptions? If he favored capital punishment, why didn't he have the courage to say so? One newspaper, after reviewing the governor's own inconsistencies, said: "A gubernatorial veto would place Mr. Rockefeller among the Neanderthals. We cannot believe that is the way he wishes to be remembered in the State's history books; but clearly the bill presents a historic challenge to him."

On May 20, the day after the legislature voted to abolish capital punishment, Governor Rockefeller spoke at a dinner sponsored by the Nassau County Republican Committee. I went, to gauge his reaction to the bill. But he avoided reporters' questions; he refused to commit himself. He kept the bill on his desk. But at public and private functions, in response both to legislators and to private individuals and civic groups who contacted him on our behalf, he voiced the same objections, maintaining that he had not made up his mind. "I'm still receiving opinions on both sides of the question. The feeling throughout the state is pretty evenly divided."

The committee called on civic leaders throughout the state to make their feelings known to the governor. Still he refused to give his position on the bill. By June 1 he would have to approve or veto it. That morning Rockefeller's press office issued a routine announcement that the governor would act on the bill that day. But when I tried to find out if this meant approval or disapproval, they refused to say. Right up to the last minute, he was calculating the political effect of a veto.

On the afternoon of June 1, 1965, Nelson Rockefeller signed without ceremony or explanation a bill virtually abolishing capital punishment in New York. Capital punishment—in effect in New York since Dutch colonial times, when it was imposed for such crimes as stealing from a garden—and the electric chair, used since 1891 to kill 614 persons, were consigned to the past as New York became the eleventh state substantially to abandon the death penalty. Michigan, Rhode Island, Oregon, Wisconsin, Maine, North Dakota, Minnesota, Alaska, Iowa, and Hawaii had been the first ten.

We were pleased at our victory—but not overjoyed. The men at Sing Sing knew why. A *New York Times* writer reported the scene there: "The New York Mets were playing the Cubs at Chicago and the game was piped in by radio loudspeaker to the long corridor of the death house at Ossining. At five minutes before five o'clock, the sportscast was cut off for a bulletin: Governor Rockefeller had signed the bill abolishing the death penalty in most cases. Then there was silence. The baseball broadcast came back on. There was no demonstration, no cheering, no yelling at each other." The men knew the bill made no provisions for those already condemned to death.

A few days later I called Rockefeller's office and spoke to one of his legal advisers. (Correa was one of the men still in the death house.) "How can the state execute any men after it has voted for abolition?" I asked, and I was told that the governor would consider clemency on a case-by-case basis and only when all court proceedings were over. The inhumanity of this went unheeded. Finally Rockefeller relented, however, and on October 11 he agreed to commute the sentences of all the condemned men who did not fall under the new bill's exceptions.

Years later he commuted the sentences of all the men who were in the death house when the death penalty was abolished.

Today, nine states have done away with the death penalty completely. In five—Rhode Island, New Mexico, North Dakota, New York, and Vermont—executions are carried on in narrowly prescribed situations only. Thirty-six states retain capital-punishment laws, but in many there are no executions. Montana has not had an execution since 1940, New Hampshire since 1939, Massachusetts and South Dakota since 1947, and Delaware since 1949.

Because there have been no executions in the last few years, public pressure to do away with the death penalty in the remaining states has diminished. There have been numerous attempts to restore the penalty where it has been abolished, however, and to broaden it where it has been limited. On February 13, 1967, Representative Frank Comer introduced a bill in the Pennsylvania State Legislature to make rape a capital offense. Seated in the gallery was Gordon Ragen, released from a Pennsylvania prison three days earlier, after serving three years for a rape someone else committed. Comer asked for speedier disposition of cases. He said lawyers were delaying executions with appeal after appeal, rendering the death sentences ineffective. When reminded of cases like Ragen's, Comer said, "Tough!" The following year Mario Procaccino, the law-and-order candidate for mayor of New York City, ran on a platform calling for the return of capital punishment.

The last few years have seen an increase in the filing of lawsuits attacking the death penalty on constitutional grounds. Some of the peripheral legal arguments we first brought to court ten years ago have won, but the larger argument—that the death penalty itself is unconstitutional—has not. And given the present composition of the United States Supreme Court, it will probably not be won in this decade.

# Five

*The People against Timothy Leary*

I FIRST MET TIMOTHY LEARY one day in April 1966. Alan Levine, staff counsel for the New York Civil Liberties Union, had telephoned to ask if I would be able to defend Leary against criminal charges pending in Poughkeepsie. The New York Civil Liberties Union had refused to take his case. I remembered the newspaper description a few days before of the spectacular raid on Leary's house and his arrest in Millbrook, New York, an upstate village.

I told Alan I'd be glad to see Leary that day. Twenty minutes later Leary walked into my office, wearing a once-elegant but now stained gray-herringbone suit and a crumpled white shirt. Looking like a country boy who had been stuffed into ill-fitting Ivy League garments, he still had the bounce of a child. His hair was curly, prematurely gray. His mobile, open face seemed at times bright and intense; at other times, wan and ravaged.

Timothy Leary was practically unknown before 1966. His arrests in Texas and New York for possession of drugs and a Texas conviction for carrying drugs from Mexico into the United States that year thrust him into national prominence. Only a few people knew about his drug experiments at Harvard and his expulsion from that school's faculty, or about his earlier experiments in Mexico.

In the five years since 1966, he has become a cultural phenomenon, a media-appointed representative of all middle-class marijuana smokers, and a "guru" to the young and alienated. A prominent New Yorker who later became active in the fight to change the drug laws said of the first of Leary's arrests, "I'd never thought about it until then. It never touched my life. But when Leary got arrested and they started to go after him, it made me wonder. He's middle-class and I am undeniably so. I really began to understand that marijuana was not just a lower-class ghetto problem."

Law-enforcement officials desperately wanted to suppress Leary and his ideas. Their tactics had the opposite effect, giving the so-called "Pied Piper of Inner Peace" a wider audience than he ever could have gotten without the arrests.

Leary told me about the Millbrook raid. In early 1966 he had invited twenty friends to a lovely 2,500-acre estate to start communal life. These twenty friends had brought forty more. On April 17, 1966, at two in the morning, while he and his many houseguests were asleep—some in the house and some in the fields surrounding the house—the police moved in from every direction. Those outside were rounded up first to make sure they would not run into the house and warn the other guests. Those asleep inside were pulled out of bed and herded into the main rooms on the lower level. "My son and a friend," Leary said, "were in the room, talking to me about a term paper my son was writing. I heard a noise outside in the hallway. My friend opened the door and shouted, 'Wow! There's about fifty cops out there!'" "You're under arrest," said the officer entering Leary's bedroom. "Get out in the hall." Leary immediately proclaimed his constitutional rights. "First let me put my pants on."

The raiding force—twenty-five deputy sheriffs with billy clubs and guns—ransacked closets, suitcases, and chests in the sixty-four-room main house. They cut the telephone wires to prevent outgoing calls, and they held Leary and his guests for three hours while they searched for drugs.

Leary described the raid further in an affidavit we later filed in court. "My guests were interrogated, embarrassed, abused, and asked whether they 'smoked marijuana' or had 'sexual relations' while guests at my home. Each of the women was stripped naked and examined. Several of the women, after they had been stripped by a police matron, were then required, in the presence of police officers, to pull their skirts all the way up while the police matron again inspected their legs for marks indicating heroin use. Women were required to take off their blouses in the presence of the policemen. Some of the witnesses were asked whether they had taken any pictures or whether there had been any tape recordings made of the events of the evening.

"During this entire time the district attorney interviewed witnesses and he and other law-enforcement officials took notes on everything that was said. The assistant district attorney took people into a separate room for questioning. The witnesses were badgered until they gave their names and addresses. They were asked how long they had known me. One of the young women was asked, in my presence, whether she had had intercourse that night. All were asked if they ever saw me take drugs and whom I slept with. They wanted to know how I treated my son Jackie and daughter Susan. Did I give them drugs? My guests were never advised that they need not answer the questions, or of their right to counsel, or of their right to be silent at that time. Our demand to call a lawyer was denied. Several of the young women were reduced to tears.

"They removed cartons of objects from the house and claimed they found marijuana. It was taken from a drawer in one of the guest's rooms. I don't know whether they had it or not. With sixty people in the house, many of whom I barely knew, it's amazing that's all they found. The inventory statement filed by the police after the raid showed that checkbooks, jackets, items from a child's chemistry set, money, the diary my daughter wrote when she was thirteen, prescription drugs, vitamin pills, Chinese jasmine tea, aspirins, tape recorders, exposed film, paintings, medicine droppers, cigarette paper, pocket knives, religious objects, tape spools, books and children's drawings, and other objects were seized."

Leary smiled wryly and said, "The sheriff told the press the raiding party found most of the occupants in the house in a state of seminudity, which sounds wild until you realize that nearly everyone in the house was in bed asleep at the time of the raid." Leary and three of his guests were arrested and were now facing indictment.

At our first meeting in my office, Leary made it clear that he wanted to reform the drug laws as much as he wanted to be acquitted. He wanted to litigate the case on the issue that would be most difficult to win on—the constitutional question whether the use or possession of marijuana, in view of its alleged harmlessness, should be a criminal offense.

I had previously represented many defendants arrested on federal and state drug charges, and I had always tried to litigate the constitutionality of the laws as well as the validity of the harsh sentences handed out to narcotics defendants. But, in nearly every case where I was unable to get the case dismissed because of defective search warrants or unauthorized searches, I had negotiated a lesser plea for my client. The long sentence that might be imposed by a judge discouraged the gamble of a trial.

Leary was all too eager to take the gamble. He was financially and emotionally prepared to go all the way. A "Timothy Leary Defense Fund" was enlisting notables (including Anaïs Nin, Robert Lowell, Steve Allen, Eric Bentley, and Norman Mailer) and dollars for his defense.

At our first meeting he showed me the briefs and arguments that had been prepared for his Texas trial. Leary, with his son and daughter and a friend of his son's, had crossed the bridge at Laredo, Texas, on December 22, 1966, intending to go to Mexico. Realizing his papers were not in order, Leary had driven back over the bridge and had told the young people in the car to be sure they did not have any marijuana because he knew there might be a U. S. Customs' search. The customs' official later testified at the trial in March 1966 that he had decided to stop the car because one of the occupants was "bearded and a hippie." The search revealed that Leary's daughter had some marijuana and that there were a few marijuana seeds under the car rug. The drugs, unquestionably, were not Leary's, and in fact he did not know there were any drugs in the car. Nonetheless, he was found guilty of unlawfully and knowingly transporting illegally imported marijuana with intent to defraud, with knowledge of illegal importation, and of failing to pay a transfer tax on marijuana brought over the border. Leary was sentenced to thirty years. The total amount of marijuana carried in the car was less than half an ounce.

Leary told me of the many amateur legal scholars who had been giving him legal advice on his appeal from the Texas conviction and who would, if I should represent him in New York, graciously give me the benefit of their expertise. They had already advised him to bypass the charge of carrying drugs and get straight to the defense of the use of marijuana on constitutional grounds, assuring him he could not lose. If he did anything less, they said, he would not be confronting "the system" head on.

I told Tim that if I did represent him, I would not bypass anything. I would conduct the same defense for him as if the charge were murder—all the procedural maneuvering, all the motions, and all the affirmative action I could take, including trying to move the case to a Manhattan federal court and attacking, if necessary, the judge who signed the search warrants and the grand jury, who must have relied on hearsay evidence in order to return the indictments. I would not be forced into a

purely defensive position, giving up all our weapons and rely-
ing solely on a defense that probably would not win. You
can confront the system as much by winning as by losing, and I
think you gain more by winning.

Tim asked me how old I was. I told him I was thirty-two.
He laughed. "Marty, even though you're over thirty, I'd like
you to represent me." We shook hands.

I wondered why the New York Civil Liberties Union had
refused to represent Leary. After Tim left, I called Alan Levine, who had first contacted me about Leary, and he told me
what had happened. A few hours before he and I spoke, he had
gone before his board of directors, asking them to authorize
the organization's representation of Leary in the Millbrook arrest. After giving the board the facts of the raid, Alan concluded, "I ask that the Union directly represent him because
the warrant seems to have been improperly issued and because
the raid seems to have been motivated by a desire to harass
Leary."

Helen Buttenwieser, a respected member of the Union board
and one of Alger Hiss's former lawyers, disagreed. "I don't
think we ought to represent Dr. Leary directly. It's a case
where we ought to submit an amicus brief in support of his
warrant claim. Dr. Leary believes, as I understand it, that the
state's attempts to stop his drug use violate his right of privacy.
He also believes his religious freedom is being interfered with.
The Union has not yet taken a position on these matters. If we
set out to represent him and fail to have the warrant rejected,
we must urge his privacy and religious claims. Our only interest is the validity of the warrant, and we need not get involved
in all the issues to raise that question."

Charles Ares, a young, quiet, soft-spoken professor of law at
New York University, supported Alan. "You can't contest the
validity of the warrant without seeing what facts existed prior
to the issuance of the warrant. This means that you can't limit
yourself only to the warrant. Search-and-seizure issues are

questions of fact, and if you want to develop the facts, we must try the case. We ought not to be halfhearted. We should represent him directly." The Union ought to reexamine its policies, Ares went on to say, and decide whether they should, at some later time, support Leary's religious and right-to-privacy claims.

Osmond Fraenkel, seventy-six-year-old General Counsel to the ACLU, was recognized and stood up to speak. Perhaps the most influential member of the board, Fraenkel had battle scars that included the Scottsboro cases and years of fighting in First Amendment cases to stop the persecution of Jehovah's Witnesses. He declared himself against Ares's position: "I join Helen's motion. We should not get involved in these other issues. It's none of our business and I personally don't consider them civil-liberties questions. We ought to go in as amicus on the search-and-seizure issue. The case is before the grand jury and we don't yet know what an indictment will charge. Leary can't vouch for what the other occupants of his house had in their possession."

Levine, Ares, and their supporters argued vehemently in support of their position. The question was debated at length, but the verdict, after Osmond Fraenkel joined Mrs. Buttenwieser, was never in doubt. Helen Buttenwieser's motion expressing the view that the Union ought not to represent Leary directly was passed by the New York Civil Liberties Union board by a vote of 12 to 6.

In the next few days I met some of the people present at the raid. They came to New York and told me what had happened. Dr. Ralph Metzner, an ascetic-looking Oxford- and Harvard-trained psychopharmacologist who had worked with Leary for years, told me: "Albert Rosenblatt, the assistant D.A., was taking people one at a time into a separate room for questioning. He asked me to go with him and the sheriff, which I did. He said he knew that I was primarily interested in the scientific aspects of this thing, but narcotics had been found and criminal activities were involved. He would, therefore, like to have some information about the use of marijuana here—whether it had been administered and to whom. He also said I did not have to answer any questions. I said I preferred not to answer any questions. He said 'All right.' The sheriff, who was listening and watching, got annoyed and said, 'Get the identification.' Mr. Rosenblatt said, 'I know all that.' The sheriff said, 'Get it anyway and write it down.' I gave my name and gave my address as Millbrook. Mr. Rosenblatt said, 'You also have an address in New York. Give us that.' And I did.

"Back in the hall, Tim suggested I try to phone a lawyer in New York. He said he had tried earlier but the phone was disconnected. I asked the man who seemed to be in charge of the raid to arrange for someone to drive me to town to call the lawyer. This was done hours later."

Marya Mannes, the social critic, had been sent by a magazine to write a story about Leary's seventeen-year-old daughter. I had last met her when we were on opposite sides of the fence in the Bruce case. My recollection of that meeting was unpleasant. I had spent several hours conducting a frustrating cross-examination.

Asleep in an upstairs room of the house when the police invaded, Miss Mannes was to write a very different story from the one she had planned. Her roommate, Helen Putnam, was awakened by a crash in the early morning and investigated the noise. She came back and said, "The police are raiding us. They want to search us." Miss Mannes's version of the raid appeared the following month in *The Reporter* as well as in an affidavit filed in court:

"I got out of bed and started to put on my raincoat over my improvised nightwear of shorts and sweater, but Helen said, 'No, they want us to strip.' A policewoman with a pleasant face, who wore a red suit and carried a shoulder bag, came in and we stood there naked while she looked at the insides of our arms and thighs for needle marks . . . We learned later that, while everyone's belongings were ransacked, only the women were stripped . . .

"It was nearly four in the morning before the police searched my room. In their haste to get through the sliding door, they pushed me against a painting on the wall back of me . . .

"People were then taken downstairs one at a time for questioning. An intelligent and gentle young woman, who looked much younger than her twenty-eight years, was asked, among other things, 'Have you had sexual intercourse here?' She said no, she hadn't, and told us later that she wondered what that had to do with anything anyway. Searching through her effects, they took her Vitamin A tablets, her Bufferin, and her prescription diarrhea pills . . .

"After the police left, all the group agreed that the troopers and sheriffs expected an orgy and found it hard to convince themselves that this time, at least, none had existed. They looked at the messy house, they looked at the mattresses and the clutter and the glittering candles and the human assortment with expressions that mirrored the aversion they must have felt as they compared it with their own tidy homes and the ordered life they knew. The mattresses alone were symbols of sin and depravity. It had probably not occurred to them that—quite apart from the shared belief, expressed at Castalia,* that lying on the floor is natural and relaxing, conducive to peace—beds cost money and Leary didn't have any; or that one of the reasons clothes were strewn on the floor was the absence of furniture to put them on or closet space to hang them in."

I made arrangements to visit Millbrook. I wanted to learn what had been going on there before the raid, for the illegality of the search would be the first defense. I wanted to see the

---

* Leary took the name from Hermann Hesse's book *The Glass Bead Game* (*Magister Ludi*).

house and speak to everyone who was in the house at the time of the raid, re-create the police activity during the search, and examine the warrants and affidavits.

My wife Ruth and I drove out on a sunny Saturday early in May. The village, two and a half hours north of New York City, with a population of 2,800 people, is not unlike other Dutchess County towns—strait-laced, affluent, and Republican. The leaders of Bennett College, a girls' school, play a dominant role in Millbrook's social and political life. Many large estates embellish the rolling hills, and a number of blacksmiths are kept busy servicing the private stables.

Leary's place, known as the Dieterich Estate, had been one of the county's grandest manors. The 2,500-acre property with six houses was lent to Leary by William Mellon Hitchcock, the son of the late Tommy Hitchcock of polo fame. It is a complete retreat.

At about 11:00 A.M. we came to the moat surrounding the estate and crossed a turreted gray-rock bridge. Beyond the bridge the road curved through fields and groves past a pond, which looked very inviting for swimming, and several small houses in the same style as the bridge. We nearly got lost trying to find the main house, but fifteen minutes later we were there. The four-story white Victorian house is liberally sprinkled with eaves and turrets and is encircled by a wide porch. As we drove up, about a dozen children were playing on the porch roof.

A young woman with an infant told me Leary was out walking with his daughter, and she invited us to wait in the kitchen. There we were greeted by a Great Dane, two black and white dogs of setter ancestry, two small poodle-like dogs, and a tiger cat. Several young women were seated on mats beside a long dining-room table cut down to a height of eighteen inches. While we ate a second breakfast, one of the mothers prepared lunch for several of the children.

We finished eating and walked through the house. Each of

the rooms was painted a different color—red, orange, purple, or green. Mattresses lined the floors of the bedrooms and the living room. Someone was painting a two-story-high god's face on the front of the house, alongside a Star of David.

Immediately after Leary's Texas trial, the people of Millbrook, using the sheriff's and prosecutor's services, had decided to clamp down on Leary and run him out of town. The Texas trial had focused on his alleged immorality and failures as a father. In his summation the Texas prosecuting attorney spent as much time calling Leary an irresponsible father leading his children down the path of sin as he did on the specific narcotics charge before the court. The working people and the "horsey set" of Millbrook were of the same mind—to get rid of Leary and preserve the Dutchess County way of life. They began to pressure John Heilman, the newly appointed district attorney, to follow up the Texas trial with his own prosecution.

The concern of the people in Millbrook was understandable and I was sympathetic to it. My wife Ruth was born and spent the first fifteen years of her life in a nearby town, and we had, this summer and for many summers, rented a house in Woodstock, New York, three quarters of an hour from Millbrook. Woodstock, was just then becoming the town that later attracted those very people that Millbrook feared, and the townspeople were up in arms.

During February, March, and April, many townspeople, as well as Leary's family and guests, had been called before a grand jury in an attempt to get evidence for an indictment. Millbrook wanted a replay of the Texas trial. Did Leary's children take drugs, the Millbrook grand jury wanted to know. Who looked after the children? Did Leary take drugs in front of the children? Was Leary ever alone with women? Rosemary Woodruff, Leary's future wife, was sentenced to jail for thirty days by the Millbrook judge because of her refusal to answer questions about whether there was "lewd conduct" at Millbrook, and other irrelevant matters. (The sight of Rosemary standing on her head every day in the cell during her yoga exercises drew an audience of jeering guards.) Leary's son and daughter were told they would be jailed and taken from their father if they did not testify against him.

Millbrook officialdom made every effort to find evidence that would insure a criminal conviction. But by April the grand jury still did not have enough facts to hand down an indictment.

Rosemary, after serving her jail sentence, was again called before the grand jury and threatened with repeated contempt charges (and further thirty-day sentences) until she would talk. The law allows a judge to sentence an individual to jail for thirty days each time he or she refuses to answer a proper question before a grand jury. The same question can be asked the day after the person is released from jail for having previously refused to answer it. The New York City district attorney, in his attempts to crack down on the Mafia and other organized crime syndicates, had developed the practice of repeatedly calling back the same witnesses before the grand jury, and they were often sentenced to ten or eleven consecutive thirty-day terms. Leary's teen-age children and his future wife were threatened with this.

At Millbrook, by interviewing Leary's guests and examining the search warrants, I was able to piece together the events leading to the raid. Early in 1966 Sheriff Quinlan had sent two informers into Castalia. The informers, both involved in pending narcotics prosecutions, were told that in exchange for leniency they were to return with enough facts so that a search warrant authorizing a raid could be obtained. The stories they brought back were disappointing.

Sheriff Quinlan, not trusting his informers, then sent in Sheriff Borchers. Borchers sneaked into the estate at night on numerous occasions, sometimes alone and sometimes with part-time deputies assigned to the Leary investigation. Borchers's Sherlock Holmes instincts were titillated by this project. He later said his men were directed to stay outside and watch from the bushes but not enter "the building known as the 'Pad.'" (To Leary and his friends it was known as the "main house.") However, all the investigation, surveillance, and infiltration revealed nothing. The pressure increased on Borchers and on the district attorney's office as the people of Millbrook saw cars with Leary's disreputable-looking visitors drive through town and turn into the Dieterich Estate.

In early March, after a seventeen-year-old boarding-school student at Bennett College in Millbrook was given a pill, supposedly by a friend, she suddenly became hysterical and was taken by ambulance to St. Francis Hospital in Poughkeepsie. After spending several weeks in a mental institution, she was reported to be recovering. No one was sure whether she had taken a pill, or if she had, what was in the pill; but there were rumors it contained LSD.

On April 9 a Millbrook mother told Dutchess County authorities that her eighteen-year-old son, after visiting the Dieterich Estate, was growing marijuana in flowerpots in her house. He was arrested and released on $500 bail pending a trial. The townspeople blamed the restlessness of their youth and the surfacing of the drug problem on Leary.

On April 11 Sheriff Borchers, with Deputy Sheriff Albert D. Travers and Acting Police Officer Harold B. Cyphers, again went to spy on the residents of the house and to look for LSD in the form of sugar cubes. Trying to obtain a search warrant, they then went to the courthouse and said they saw enough to justify a warrant permitting a raid. What did they see that justified a raiding party at two in the morning six days later?

Borchers, under oath, said he saw "numerous vehicles bearing out-of-town license plates," "known drug users," and "females actually or apparently under the age of eighteen years" who did not "reside" at the "Pad." Borchers later tracked down the owners of the cars but could not find any known drug users among them. Borchers explained to the court that he knew of illegal goings-on because his informer told him there was a party on April 2, 1966, "run by a person who is in the field of entertainment," and "the persons in attendance at said party were seated on the floor and on mattresses and they were behaving in an abnormal fashion, and there was conversation among the people at the party about their using drugs." Borchers then told the court he needed a warrant immediately because he knew of another party, set for April 16, which "forty persons will attend," and from what another undisclosed informant said, Borchers thought that "certain narcotic and hallucinogenic drugs will be used at said gathering."

The warrant was issued on April 12. It permitted Borchers to enter Leary's property and house whenever he wanted, at any time of the night or day. Borchers was "commanded" by Judge Joseph J. Hawkins "in the day or night time to make an immediate search of the premises described herein and of any other person who may be found therein to have such property [drugs] in his possession or under his control, and if you find such property or any part thereof to bring it before me at the Dutchess County Court House, Criminal Court, Part I, in and for the County of Dutchess." The warrant further stated, "The Officer executing this warrant may break open an outer or inner door or window of the building, or anything therein to execute the warrant, without notice of his authority and purpose, inasmuch as the property sought is a quantity of narcotics drugs, which may be easily and quickly destroyed or disposed of if such notice was given."

Five days later Borchers and his fearless twenty-five deputy sheriffs descended on the estate. Sheriff Quinlan stayed behind but afterward spoke to the press of "nude women dancing around the fire and sex orgies." One raider reported he saw "girls sitting around without bras." Another said that "weird statues" made him think it was "another world." The officers were obviously proud of the role they played in stopping immoral conduct in Millbrook.

I spent several days at Millbrook. One day Tim and I had a lengthy conversation which began in Tim's office, a long room with ceiling-to-floor windows facing the front of the house. Tim, barefoot, his neck garlanded with chains of beads and bells, was dressed in white—white collarless shirt with white pants that were a bit too tight-fitting and short. From time to time we were joined by various guests who strolled in, listened for five or ten minutes without speaking, then strolled out. We stepped out through an open window and sat on the porch roof.

Tim told me about his first involvement with drugs. "During the summer of 1960 I ate the sacred mushrooms in Mexico. Prior to that, I had been enormously interested in religious and mystical writings. The mushroom experience was incredible. It was as though God had taken me by the hand and let me come into his workshop to see and directly experience the incredible wonders, beauty, and intelligence of the timeless energy process. Everything I've done since that afternoon has been devoted to an understanding of this experience, to a communication of it to others, and to a systematic study of how these experiences can be used to make man more harmonious and healthy in his relationships with other men and nature. That September I read everything I could on experiences like mine. Religious leaders of the past, particularly in Eastern religions, had similar revelations. Psychologists and psychiatrists had little to say about those experiences, except that they were psychotic and abnormal."

I understood Tim's reaction to the eating of the mushroom. Several years before we met, I had taken LSD. I had not forgotten the richness of that "trip," full of new experiences and new self-perceptions. I remember sitting in the country after taking the drug, hearing music in a way I had never heard it before, seeing the trees, the dark night, and stars with new eyes, and feeling close to myself and my family in a unique and wonderful way. A few of the lawyers who got involved with Tim became drug users for the first time and were seduced by the attractiveness of the style of life Millbrook seemed to offer. Several of them gave up their legal practices as their lives took different directions. I did not, perhaps because my personal goals and concepts of social commitment were not consistent with dropping out. Or it may have been that my life style up to that time had conditioned me against such a radical change. However, in many ways I envied Tim's change of direction.

Tim continued describing his experiments with drugs. "I discussed my experiences with some of my colleagues in the psychology department at Harvard, as well as with some graduate students. Some of us decided to do systematic studies, for there was very little scientific writing on the use of drugs. At the time, Aldous Huxley was in Cambridge, and we invited him over. He helped with our planning sessions, which were attended by over two hundred professional religious leaders. We were not, at this time, using marijuana—only psilocybin, the essence of the sacred mushrooms of Mexico; mescaline, which comes from the peyote cacti; and LSD. We could not get marijuana for experimental purposes, but we could get the others. A high percentage of those attending reported that using the drug or plant produced the most intensive and deepest religious experiences of their lives."

Tim and I left the porch and walked across the fields.

"When did you first start using marijuana?" I asked.

"In 1964, the year before I became a member of a Hindu sect. I met Swami Kalidas at his religious center, a Hindu temple, at a seminar on religious experiences, held by Dr. Alan Watts. One of the first things that impressed me about this Hindu temple was the sight of the stained-glass windows on either side of the room—portraying the Christian cross, the Jewish Star of David, the crescent of Islam, the fire of Zoroaster, a Japanese Shinto shrine, the wheel of Buddhism, and the lotus of Hinduism. It was impressive to see that this Hindu sect, far from being in conflict with other religions, embraced them and recognized the validity and divine origin of these other religions. This Hindu group celebrated Christian holy days, such as the feast of Christmas—the birth of Christ. They celebrated Easter, the occasion of the death and resurrection of Christ. They also celebrated the birth of Buddha and holy days of other Eastern religious figures such as Brahma, Krishna, and Siva."

Tim showed me Millbrook's one-story stone house set aside for prayer. It too had stained-glass windows, and each day one or more of Leary's guests used the stone house for meditation. He showed me the "shrines" in the woods—cleared spaces, each with a statue and a prayer rug (the "weird statues" that Quinlan's men had wrecked while probing in the dark). Behind the main house we came upon a grove of pine trees laid out in the shape of a mandala, a symbol common to the major Oriental religions. Work was underway on a one-room house and half a dozen men and women were clearing out underbrush. Two men were discussing the technical aspects of shoring up the roof. Tim told me that another meditation house was being built.

I remembered that some of the sheriff's men had admitted to Noel Tepper, a Poughkeepsie lawyer who later became the attorney for Leary's Millbrook codefendants, that they were frightened to death during the raid: "Mysticism, magic, and all that stuff—we didn't know what to expect." Their worst fears were confirmed when they saw "little men" (the statues) standing in clearings "all over the woods."

Tim continued: "In December of 1964 I took a trip to India. On the way I stopped in Japan to talk with several Zen masters and visit monasteries. On January 1, 1965, I arrived in Calcutta, India. There I met a holy man whose name is Sri Asoke Fakir. Sri Asoke is the head of a religious sect which uses narcotics and hallucinogens. He became extremely interested in conversing with me because I was one of the first Americans he had ever talked to who recognized what he and his large group understood—namely, the sacramental importance of psychedelic plants. He asked me if I had ever used marijuana for religious purposes and I told him I hadn't. So he took me, a day or two later, down to a government-licensed store, where I purchased marijuana. He subsequently trained me in the method he used for meditating while taking marijuana.

"That was the first time I smoked marijuana. On the banks of the Ganges River, which is holy to the Hindus, there is a spot called the 'burning ghat,' where bodies of dead people are brought. They are put on pyres of wood and cremated, surrounded by devotees of religion. The funeral pyres stimulate contemplation about the transience of human affairs, the inevitability of death, and the cycle of life. I joined them and took part in the contemplation to the extent that I could. I attended such ceremonies and studied religion and meditation for many months.

"I then went to Benares and saw marijuana being smoked by the sadhus but didn't join them. Next I went to the Himalaya Mountains, where I lived for three months in a shack without water, gas, or electricity, five miles from the nearest town. There I studied with Lama Gauinda, a Tibetan Buddhist. He would be the equivalent of a cardinal in the Catholic Church. I did not smoke any marijuana during that period. Marijuana was not one of his techniques for producing a psychedelic experience."

As he told me of his visit to India and what he had tried to achieve, he took on an air of melancholy. He was afraid he would never again have the time or freedom to continue his investigations. As indictment after indictment came down against Leary, I thought of the freedom he had had and lost.

"After leaving Almora, in the Himalayas," Leary went on, "I traveled up near the headwaters of the river Ganges and spent about ten days with his holiness, the Sakya Lama. The Sakya Lama is the head of one of the large Buddhist sects in Tibet. I stayed three weeks and then went to a holy city on the banks of the Ganges, called Risikesh.

"Living at Risikesh at that time was none other than Sri Kalikananda, who had come to my house three years before, when I was teaching at Harvard. Sri Kalikananda had come over with Dr. Ralph Metzner and their goal was the setting up of an East-West, American-Indian ashrama on the banks of the Ganges. Sri Kalikananda had been living alone in a little hut near the Ganges, helping to get things organized for the construction of a new monastery.

"During that period at Risikesh, we all lived in a monastery called Sivananda. I was with my wife, so it wasn't possible to live in the little shack with Sri Kalikananda. I did a good deal of scientific writing and put together a book containing prayers and instructions for running a psychedelic drug session. It was based on one of the classic Tibetan Buddhist works, *The Tibetan Book of the Dead*. Articles about my religious experiences later appeared in many magazines, including *The Journal of Religious Education*, and I also gave a paper on them at a Lutheran conference."

At Millbrook we had a lunch of salad, soup, buckwheat cakes, and home-canned peaches. As we sat in the kitchen and spoke, visitors told us about the police stopping and questioning them. Throughout the month roadblocks had been set up around the main house, sometimes for as long as six hours. Visitors were searched and insulted when they entered town, then charged with such heinous crimes as driving with defective tires or having improper equipment in their cars. They were interrogated at length about past and present Castalia activities. But the police found no drugs among Leary's visitors.

Helen Putnam, a guest at the time of the raid, told me at lunch what happened the night before the raid: "Shortly after dinner Dr. Leary suggested that we go out to the 'sacred grove,' as he called the clearing among the pines, and sit around a campfire. We gathered flashlights together and all but one of us walked through the woods to the clearing. We sat down on logs that had been placed around the fire site, while Dr. Leary and some of the men fed the fire with shrubs that had been cleared during the afternoon. Leary's son Jack suggested that we close the circle by holding hands, which we did. Apart from an occasional whisper, nothing was said. At one point, Jack broke the connection by moving away from his seat next to his father. He was asked to rejoin the circle, which he did until he grew tired of sitting still. We sat there a little longer, contemplating the fire and thinking our own thoughts until Dr. Leary suggested that we move back to the house and use the library, where another fire could be lit. As this room had been turned into a bedroom for two of our party, one of whom had already gone to bed, the setting had to be changed and the others went to the third-floor room occupied by Dr. Leary and lit the fire there. I went to bed in the library. We put out the light and I drifted off to sleep to the accompaniment of soft banjo playing in Dr. Leary's room above."

The day Tim and I had our long conversation, the *Poughkeepsie Journal*'s front page proclaimed in three-inch type: "Millbrook Residents Seek to Oust Leary." Even as we were talking, members of the Committee of Prominent Citizens were holding a meeting about Leary. Rev. Malcolm Sawtelle, the six-foot eight-inch minister of Grace Episcopal Church, said, "We want to do everything right, but I wouldn't be honest if I didn't say the hope is to run him out of town." A Millbrook resident wrote a letter that appeared the next day in the community newspaper: "Millbrook watch out. Leary will draw drug addicts to Millbrook. When their money runs out they will murder, rob, and steal to secure funds to satisfy their craving. Then the crime wave will have reached Millbrook." Sheriff Quinlan, who wore a ten-gallon hat and walked like a Western sheriff, said to three hundred residents at a meeting later that week, "I'll do anything we can to drive Leary out of town."

Bennett College students were treated to a slide show featuring close-ups of Leary and pictures of him and his friends walking in the village. They were warned that fraternizing with Leary or his friends meant expulsion. Three new citizens' groups (one of which was headed by Hamilton Fish, Jr., the son of the noted World War II isolationist and Congressman) tried to find out if Leary was violating health, drug, or zoning regulations, so that he could be removed from the estate.

As Leary and I spoke that afternoon, we were continually interrupted by phone calls: Max Lerner wanted to have lunch with Tim the following week; the Playboy Club in Chicago wanted him to lead its patrons in prayer; a publishing company wanted a book written; a college student requested help after returning from a bad "trip."

Aware of his growing notoriety, Tim refused many such requests, while at the same time he enjoyed the attention. Unable to work as a psychologist, compelled to make public appearances to raise funds to pay for all his lawsuits, he found it necessary, and in some ways gratifying, to keep himself in the public spotlight.

With Tim's increasing public exposure, strangers and hangers-on started to flood Millbrook. Many of the people who travel from one culture hero to the next were there. Leary tried to keep them away. He explicitly told people who called not to bring any drugs and for a while he had people he did not know searched. Nonetheless, he was being overwhelmed by visitors, many of whom, because of their appearance, the police could reasonably suspect of carrying or using drugs. His attempts to keep out persons whose presence would harm him met with varied success. Ultimately, he banned all new guests.

Tim asked that afternoon in Millbrook what I thought about the religious-freedom argument. I told him religious practices cannot be restricted unless there is an overriding public necessity. We could argue that only the certainty of harm to the marijuana user would justify the state's prohibition, and that certainty does not exist. But it would be a difficult argument, and I didn't think we would win. Today, five years after our talk, no court has yet upheld arguments such as these, justifying the use of marijuana.

Our long conversation was ended by a shout from the house: "Dinner in twenty minutes." But first the new Castalia engineering feat—the installation of strobe lights to play on the fountain in the center of the lawn—had to be watched by everyone. The forty residents of the house gathered at dusk around the ornate stone fountain. The water appeared cool and delicious. Leary threw off his clothes and dove into the pool. Others followed. Hilarity grew as the number of swimmers increased. The Castalia children danced around—some dressed, others not. The world seemed sane and simple, and law courts were a million light-years away. Later, dinner was cooked communally in the enormous white-walled kitchen.

After dinner we went to a rectangular stone house and I saw for the first time a psychedelic light show. The modern kaleidoscopic patterns of color contrasted with the old gray stone house. As raga music provided a background for changing color patterns, Tim whispered to me, "Psychedelic art, new colors and shapes will help change society. The next time you buy linoleum, you may end up walking on someone's vision."

My wife and I slept that night in a paneled room which opened out onto the roof of the front of the house. Half a dozen strobe lights flashing red, blue, and green had been placed beside the fountain. Illuminating the lawn, the house, the dark sky, and then the water, they contrasted with the country quiet.

Bagpipes awakened us the following morning. At precisely eight o'clock Leary and three of his guests, wearing kilts and playing bagpipes, walked across the lawn and through the halls of the house, awakening the occupants. Within fifteen minutes, half the guests were out on the front lawn doing exercises. Children, some with their mothers or other children's mothers, ran past the exercisers to play with the goats or to get in a quick swim before breakfast.

Tim told me of his plans to have a summer school teaching religions, primarily Oriental, and the wonders of drug taking. Most of the people at Millbrook—doctors and stockbrokers, actors and housewives—planned to stay for the summer and, depending on that experience, perhaps remain for an indefinite time. Many were thinking about severing their outside ties and working on the farms of the estate while they went to the school. Acknowledged experts in Oriental cultures and psychiatrists knowledgeable in the uses of LSD and other drugs had committed themselves to teach. Tim's immediate plans were to stay in Millbrook and make his center self-supporting. A fee schedule had been set up for those who wanted to take the courses. It included room and board for two-week sessions. Health foods were to be available for those who wanted them, and day-care centers were set up for the children—all this in lovely surroundings, with intelligent, attractive people.

Ruth and I were excited about it and planned to visit Millbrook when the school came into being. It never did.

The following day an indictment was handed down against Leary. It began:

THE GRAND JURY OF THE COUNTY OF DUTCHESS by this Indictment accuses TIMOTHY LEARY of the crime of VIOLATION OF PUBLIC HEALTH LAW WITH RESPECT TO NARCOTIC DRUGS, A FELONY, committed as follows:

The Defendant, on or about the 17th day of April, 1966, in the Town of Washington, County of Dutchess and State of New York, unlawfully and in violation of Article 33 of the Public Health Law, had in his

possession and under his control one quarter of an
ounce and more of a preparation, compound, mixture and substance containing cannabis.

Other crimes were charged against Leary. Barry Kaplan and
Nancy and Fred Swain, three of Leary's guests, were charged
with felonious possession of drugs; and the district attorney, on
the theory that anything found in the house was presumptively
Leary's, threatened to charge Leary for that "possession." All
in all, Leary could have been sentenced to jail for sixteen years.

Fred and Nancy Swain, Tim, Noel Tepper (the Swains' lawyer), and I met to discuss priorities a few days after the indictment was handed down. We had to stop the grand jury from
continuing to hear witnesses and putting Leary's friends and
family in jail. We also had to prepare for a pretrial hearing to
show that the search warrant was illegal and that any evidence
obtained on the raid would, as a result, be inadmissible in court.
Most important, we had to take the offensive by attacking
every aspect of the state's procedure in handing down the indictment and charging Leary with a crime. Lastly, we had to
prepare for the trial, which the district attorney said would be
held before the summer was out.

Local hysteria made it impossible to get Leary a fair trial in
June or July. Any jury would be prejudiced by the lurid
newspaper stories then being written about Leary. But there
were no grounds for any substantial adjournments and we
would be forced to trial whenever the district attorney was
ready. Leary and drugs had become a political football for the
fall election for district attorney and judge. The Democrats
claimed the Republicans had not done enough to keep the
"hippies" and "drug people" from pouring into the Poughkeepsie area "like bees to honey" because the "center of
Leary's drug activities is at Millbrook." The Republicans were
going to prove their toughness at Leary's expense.

John Heilman, newly appointed as district attorney to finish out the term of his predecessor, Raymond Barratta, wanted to prove himself Barratta's equal. Leary's conviction could assure his election in November.

Barratta, a former Republican district attorney who had previously investigated Leary on drug charges, was now the county judge who most likely would hear the case. A man quick to anger but equally quick to calm down, Barratta had earned a reputation as a tough prosecutor by the time he left the district attorney's office early in 1966 after working there for fifteen years. Barratta wanted an appointment to the New York State Supreme Court. The notoriety of the Leary trial could advance his career.

I decided to try to transfer the case to the federal court in Manhattan to get away from the local political pressures and the local provinciality. A Manhattan jury would be more sympathetic to Leary—it might even include some marijuana smokers. Heilman's office could be expected to oppose the move and say that, if there was anything improper in the Poughkeepsie trial, a conviction could be reversed on appeal. But an appeal would take years. If Leary was being wrongfully prosecuted, he should be acquitted immediately. The Supreme Court, in a case decided a few months earlier, stated that constitutional rights may be "irreparably injured" during a lengthy appellate process.

Removing a case to federal court is not easy. Federal judges are reluctant to grant removal applications because they are committed to maintaining state and federal judicial systems independent of each other. I would have to prove to the satisfaction of a federal judge in Manhattan that Leary could not get a fair trial in the state court in Poughkeepsie. I had other purposes in trying to transfer the case, however, and they would be served whether or not the effort was successful.

In trying to transfer the case to the federal court, we would be on the offensive. Poughkeepsie District Attorney Heilman would have to defend against our removal application in the

federal court in Manhattan. We would show him that we had
something (although it was very little) to say about the conduct of the litigation, and this would give us a psychological
advantage. More important, Heilman could probably be ordered to stop harassing Leary and his friends until the federal
court decided whether or not to take jurisdiction. Still more
important, by making the removal application, I could post-
pone the trial, probably until fall, when local passions had time
to cool. Political pressures would be reduced when Millbrook's
more affluent residents left town for the summer. I could file
papers and have our court hearing early in June. It would be at
least three weeks before we got a decision. And the Poughkeepsie trial court usually does not sit during July and August.

Noel Tepper and I submitted briefs and affidavits to the federal court in Manhattan, spelling out the pattern of abuse of the
search powers by the sheriff's and prosecutor's offices. The
Poughkeepsie legal procedures were stopped, pending the argument in the federal court.

Heilman, after receiving our papers, asked for a delay. I argued the application in the Manhattan Federal Court on June
22, and three weeks later the judge handed down his decision.
We lost, but we had delayed the case until the middle of July.

I did not want to give the state time to gain momentum in its
prosecution, and by the end of July I was back in the state
court ready to litigate new motions. The grand jury had been
called back into session after the federal judge's decision denying the removal application. First I filed a motion to stop the
grand jury from considering any evidence that was discovered
during the illegal raid. This and all subsequent motions would
be heard immediately before the trial.

The district attorney had probably taken statements from
informers and forced them to go before the grand jury. I asked
the court to direct the district attorney to give me the grand-
jury testimony of each witness who appeared before it and any
statements taken from informers.

The use of informers in narcotics investigations is wide-spread. Most informers, themselves under indictment, are motivated to lie. They know that the more information they give and the more names they name, the more leniency they may expect in return. Often, though, the promise of leniency made by the district attorney cannot be kept because the judge, who makes the final decision on the degree of punishment, may not go along with the prosecutor.

Besides any statements taken from informers, I also asked the court to give me the names and addresses of everyone who had direct knowledge of the raid or arrests, and I asked to have the district attorney, to the extent that he could, produce these people for me to interview, including all the deputy sheriffs. If they refused to meet with me, or if they met with me and were evasive, I could put that information to good use on my cross-examination during the trial—after getting them to admit they had had many meetings and full talks with the prosecutor.

Assistant District Attorney Rosenblatt had interviewed Dr. Ralph Metzner and many others at Millbrook. He had made attempts to get written statements. Most of those questioned had refused to sign any statement, but they did answer Rosenblatt's questions. It would not be surprising if Rosenblatt and the three sheriffs who were always in the room during the interviews testified at the trial that Metzner and Leary's other guests had made "admissions." Metzner denied having said anything incriminating, but the jury might not believe a witness's denial of statements that four law-enforcement officials said he had made. It was necessary to get every statement allegedly made by Leary, Metzner, or any of the other guests. I asked the court to direct Heilman's office to give them to me.

If all else failed, we could fall back on the constitutional argument, and so I began to prepare a brief challenging every aspect of the marijuana laws. There were many different arguments based on constitutional rights to be considered. Some arguments are solely legal and require no proof, while others require medical proof. One argument is that marijuana statutes violate the right to privacy by prohibiting harmless private acts. Another is that the police power of the state is abused when the marijuana statutes curtail the rights of an individual to conduct (possession of marijuana) which in no way infringes on the rights of others. Since marijuana is not a narcotic, is not addictive, and its use does not lead to the commission of crimes or violence, we could claim the possessor or user should not be subject to punitive criminal laws. A third argument against the marijuana laws, which rests on the Eighth Amendment to the Constitution, asserts that it is cruel and unusual to punish one who is an addict or user. Our brief also claimed that the marijuana penalty structure was unconstitutional because available scientific evidence showed that marijuana was less injurious than alcohol or cigarettes.

State and federal narcotics sentences have always been intolerably severe. Twenty-year sentences were common in the fifties and early sixties. Illinois permits a judge to sentence a first offender against its drug laws to life imprisonment. Many states impose enormous minimum punishments. Michigan, Nevada, Rhode Island, and Ohio demand imprisonment of "not less than twenty years" for a first offender convicted of selling drugs. Louisiana is more generous: the minimum is ten years' imprisonment. In Nevada the drug seller can be imprisoned for life if the purchaser is under twenty-one years of age, and a second offender faces a minimum punishment of forty years.

The federal punishment scheme is similar to the penalty scheme imposed by the marijuana laws of Alabama, Alaska, Colorado, Iowa, Mississippi, Missouri, New Hampshire, and Pennsylvania. A first offender charged with selling or acquiring marijuana faces not less than five years or more than twenty years in prison. The punishment for the second offender is double. The mere possession of marijuana, without any evidence of use or intent to sell, renders the defendant liable to not less than two years' or more than ten years' imprisonment. The second offender can get from five to twenty years for mere possession, and the penalty is doubled for the third offender.

I used responsible legal and medical authority to show that laws placing marijuana in the same category as cocaine and heroin are arbitrary and irrational. I quoted those federal and state officials who, beginning in the mid-sixties, saw that the present marijuana penalties were based on Congressional misapprehension in the thirties that marijuana was a dangerous hard-core drug. I began reading all the material I could find on the use of narcotics—including White House Conference reports, medical texts, and pamphlets issued by Allen Ginsberg and his organization, Lemar, a group devoted to the abolition of criminal sanctions against marijuana. Our brief quoted all these authorities.

I knew the argument we had to make centered on the possible physical harm in taking drugs. But marijuana was not being banned primarily because of its physical effects. Nearly everyone admits either that marijuana is not harmful or that there is not enough information to draw a conclusion one way or the other. Drugs are being banned primarily because of the ideology that seemingly arises from the drug culture.

I also wanted to argue Leary's claims that the state's marijuana statute infringed on his religious freedom, but the legal underpinnings for the argument were weak. The marijuana issue had never been presented in this context. The traditional cases discussing the extent to which religious freedom could be protected against legislative enforcement did not offer solace. Supreme Court decisions had upheld restrictions on polygamy against the Mormons, whose church taught and required the practice. The court had also rejected the claim made by Jewish businessmen that Sunday closing laws violated their religious beliefs. Society's interests could indeed infringe on religious freedom, even the freedom of established religious groups.

On the other hand, the Supreme Court of California, in two

1964 cases, held that the religious use of peyote (a hallucinogen derived from the peyote cactus and much more potent than marijuana) was constitutionally protected. The court found that the use of peyote by members of the Native American Church was central to the religious beliefs and practices of the church and hence could not be stopped by the state. "Peyote works no permanent deleterious injury to the Indian," the court observed, and found "no evidence to suggest that Indians who use peyote are more liable to become addicted to other narcotics than non-peyote-using Indians." But the California court went to great lengths to note that peyote was not used by youths; it was an important part of a religious ceremony. The general unavailability of peyote also was a significant factor. The decision of the California court was not making peyote available to twelve million Americans—the present number of estimated marijuana users. Courts in Montana and North Carolina had rejected entirely the claim that the use of peyote was entitled to constitutional protection. All in all, the religious-freedom argument was not a promising base to build on.

As time passed, Leary's face became more wan; it showed the pressure of his being involved in continual criminal prosecutions. His creative energies were being subverted into publicity stunts; the prospect that he would be arrested at the slightest provocation was intimidating. He might win one case and later another, but ultimately he would lose, face jail, and be destroyed.

Life at the Dieterich estate had changed radically in the months since the arrest. Leary's expectations for a rich, varied communal life at Millbrook were over. Nearly all the people I had seen there in May and June were gone by fall. The pressures of the townspeople, the constant fear of the police and of continual arrests, and internal bickering had driven them away and discouraged others from coming. Furthermore, Leary was getting (and giving) a bad press. A *Playboy* interview in which he talked about thousands of orgasms while "tripping" made him appear silly.

I spoke to witnesses who could testify to the harmlessness of marijuana and through whom I could introduce medical evidence and various scientific reports. Dr. Ralph Metzner, who held a degree in pharmacy with honors from Oxford and a Ph.D. in clinical psychology from Harvard, would make an excellent witness. Unfortunately, his close professional and emotional ties with Leary and the fact that he was present on the night of the raid would make him seem unobjective. I decided not to call him as a defense witness on the issue of police conduct during the raid but to save his testimony for the drug issue.

Another potential witness was Dr. Joel Fort, a faculty member of the University of California at Berkeley and a specialist in psychiatry and drug addiction. He had set up the San Francisco Center for Social Problems—the only organization in the world then providing treatment for all kinds of drug-related problems, including criminal behavior, sexual maladjustment, and suicidal depression. Besides writing on drugs, Fort had served twice as a consultant on drug abuse to the World Health Organization and once as an adviser to the United Nations Division on Narcotic Drugs. Fort agreed with our defense and had new, unpublished medical data of his own to back it up.

Fort and Metzner were investigating the possibility that the use of marijuana could lead to criminal activity. Fort, an expert witness, would testify that these studies showed a negative correlation between crime and the use of marijuana. In fact, marijuana users are shown to be less violent than the general population.

In early August I called Assistant District Attorney Rosenblatt to discuss a timetable for the arguments to be presented at the pretrial hearing. After some preliminary conversation he said, "Why don't you come to our office, meet John Heilman, and we'll see if something can be worked out?" I agreed, not knowing what this meant, and the next week I met with Heilman and Rosenblatt in the district attorney's office in Pough-keepsie.

After exchanging niceties, Heilman declared, "If Leary will plead guilty to one of the charges in the indictment, we'll drop all the other charges. I'll also discharge the grand jury and we won't return any more indictments for things that happened before. We want each one of the defendants to plead to one count. I'm reasonably sure Leary's codefendants won't be jailed. You'd better decide."

I was astonished. Faced with trial, the prosecution had apparently taken stock and found themselves short of enough evidence to obtain a conviction. But how short?

Heilman nervously tried to convince me that his suggestion was the best course of action for Leary. I replied that I didn't think the prosecution could get a conviction and that I was going to file false-arrest damage suits on behalf of Leary and some of the guests in the house. I asked what proof Heilman had of a crime, whether he had any confessions, whether his informers would hold up under cross-examination. I watched Heilman's and Rosenblatt's faces as I spoke but learned nothing. "We've got enough to convict him for this and other crimes—no problem about it," the district attorney replied.

"I'll have to talk to my client," I told Heilman, and I then drove to Millbrook to meet with Leary.

Why was Heilman willing to stop with a plea to one charge, which would give Leary at most one year in jail? And what should I advise Tim? "If I had the feeling you'd be treated fairly if you pleaded guilty to one count, I wouldn't hesitate to recommend that you do so," I told him. "If the case goes to trial, they probably have informers who will tie you into drugs. You'll get a long sentence, maybe ten to fifteen times as long as if you take the plea. And the grand jury has been sitting for several months. They must have something there. If we turn down the guilty plea, other indictments will probably come down from the grand jury."

Defending the case on all the counts would occupy Tim for at least another year. The search-and-seizure hearing would take ten days, the trial itself twice that, and then, after conviction, there are two years of appeals. It would be costly. Witnesses would have to be rounded up twice—once for the hearing and once for the trial. Most of the people who were guests in the house on April 16 were not from the Poughkeepsie area, and none of them really wanted to testify.

On the other hand, we were in a bargaining position. We might be able to prove to the jury that the sheriff, the district attorney, Judge Hawkins (who had issued the search warrant), and perhaps Judge Barratta (who had been district attorney when the investigation started) had acted improperly in searching Millbrook and had used the grand jury improperly.

Public opinion in Millbrook had changed in our favor. The summer had passed; the town had not been ruined by an influx of hippies. We could push for a trial before election and let the prosecutor's office know the trial would provide daily publicity about Millbrook's style of law enforcement. Or, if the prosecution tried to adjourn the trial to get past election day, we could keep up a steady barrage of publicity claiming that they were trying to avoid a trial before election because they didn't have a case.

Tim's belligerent Irish nature was aroused. He wanted to use his case to strike at all marijuana laws. He was strongly opposed to accepting a lesser plea and leaving the law unchallenged. But he left the decision up to me. "Let's turn down the guilty plea and go ahead," I said. "If we want to change our minds later, if we lose the search-and-seizure hearing, we can probably accept." That was what he wanted to hear.

Trial was set for October 3. I began putting together our

evidence, organizing the medical testimony, and rereading the medical and religious texts I planned to introduce. I ordered a mock-up of the main house, meditation house, and pine groves and the sourrounding area; floor plans of the main house; and five-by-seven-foot blowups of aerial photographs of the estate.

If Leary testified and the jury believed that the drugs found at Millbrook were not his and he knew nothing about them, or they believed that in any event he had the right, as a scientist and a religious figure, to use drugs, he would probably be acquitted. If he was not believed, he would be imprisoned. It would all depend on his credibility and his credibility would depend on what kind of man the jury thought Leary was. I wanted his personal and professional background brought to the jury's attention. It would astonish many of them.

Leary was born a Roman Catholic of Irish-French ancestry. One of his uncles was a monseigneur. He went to Holy Cross in Massachusetts, then to West Point (his father was an army officer), where one of his most searing memories was being prohibited for a year from any social conversation with the other cadets for a minor infraction of West Point discipline. After he proved he could bear the social isolation, Leary left West Point the day his punishment ended. He went on to major in psychology at the University of Alabama, graduated in 1942, then enlisted in the Army and served as a military psychologist at a Pennsylvania hospital. After being discharged, Leary earned his doctorate in clinical psychology from the University of California and received an appointment as assistant professor at the University of California's School of Medicine in San Francisco.

He spent a good part of his next fifteen years treating the mentally ill. During hospital and teaching jobs at Cambridge, San Francisco, and Oakland (where he helped found the progressive Kaiser Psychiatric Clinic), he published thirteen scientific articles (contending traditional psychiatric methods were hurting as many patients as they helped) and two books, formulated important diagnostic tests, and earned a reputation that resulted in an invitation to join the Harvard University faculty to teach and explore new methods of treating mental illness.

Leary joined Harvard in 1959, and despite his growing doubts about his profession ("I thought psychology was now a trade union"), he was recognized by the faculty as one of the brightest and most committed men on the staff. It was there that he and Richard Alpert began experimenting on themselves and hundreds of volunteers with measured doses—first of psilocybin (the chemical derivative of the "sacred mushroom") and later of LSD.

Leary's brightness was matched by his charm and the students were attracted to him. Soon there were rumors that he and his students were jointly involved in drug experiences, and in 1963 Harvard asked him to leave. This upset many faculty members, not only because of the harm done to Leary personally but because the expulsion might put an end to his professional contributions.

I was prepared to ask the Dutchess County sheriffs about every visit they had made to the estate—what they saw and where they stood. I was sure that Borchers, Quinlan, and company would not be able to answer detailed questions and could therefore be cross-examined to great advantage. I was confident that if I produced several witnesses to dispute each officer's version of what had happened the night of the raid and in the previous months, an appellate court would conclude the state had not had "probable cause" to issue the warrant.

In the second week of September Rosenblatt phoned me and suggested I go up to Poughkeepsie to "talk about the case." We had rejected their deal. I guessed they were going to try to persuade me to reconsider by showing me some of their evidence against Tim. I was half right.

"You're being foolish," Heilman told me. "A guilty plea without a jail sentence is better than a long trial that will undoubtedly result in conviction and a long sentence." I restated my commitment to try the case, adding that I thought we would ultimately win on the search-and-seizure issue, perhaps even at the first appellate level.

As I spoke, Heilman and Rosenblatt exchanged glances. "I won't allow my client to plead guilty to anything," I continued. "And since I've gotten into the marijuana argument, I feel better about it. I didn't think we'd push it when I first started, but now we have a dozen good witnesses attacking every aspect of the New York law. It will be the first case of its kind in the country. The country will be watching; there'll be daily publicity. You'll be in the papers every day. I don't think the state has sustained its burden of proving the drug is dangerous. I think the government's regulation of a private act violates the right of privacy."

Rosenblatt and Heilman were giving each other signals. I kept at it: "I'd like the hearing on the validity of the search warrants and the admissibility of the evidence obtained on the raid to start in the afternoon. I have six days of testimony. I'd like to start the trial the following week. I'm getting witnesses in from all over the country and I don't want to have to bring them back and forth. I've arranged my schedule so that I'm free all of October for both the hearing and the trial. I know that may tie up your electioneering schedule and we ought to resolve it now. How long will your proof for the hearings take? I'd like to know how to arrange my witnesses' schedule."

Neither Rosenblatt nor Heilman answered.

I repeated my question.

"Will Leary leave Millbrook?" Rosenblatt asked me. "What are his plans? We're interested in seeing that he leaves. That's what the people of this town want. We don't want to hurt him but only to get him to leave town. He's responsible, whether he wants to be or not, for a lot of undesirable elements coming into town."

"I don't know. Even now he's spending less time here than

he did this summer. He's in New York a good deal. But I'll ask
him if you want."

"We'd like you to ask him," Heilman said.

"Fine. I'll ask him. Why?"

The words rushed out of Heilman's mouth, almost against
his will. "We've concluded that because of *Miranda* we probably can't sustain a conviction. We feel we can get a conviction at trial, but even though Leary is guilty, it might be reversed on appeal—if not at the first level, then in the Court of
Appeals or in the United States Supreme Court. But we want
Leary out of Millbrook in exchange for our dropping the
charges."

I nearly jumped out of my chair. I was totally unprepared
for this. I had assumed that there were informers ready to say
they saw Leary taking and handing out drugs. I thought the
prosecution held all the cards, and now they were talking
about dropping the charges—charges that could have sent
Leary to prison for a long time.

On June 13, 1966, the United States Supreme Court had decided, in a series of four cases now referred to by the name of
the first case, *Miranda v. Arizona*, that police interrogation
must conform to certain explicit standards designed to protect
the suspect's constitutional privilege against self-incrimination.
Whenever a person is about to become the object of "custodial
interrogation," the police must inform him that he has a right
to remain silent, that anything he says can be used against him,
that he has the right to presence of counsel, and that counsel
will be provided by the government if he is indigent. Before he
can confess, the suspect must knowingly, intelligently, and voluntarily waive the right to remain silent and to have counsel
present, and even after the waiver the police must respect a
suspect's desire to discontinue his confession.

In Leary's case the *Miranda* issue was a false one. Leary told
me he had not said anything that could be construed as a confession. Leary's version of what he said to the sheriffs and

Rosenblatt on April 17 was confirmed by every guest who had been present when he spoke to the police.

Heilman continued, "And we want all the defendants to sign releases. We'll prepare them. Can you give me an answer today? I'd like to do this quickly if we are going to do it before the press finds out about it. I'll make the motion to dismiss so that the case will be dismissed on the state's motion."

The indictments would be dismissed if we agreed that Tim would leave Millbrook and if we could work out a way for the district attorney to save face.

I went to see Leary. His excitement surpassed mine. I hadn't seen him so happy in months.

"Why are they doing it?" Tim asked.

I told him I believed that Judge Barratta could not afford to go through a long, brutal trial and hearing the month before elections. Also, if the district attorney's case was defective, Barratta would be in a tough spot. If he dismissed the case on our motion, the townspeople would criticize him. If he didn't, he'd be reversed and might be criticized by the appellate court. But I told Tim I didn't think he should be forced to leave Millbrook under a cloud. I thought we could give them less than they asked for, since they obviously were determined to avoid the trial.

"Marty, I'll leave it up to you," Tim said. "If I have to leave, I have to leave. I'd rather stay. I don't like not testing the laws and I don't like to be run out."

"There'll be other cases for that," I replied.

As we finished our talk, some young people drove up the circular driveway to the main house. They had come to hear about the wonders of LSD. I stayed for a few minutes and listened to Tim, who had never seen them before, tell them about the dangers of drugs. He first asked them questions as he tried to learn something about the psychological state of the potential user. At this and other times when I saw him in similar situations, he more often than not warned against the taking of any hallucinogen at any time. He admonished against the taking of drugs in an unfamiliar setting and he urged potential drug takers to have a doctor or psychiatrist's phone number at hand and not to take the drugs unless another person is present. The young people that day listened to his warnings; they probably would not have paid attention to anyone else who said what Leary was saying to them.

I went to the pay phone behind the stairs on the first floor and called Heilman. "We won't agree to leave. However, Leary has already closed down the psychedelic workshops because you were arresting anybody who came near Millbrook. We'll agree to continue to curtail his activities."

"Okay," Heilman said. "I'll prepare the releases. I want them signed before we go to court. We'll have the indictments dismissed in open court. I haven't spoken to the judge yet, but I think it will be as I say."

Heilman insisted that Leary sign a "general release." Leary's signing of the release meant he would not sue for false arrest or for the raid on his home. This release, Heilman and I agreed, would be held in escrow until we appeared before Judge Barratta. If Barratta refused to dismiss, the release would be returned to us and the trial would start.

Two days later the *Poughkeepsie Journal* headlines announced: "Grand Jury Discharged after Leary Indictments— No Further Indictments." The article said, "District Attorney John R. Heilman said today that County Judge Raymond C. Barratta had discharged the grand jury which brought indictments against Dr. Timothy Leary, accusing him of possession of marijuana. Morgan Mackey, former basketball star, was foreman of the grand jury which handed up indictments against Dr. Leary. 'All available witnesses were called, and the grand jury was satisfied that there were no violations of any criminal laws other than those for which the indictments were handed up,' said Mr. Heilman." He congratulated the grand jury for "its long and thorough service to the people of the county and the cause of impartial justice," adding that the "grand jury and Judge Barratta are satisfied that all evidence within the area of investigation was heard."

We went to court on Friday morning, September 23, Tim with an orange flower in his lapel. Heilman had asked us not to tell the press that the case would be called. He told me if there was any publicity surrounding the dismissal, he might not be able to go through with it. The dismissal would be sprung on the citizens of Millbrook before they had a chance to stop it. So secretive was Heilman that the case was not even listed on the court calendar.

Judge Barratta disposed of all the other cases before him and, when the courtroom was nearly empty, called *"People v. Leary."* Heilman, Leary, Fred and Nancy Swain, Noel Tepper, and I walked inside the railing separating the spectators from the judge's bench.

"I understand the People have a motion," the judge said.

Heilman, nervous and tense, appearing as if he had more at stake than the Leary case, addressed his former boss. "Yes, Your Honor." He then read from a long prepared statement that he later issued to the press:

"The *Miranda* decision came out after the arrest and indictments of Doctor Leary. The authorities were acting under then existing laws and could not have foreseen that this later decision would apply retroactively to their actions, nor could they have anticipated the exact language and conditions specified by the court. Thus, the statement of Dr. Leary is governed by the *Miranda* rule and is not admissible against him."

Tim and I began to relax. Heilman would not have gone this far if there were any doubt about the judge's intentions. Leary's face shone. This was about to be his first court victory and he took it as an omen of things to come. Heilman continued:

"With members of my staff, I have carefully analyzed the entire evidence in the light of the Supreme Court decision. I am of the opinion that without the statement of Dr. Leary there would be insufficient evidence in possession of my office to bring about a verdict of guilty beyond a reasonable doubt, or to assure that such a verdict would survive appellate scrutiny.

"I sought, through his counsel, to have Dr. Leary dissolve the Castalia Foundation and to discontinue the Foundation's activities in Dutchess County. I have received assurance that such action will be announced and carried out immediately.

"Under the present status of the law and the changes which dictate the inadmissibility of Dr. Leary's statement, it is my considered judgment and I so move, Your Honor, that the indictment against Dr. Leary and his codefendants be dismissed.

"There was other evidence against these defendants which could have been used to obtain a conviction after trial. This other evidence was the product of a search and seizure under a search warrant. Unfortunately, certain evidence available at the time that the search warrant was issued now is no longer available to the people. This court is aware of the troublesome area of search and seizure and the rigorous rules which have pervaded that phase of criminal law, often requiring the dismissal of a case or the exclusion of evidence, such as narcotics and contraband, because of technical defects in a search warrant or arrest."

My eyes went from Barratta to Heilman: would there be any obstacles? Leary was making playful faces at Cassie, my one-year-old daughter sitting in the back of the courtroom with my wife.

After Heilman finished, the judge turned to me. "With respect to the dissolution of the Castalia Foundation, I understand then that he intends to continue residing in Dutchess County?"

"He does," I answered.

Judge Barratta flushed with anger. "Well, any decision that I make here this morning certainly would have no effect upon Doctor Leary or any of the other defendants whether or not they wish to continue in Dutchess County. There is no mandate that I might issue to compel him either to live in Dutchess County or to move out of Dutchess County.

"Frankly, it is the opinion of this court that I would like to see him out of Dutchess County, both as a resident and as a participant in the advocacy of any drugs. Since the inception of these criminal proceedings various motions have been brought on behalf of the defendants, including individual motions for inspection of the grand jury minutes. This has given me an opportunity to read and study these minutes and thus familiarize myself with many of the facts which are the basis of the prosecution of each defendant. The evidence seems to be clear that certain narcotic drugs were found on the premises of the Castalia Foundation and certain incriminating admissions were made in connection therewith.

"As stated by the district attorney, under the *Miranda* decision, which postdated the arrests made, this prosecution would not permit the use of these admissions in evidence. With respect to the other grounds as set forth by the district attorney, this court is constrained to agree that the indictments against each of the defendants must be dismissed. Therefore, for these reasons and those stated by the district attorney, I grant the motion to dismiss the indictment.

"I might add that, fortunately for you defendants, and particularly for you, Timothy Leary, the laws of this great nation and the interpretation of the individual's rights within the concept of our Constitution protect not only the innocent but from time to time those who might be proven guilty at trial."

Heilman spoke. "Your Honor, please, I move to exonerate bail on all four defendants."

"Motion is granted," said Judge Barratta.

As the judge, still angry, picked up his papers to leave, I said,

"Thank you, Your Honor." He gave Leary a final withering glance and stormed out of the courtroom.

Tim and I both literally skipped down the stairs. His excitement at having the charges dismissed was not diminished by the fact that his chance to challenge the state's marijuana laws was lost.

The front page of the *Poughkeepsie Journal* that evening was devoted almost entirely to the morning's happenings in court. Its headline—"Leary Case Dismissed in County as He Agrees to Curb Activities"—was followed by the statement that Dr. Leary "agreed to discontinue all Castalia Foundation activities in Millbrook. Leary, faced with criminal charges that could result in forty-five years of imprisonment, was, today, set free because of recent Supreme Court decisions."

Heilman, then running as the Republican incumbent for the office of district attorney, was attacked by his Democratic opponent, Bernard Kessler, who said, "The whole thing was fishy." Heilman answered that he had saved the people the expense of a trial because he decided his evidence would not sustain a conviction.

My comment to Tim that there would be other chances to test other aspects of the marijuana laws was immediately proven true.

Murderers and rapists who have served their time can travel where they wish without restriction; a person convicted of possessing (not using or selling) the smallest amount of marijuana, however, is guilty of a felony punishable by three years' imprisonment if he does not register with customs when he leaves the country. In September 1966, while the Millbrook proceedings were still pending, Tim committed himself to a television appearance in Canada with Marshall McLuhan. Leary flew to Canada from New York on October 12, 1966, and returned the following day. He was arrested as soon as he

stepped off the plane at Kennedy Airport, taken before a
United States Commission in the Brooklyn Federal Court, and
charged with violating a federal law because he had not registered with customs officials when he left the country. The penalty for failure to sign a piece of paper: three years in prison.
Until Leary's arrest, practically no one had heard of the
statute.

Leary would hear of it again. Allan Kamin, a student at the
University of Toronto, called Leary in December 1966. The
University of Toronto wanted Leary to appear in a faculty-
sponsored symposium on February 10 and he wanted to go.
Allan and I discussed Tim's legal status and his obligation to
register with customs. But on February 8 Kamin was advised
by the Canadian Department of Immigration that Leary would
not be allowed to enter the country. A rule, rarely invoked,
prohibited anyone with a narcotics conviction from entering
Canada. Kamin and I contacted the Minister of Immigration,
who could issue a permit exempting Leary from the rule. We
were denied the permit.

So Tim and Kamin worked out another arrangement. Tim
had a speaking engagement at a college in Detroit. He agreed to
meet Kamin at the customs office on the Canadian-American
border and give him a tape-recorded statement for the conference. Leary boarded a tunnel bus at Detroit, went through the
tunnel, and met Kamin at the Canadian side of the tunnel. He
stepped out of the bus and gave Kamin the tape without entering the Canadian Customs Bureau. Kamin's father, a lawyer, and
several students were present to meet Tim. They spoke briefly.
Tim then started walking toward the bus. He was arrested before he got there. The customs official said Tim would be
charged with trying to enter Canada illegally; the border line
separating Canada from the United States, he said, was somewhere in the tunnel.

Leary was taken before Judge Kaess of the United States
District Court for the Eastern District of Michigan, Southern

Division, sitting in Detroit. The following day a complaint was issued for violation of the customs-registration law, based on facts given by Noel Pickering, immigration officer for the Dominion of Canada, and Kenneth Aschim and Paul Hudsutt, United States Customs agents. I was trying a criminal case in New York and tried to arrange for a Detroit lawyer and bail.

The news media played up the arrest. The *Detroit News* on February 14, 1967, in its article captioned "LSD 'Holy Man' Leary 'Tuned Out' Seized Here," said, "The federal 'fuzz' put the arm on Timothy Leary, the high priest of LSD, again today. After what could be called a 'bad trip' to Windsor, which ended when Canadian immigration authorities firmly turned him around at the other end of the Detroit-Windsor Tunnel and sent him back, the self-proclaimed 'holy man' was charged here with trying to leave the country while under federal bond. . . . Last night, sitting cross-legged on a stage with a candle beside him in Ann Arbor, he told a University of Michigan student audience, 'Turn on, tune in and drop out.' That was just what Canadian immigration agents had done yesterday afternoon when Leary showed up on the tunnel bus to Windsor. 'Tuned in' that he was coming, they 'turned on' the pressure and made him 'drop out' of the country."

There was no claim in the complaint that Leary knew he had crossed the border. Avern Cohn, the Detroit lawyer, and I spoke to the federal authorities, contending that the law was unconstitutional because it did not require proof that the violator knew he was committing a criminal act. They agreed with us, realizing that if Leary were prosecuted, the statute would be struck down. On May 11, the United States attorney for the Michigan federal court filed a motion seeking to dismiss the complaint. The motion was granted and the case ended. The New York criminal proceedings for failure to register eventually were dismissed, too.

On May 19, 1969, the Supreme Court, in an opinion written by Justice John M. Harlan, unanimously overturned Leary's

Texas conviction. The press, and even some noted constitutional lawyers, reported that Leary's victory had ended the federal ban on narcotics. They were wrong. Although the case was important in other respects, it did not substantially affect the drug laws.

The Supreme Court's decision in *Leary v. United States* held that two key provisions of the federal tax law were unenforceable. One provision made it a crime to transfer, acquire, or possess marijuana without paying a $100-per-ounce transfer tax. The court reasoned that Leary and others would incriminate themselves if they declared to the customs officials at the border that they wished to pay the tax and comply with the federal statute. This declaration could be turned over to state officials, who could prosecute for possession of marijuana.

A second provision of the tax law governed the illegal importation of marijuana. The law provided that possession of marijuana creates a presumption that the possessor knows it is imported. The Supreme Court said that such a presumption is unconstitutional: one cannot presume that a man arrested for possession of drugs knew the drugs were imported. They referred to statistics indicating that many of the drugs in this country are produced here. However, the court said nothing to upset the other state and federal narcotics laws, which remain in force.

Leary was retried for the Texas offense on January 19, 1970, was convicted, and one month later was sentenced to ten years in prison. On March 20, 1970, he was sentenced by a California State Court to a six-month to ten-year term. He began to serve the California sentence, knowing that when he was finished he would start serving time on the Texas conviction. Then, because he was again arrested in Millbrook in 1967 on charges similar to those previously dismissed, he would have to face further New York indictments.

One September day in 1970, while driving, I heard on the car radio that "Leary had taken another illegal trip." He had escaped from prison. I was overjoyed. I wish him all good things and hope he finds sanctuary. Had he not escaped, he'd have spent the rest of his life in jail.

Today courts and prosecuting officials are tougher on drug users than ever before. But there is good reason to expect that this will soon change.

Richard Lyons, writing in *The New York Times*, named the week following Leary's second conviction "National Marijuana Week." On Sunday, January 26, 1970, John P. Cahill, son of the recently elected Governor of New Jersey, was arrested and charged with felonious possession of marijuana. That same morning, Pasadena police burst into a party given by space scientists from the jet-propulsion laboratory facility run by California Institute of Technology. Twenty persons, including seven scientists, were jailed for possession of marijuana and its more potent form, hashish.

On Monday of that week Harvey Fleetwood III, son of a New York banker, was charged with smuggling $200,000 worth of hashish from India into Puerto Rico inside a scuba tank and a stuffed horse. On Tuesday, Jonathan Freedman, the seventeen-year-old son of Hartford's city manager, was charged with selling LSD. On Wednesday the United States Senate astounded everyone with an 80 to 0 vote to relax federal penalties for marijuana use. On Thursday, New York's Governor Rockefeller announced the formation of a new committee to recommend changes in the state's penalties for drug use. And on Friday, Howard Samuels, Jr., seventeen-year-old son of the New York gubernatorial contender, was arraigned on charges of possessing hashish.

In the following month dozens of the children of governors and congressmen, including some of the Kennedy children, were arrested.

The next generation of lawmakers is smoking pot. Leary

knew what the real dissatisfactions of the young were, often before they themselves did. He understood the role he played in telling the country why the alienated young were rejecting its morality and in broadcasting the freedom of the psychedelic and marijuana experiences. Although many others had said the same things before, Leary, because he had middle-class credentials, was more credible. First the alienated young, and then others, convinced that the country was spiritually bankrupt, listened to him because he had acted out his beliefs. He gave up his previous life-style for a more experimental and, to him, rewarding one, which, by its nature, subjected him to the pressure of state and federal law enforcement. Having spent years of study as a psychologist, he exhorted his audiences to devote themselves to a life of feeling, sensing, and touching as a means of knowing themselves.

What may not have been immediately apparent—or important—to his fans was Leary's gradually revealed ambition to lead and influence his followers and the country. The surfacing of this ambition, prodded by his financial needs, along with criticism of his "religious exercises" (which were shown at New York's Village Theatre for $6 a person), made Leary seem less than saintly. He had never claimed to be saintly.

Leary's actions have led to a radical rethinking of drug laws. But, more importantly, the style of life at Leary's house in Millbrook may well become the norm of the future. If so, every aspect of this country's structure will be changed and Leary will be remembered as having led the movement for that change.